A CELEBRATION
OF POETS

EAST
GRADES K-3
SPRING 2010

creativeCOMMUNICATION
A CELEBRATION OF TODAY'S WRITERS

A CELEBRATION OF POETS
EAST
GRADES K-3
SPRING 2010

AN ANTHOLOGY COMPILED BY CREATIVE COMMUNICATION, INC.

Published by:

creativeCOMMUNICATION

A CELEBRATION OF TODAY'S WRITERS

1488 NORTH 200 WEST • LOGAN, UTAH 84341
TEL. 435-713-4411 • WWW.POETICPOWER.COM

Copyright © 2010 by Creative Communication, Inc.
Printed in the United States of America

ISBN: 978-1-60050-355-9

FOREWORD

I am often asked why we create a book of the best entries to our contest. We started this project when the internet was in its infancy. It was a time when the written word was less electronic and recorded the old fashioned way: written on paper. Now in 2010, with email being the primary form of personal communication and classroom assignments often existing only between computers, this project takes on new meaning. We often say that our project helps record literature that would have been lost in the bottom of a locker or a backpack. However, with electronic books becoming increasingly popular, our books also create a historical and permanent record. We create an actual book that can be handed down and read and re-read for generations.

I also reflect upon the letters from poets, parents and teachers I receive each year. This year the most meaningful letter came from a teacher who had a student that was not interested in school and was a member of a gang. This student had received little recognition in school. However, she wrote a poem, sent it into our contest, and it was accepted to be published. With this small bit of recognition, the teacher stated that this student quit her gang, changed what she was wearing to school, and now has an interest in writing.

Why do we create a book of the best entries? We create a book to motivate and inspire today's student writers. We create a book to record poems that would be lost to history. We create a book, and in the process, change lives.

Enjoy what these students have created.

Thomas Worthen, Ph.D.
Editor
Creative Communication

WRITING CONTESTS!

Enter our next POETRY contest!
Enter our next ESSAY contest!

Why should I enter?
Win prizes and get published! Each year thousands of dollars in prizes are awarded throughout North America. The top writers in each division receive a monetary award and a free book that includes their published poem or essay. Entries of merit are also selected to be published in our anthology.

Who may enter?
There are four divisions in the poetry contest. The poetry divisions are grades K-3, 4-6, 7-9, and 10-12. There are three divisions in the essay contest. The essay divisions are grades 3-6, 7-9, and 10-12.

What is needed to enter the contest?
To enter the poetry contest send in one original poem, 21 lines or less. To enter the essay contest send in one original non-fiction essay, 250 words or less, on any topic. Each entry must include the student's name, grade, address, city, state, and zip code, and the student's school name and school address. Students who include their teacher's name may help their teacher qualify for a free copy of the anthology. Contest changes and updates are listed at www.poeticpower.com.

How do I enter?
Enter a poem online at:
www.poeticpower.com
or
Mail your poem to:
  Poetry Contest
  1488 North 200 West
  Logan, UT 84341

Enter an essay online at:
www.studentessaycontest.com
or
Mail your essay to:
  Essay Contest
  1488 North 200 West
  Logan, UT 84341

When is the deadline?
Poetry contest deadlines are December 2nd, April 5th and August 16th. Essay contest deadlines are October 19th, February 15th and July 19th. Students can enter one poem and one essay for each spring, summer, and fall contest deadline.

Are there benefits for my school?
Yes. We award $15,000 each year in grants to help with Language Arts programs. Schools qualify to apply for a grant by having 15 or more accepted entries.

Are there benefits for my teacher?
Yes. Teachers with five or more students published receive a free anthology that includes their students' writing.

For more information please go to our website at
www.poeticpower.com,
email us at editor@poeticpower.com or call 435-713-4411.

TABLE OF CONTENTS

STATES INCLUDED IN THIS EDITION:

Connecticut
District of Columbia
Maine
Maryland
Massachusetts
New Hampshire
New York
Pennsylvania
Rhode Island
Vermont

Spring 2010 Poetic Achievement Honor Schools

Teachers who had fifteen or more poets accepted to be published

The following schools are recognized as receiving a "Poetic Achievement Award." This award is given to schools who have a large number of entries of which over fifty percent are accepted for publication. With hundreds of schools entering our contest, only a small percent of these schools are honored with this award. The purpose of this award is to recognize schools with excellent Language Arts programs. This award qualifies these schools to receive a complimentary copy of this anthology. In addition, these schools are eligible to apply for a Creative Communication Language Arts Grant. Grants of two hundred and fifty dollars each are awarded to further develop writing in our schools.

Asa C Adams School
Orono, ME
Heidi Thurston*

Brant Elementary School
Brant, NY
Angela Karpinski*

Buckley Country Day School
Roslyn, NY
Joanna Cooper
Hillary Janik*
Lynn Knox*
Denise Powers
Stefani Rosenthal*
Laura Uhr

Carlyle C Ring Elementary School
Jamestown, NY
Deborah Bolling*

Caryl E Adams Primary School
Whitney Point, NY
Charlene McDonald
Chris Ruggiero

Central Elementary School
Elizabeth, PA
Lois Leggett*
Amy Tilberg

Chestnut Street Elementary School
Kane, PA
Robynn Boyer*

Clinton Street Elementary School
West Seneca, NY
Mrs. Croglio*
Shannon Schmidt*
Mrs. Verbeck*

Colebrook Primary School
Rochester, NY
Deborah Smith*
Jeff Stenglein*

Cornerstone Academy
Northborough, MA
Mary Simoneau*

Craneville School
Dalton, MA
Mrs. Araujo
Teresa Bills
Christie Mallet

E Ethel Little School
North Reading, MA
Nancy Badavas*
Ellen Devecis
Beth Leavitt
Donald Simmons

Ellicott Road Elementary School
Orchard Park, NY
Michael Cohoon*

Evergreen Elementary School
Collegeville, PA
Mrs. Beisswenger*
Kathy Long*

Fairview Elementary School
Midland, PA
Mrs. Bobin
Donna Harn
Rose Onuska

Fonda-Fultonville Elementary School
Fonda, NY
Rita Garguilo*

Fountaindale Elementary School
Hagerstown, MD
Melanie Verliin*

Helen B Duffield Elementary School
Ronkonkoma, NY
J. Griesmeyer*
Ms. Maggio*
Ms. Mare*
AnneMarie Quillo*

Indian Lane Elementary School
Media, PA
Abby Burke*

Jacksonville Elementary School
Phoenix, MD
Mrs. Fink
Tara Harmeson
Ms. Ryan
Mary C. Vananzo*

Jeffrey Elementary School
Madison, CT
Jennifer Hall
Esther R. Magee
Pam Whalen

John L Edwards School
Hudson, NY
Deb VanDyke*

John T Waugh Elementary
School
Angola, NY
Kathy Dole*

Klein Elementary School
Erie, PA
Elizabeth Brown*

Lincoln Street School
Northborough, MA
Mrs. Caldicott
Mrs. Foely
Susan Grady
Mr. Olson
Catherine Simisky

Long Meadow Elementary
School
Middlebury, CT
Dawn G. Dinallo*

Meeting House Hill School
New Fairfield, CT
Pam Quist*

Memorial School
Bedford, NH
Courtney Hannah*

Milton Terrace South
Elementary School
Ballston Spa, NY
Vicki Savini*

Mystic Valley Regional Charter
School
Malden, MA
Arleen Burke
Judy Courtney
Ashley Morris*

New York Institute for Special
Education
Bronx, NY
Edward Flynn
Lillian M. Ludwig
Dr. Franklin D. Raddock*
Melissa Reed

Number 2 School
Inwood, NY
Michele Cohen
Kim Yochai

Our Lady of Hope School
Middle Village, NY
Martha Madri*
Ellie McAuley*
Michael McHugh

Our Lady of Mercy Regional
School
Cutchogue, NY
Alicia Hunt
Mrs. Wachtel
Jennifer Wagner

Penn-Kidder Campus
Albrightsville, PA
Howard Gregory*
Jill Klotz
Angelina O'Rourke*
Diane Reese*

Pine Tree Elementary School
Monroe, NY
Mrs. Brown
Mrs. Leach

Public School 114 Ryder
Elementary
Brooklyn, NY
Fran I. Cohen*
Elaine E. Rowe*

Public School 115
Alexander Humboldt
New York, NY
Carlos Estrada*

Public School 131
Brooklyn, NY
Anita Betances*

Public School 206
Joseph F Lamb
Brooklyn, NY
Mrs. Horn
Eryn Kaplan

Public School 232
The Walter Ward School
Howard Beach, NY
Christina Armenia
Mrs. Blum
Patricia Kander
Deborah Mayerson

Public School 40
Samuel Huntington
Jamaica, NY
Ms. Hicks
Mrs. Marc
Mrs. Ogunade-Mitchell
Ms. Quinones
Mrs. Rizzo

Sacred Heart School
North Quincy, MA
Margaret Hanna
Fran McGillicuddy*
Patricia McGowan
Carmela O'Connell
Cathy Santangelo*

Sarah Dyer Barnes School
Johnston, RI
Debbi Sgambato*

Shelter Rock Elementary School
Manhasset, NY
Patricia Bacchioni*
Charles Collyer
Pamela Lawrence
Joyce Rappaport
Steve Sirof
Mrs. Watts

Southold Elementary School
Southold, NY
Mrs. Andersen
Georgia Gabrielsen

St Agatha School
Brooklyn, NY
Rosemarie Paredes*

St Clement Mary Hofbauer School
Baltimore, MD
Christine Godlewski
Linda House*
Wendy Parker*

St Joan of Arc School
Hershey, PA
Frances E. Darcy*
Cynthia Miskinis

St Louis Elementary School
Lowell, MA
Erika Joyce*
Jayne King
Loretta Lowry*

St Madeleine Sophie School
Schenectady, NY
Deborah
    Flaherty-Kizer*

St Rose School
Newtown, CT
Bobbie Blizman
Mary Jo Bokuniewicz*
Rita Garrett
Cortni Kemlage*
Tamra Russo*
Jeanne Vitetta*
Laura Whitacre*

St Stephen's School
Grand Island, NY
Kristy Pasko
Daniela Schmidt*

Strodes Mills Middle School
Mc Veytown, PA
Mrs. K. Dixon
Lani Reese*

Tashua School
Trumbull, CT
Amy Congdon
Nancy Grosso*
Lisa Pope

The Burnham Elementary School
Bridgewater, CT
Lorinda DeSantis*

The Edgartown School
Edgartown, MA
Alicia Knight*
Cindy Smith*

The Tobin School
Natick, MA
Elisabeth Andersen
Rosalind Pelletier

Thoreau Elementary School
Concord, MA
Brad Bennett
Nancy Dillon
Susan Erickson
Merrie Najimy

West Branch School
Williamsport, PA
Sandra H. Elion*

Wyoming Area Catholic School
Exeter, PA
James Renfer*

Yeshiva Ketana of Long Island
Inwood, NY
  Susan Goldberg
  Mrs. Sussman

Language Arts Grant Recipients 2009-2010

After receiving a "Poetic Achievement Award" schools are encouraged to apply for a Creative Communication Language Arts Grant. The following is a list of schools who received a two hundred and fifty dollar grant for the 2009-2010 school year.

Arrowhead Union High School, Hartland, WI
Blessed Sacrament School, Seminole, FL
Booneville Jr High School, Booneville, AR
Buckhannon-Upshur Middle School, Buckhannon, WV
Campbell High School, Ewa Beach, HI
Chickahominy Middle School, Mechanicsville, VA
Clarkston Jr High School, Clarkston, MI
Covenant Life School, Gaithersburg, MD
CW Rice Middle School, Northumberland, PA
Eason Elementary School, Waukee, IA
East Elementary School, Kodiak, AK
Florence M Gaudineer Middle School, Springfield, NJ
Foxborough Regional Charter School, Foxborough, MA
Gideon High School, Gideon, MO
Holy Child Academy, Drexel Hill, PA
Home Choice Academy, Vancouver, WA
Jeff Davis Elementary School, Biloxi, MS
Lower Alloways Creek Elementary School, Salem, NJ
Maple Wood Elementary School, Somersworth, NH
Mary Walter Elementary School, Bealeton, VA
Mater Dei High School, Evansville, IN
Mercy High School, Farmington Hills, MI
Monroeville Elementary School, Monroeville, OH

Language Arts Grant Winners cont.

Nautilus Middle School, Miami Beach, FL
Our Lady Star of the Sea School, Grosse Pointe Woods, MI
Overton High School, Memphis, TN
Pond Road Middle School, Robbinsville, NJ
Providence Hall Charter School, Herriman, UT
Reuben Johnson Elementary School, McKinney, TX
Rivelon Elementary School, Orangeburg, SC
Rose Hill Elementary School, Omaha, NE
Runnels School, Baton Rouge, LA
Santa Fe Springs Christian School, Santa Fe Springs, CA
Serra Catholic High School, Mckeesport, PA
Shadowlawn Elementary School, Green Cove Springs, FL
Spectrum Elementary School, Gilbert, AZ
St Edmund Parish School, Oak Park, IL
St Joseph Institute for the Deaf, Chesterfield, MO
St Joseph Regional Jr High School, Manchester, NH
St Mary of Czestochowa School, Middletown, CT
St Monica Elementary School, Garfield Heights, OH
St Vincent De Paul Elementary School, Cape Girardeau, MO
Stevensville Middle School, Stevensville, MD
Tashua School, Trumbull, CT
The New York Institute for Special Education, Bronx, NY
The Selwyn School, Denton, TX
Tonganoxie Middle School, Tonganoxie, KS
Westside Academy, Prince George, BC
Willa Cather Elementary School, Omaha, NE
Willow Hill Elementary School, Traverse City, MI

Grades K-1-2-3
Top Ten Winners

List of Top Ten Winners for Grades K-3; listed alphabetically

Kevanna Babyak, Grade 2
Carlyle C Ring Elementary School, NY

Taylor Bond, Grade 3
Elmer Elson Elementary School, AB

Matthew Geurtsen, Grade 1
St Zachary Elementary School, IL

Evangeline Gilmer, Kindergarten
Mary Burgess Neal Elementary School, MD

Samantha Jabra, Grade 3
St Joseph School, NJ

Taryn Jackson, Grade 3
Midland Academy of Advanced and Creative Studies, MI

Alexandra Lorentzatos, Grade 3
Wilchester Elementary School, TX

Sydney May, Grade 3
C Hunter Ritchie Elementary School, VA

Bonnie Nguyen, Grade 3
Oak Park Elementary School, CA

Mackenzie Stewart, Grade 1
St Mark's Day School, TX

All Top Ten Poems can be read at www.poeticpower.com

Note: The Top Ten poems were finalized through an online voting system. Creative Communication's judges first picked out the top poems. These poems were then posted online. The final step involved thousands of students and teachers who registered as the online judges and voted for the Top Ten poems. We hope you enjoy these selections.

Lunch

Lunch, lunch —
It's the best part of the day!
You can talk to your friends,
and everyone!
You can't do that in class —
You have to do your work.
Lunch, lunch —
I love ya lunch!

Makayla Yelenak, Grade 1
Milton Terrace South Elementary School, NY

Gold

Gold is the color of a goldfish swimming in water.
Gold is the color of stars, Saturn, Venus and Mars.
Gold is the mother of the color yellow.
Gold is the color of the Sunlight going down.
Gold is the color of a sunset beaming.
Gold is the color of a shooting star flying.
Gold is the color of a gold robot gleaming.
Gold is the color of an artist painting with gold glitter.

Kyle Taylor, Grade 3
Colebrook Primary School, NY

Making the Earth Better

I would ask my friends to carpool
And put recyclable cans in bins at school.

In national parks there would be more rangers
To help animals that are endangered.

Instead of throwing away paper, recycle it.
No matter how much you recycle it helps each little bit.

Hannah D'Egidio, Grade 3
Fairview Elementary School, PA

Blue

Blue looks like my sister's eyes
And the sky above,
Blue sounds like the waves washing on the shore.
Blue tastes like blueberries.
Blue is David's winter coat.

Preston Kelly, Grade 2
St Anna School, MA

I Like to Add
I like to add
You end up with more
I like to add
It is so easy
I like to add
I put the numbers
All together
I like to add
Because it's fun!

Anthony Dilone, Grade 2
Public School 40 Samuel Huntington, NY

Come, Come Santa
Come, come Santa
Fill our house with toys
Slide down our chimney
Eat our yummy cookies
And spread the house with joy
Come, come Santa
Guide the deer here
Give us lots of toys
And spread Christmas cheer

Genesis Ramos, Grade 3
Public School 115 Alexander Humboldt, NY

Peaceful
Peaceful is pale pink.
It tastes like warm cocoa.
It smells like a baby after a bath.
It feels like a furry little puppy.
It sounds like a bird on a warm spring morning.
Peaceful is the first snow of winter.

Maddie Culina, Grade 3
Asa C. Adams School, ME

Summer Sounds
Splish, splash go the dolphins.
Whistle, whistle sing the birds.
Crunch, crunch goes the wood chips.
Buzzzzz went the bee,
As I licked my ice cream.

Brandon Stedry, Grade 1
Milton Terrace South Elementary School, NY

My Feelings
I have all kinds of feelings.
I feel afraid when there is a test.
I feel scared because I might not do well.
I feel proud when I get a good grade on a test.
I feel surprised when I pop a balloon.
I feel sad when my brother is in Mexico
And everyone is having fun without me.
I feel excited when I learn something new.
I feel happy when my mom gives me a hug.
I have all kinds of feeling inside of me.

Nancy Marmolejo, Grade 3
Public School 131, NY

When the Wind Blows
When the wind blows,
the trees sway.
When the birds fly south,
snow falling is near.
When bears sleep,
the squirrels hunt for nuts.
When the plants grow,
the plants' tender cries of joy for the growing sapling
to someday have the life of a mother.
When thunder clashes, hope God gets all 10 pins.

Olivia Morana, Grade 3
St Mary's Catholic Elementary School, VT

Alarm Clocks
Alarm clocks, alarm clocks,
Don't like them one bit.
Alarm clocks, alarm clocks,
give me a fit.
Alarm clocks, alarm clocks
Weigh more than a pound.
Alarm clocks, alarm clocks,
I don't want them around.
So next time I go
To the alarm clock store,
I'm bringing a hammer
To make alarm clocks no more!

Sam Schwartz, Grade 3
John Ward Elementary School, MA

Green

Green is blowing in the grass.
Green is a cool color.
Green is a color in the rainbow.
Green is a peaceful color.
Green smells like a lime.
Green tastes like a mint.
Green sounds like leaves blowing in a tree.
Green looks like a flower stem.
Green feels like a soft color.
Green makes me happy and calm.
Green is my favorite color.

Robert Lewis, Grade 3
Evergreen Elementary School, PA

Gray

Gray is the color of the clouds on a stormy day.
Gray is the color of a timber wolf rushing through the snow.
Gray is the color of a hurricane on the Weather Channel.
Gray is the color of Brett Favre's hair in 10 years.
Gray smells like dull cars in a garage.
Gray tastes like oysters in the ocean.
Gray sounds like metal scraping metal.
Gray looks like the color of a tornado on the ground.
Gray feels like metal on a train.
Gray makes me feel cold.
Gray is my favorite color!

Douglas Azzalina, Grade 3
Evergreen Elementary School, PA

My Bike

I like to ride my bike, I think it is fun.
I like to ride my bike, I go faster than when I run.

I would poke myself with a spike,
Just to ride my awesome bike.

If I had a choice to ride my bike or go to the pool,
I would choose my bike cause my bike is really cool.

As you can see I really like,
My super cool, really awesome, very fast bike.

Declan Watson, Grade 3
Ellicott Road Elementary School, NY

Mr. Goodbar

M eet the chocolate in him.
R ecipes are great in him.

G ood taste he has.
O n the front so much chocolate.
O n the back so much crunch.
D o people put double chocolate in him because I can taste it?
B ecause of the chocolate, number one.
A t the store he is there.
R ed and yellow wrapper.

John Joyce, Grade 3
Sacred Heart School, MA

My Best Friend

My best friend

My best friend is always there for me
My best friend is caring when someone is mean
My best friend is nice to others
My best friend is confident about others with a "you can do it" attitude
My best friend helps me when I'm hurt
My best friend always listens to me when I say things
My best friend Eric
My best friend

Brandon White, Grade 3
Sarah Dyer Barnes School, RI

Watermelon

W atermelon what a great treat.
A sweet and tender taste.
T he great taste makes you hungry.
E veryone in the world likes watermelon.
R ough skin is around the watermelon.
M elon is good, always
E veryone knows it's yummy.
L et's go get some melon!
O h my, the watermelon is so big, I hope I can finish!
N o, you don't know how good it is!

Marrilyn Tseng, Grade 3
Sacred Heart School, MA

My Aunt

My aunt is beautiful
She is nice and kind
I love my aunt
She takes care of me and is always by my side
She helps me with Math
She is smart
My aunt is kind
My aunt is amazing
She can do wonderful things

Kristina Romero, Grade 3
Public School 232 The Walter Ward School, NY

A True Friend

A true friend is always respectful
A true friend cheers me up when I'm down
A true friend always tells the truth
A true friend lets me call her anytime of the day
A true friend always listen to me when I talk
A true friend helps me when I'm hurt
A true friend doesn't talk behind my back
A true friend accepts me the way I am
A true friend like Amber

Shania Dennison, Grade 3
Sarah Dyer Barnes School, RI

Winter

Winter, winter is the time
It is Christmas time
Cold cold days all the time
the weather changes,
wear warm clothes
It is cold outside
Time for Christmas
Is when it is cold outside

Laquanna Outerbridge, Grade 2
Public School 40 Samuel Huntington, NY

Video Games

Video games rock.
Crash will be my favorite game.
I play X-box games.

John Mancini, Grade 2
Fonda-Fultonville Elementary School, NY

Thanksgiving

The leaves are falling
With lots of colors
It is almost Christmas
Lots of happiness and friends
Parents and good food
What a great holiday!

Jeremy Santos, Grade 3
Public School 115 Alexander Humboldt, NY

Happiness

Happiness is a rainbow of colors.
It tastes like never-ending glory.
It smells like pumpkin pie ready to be eaten.
It feels like you're on top of the world!
It sounds like a happy laugh.
Happiness looks like light.

Caelen Peterson, Grade 3
Asa C Adams School, ME

Monkey

M onkeys live in the rainforest.
O ver eight monkeys are pets.
N ice monkeys don't hurt people.
K ing monkeys tell other monkeys what to do.
E very monkey is scared of other animals.
Y ou will find that they eat leaves.

Juliet Golden, Grade 2
Long Meadow Elementary School, CT

Peaceful

Peaceful is bright sun yellow.
It tastes like rich vanilla ice cream.
It smells like cookies straight from the oven.
It feels like a horse's smooth coat.
It sounds like chickadees singing.
Peaceful is a rainbow of goodness.

Chana Wingard, Grade 3
Asa C Adams School, ME

Heart and Soul

My mom is the moon, and I am the stars.
My mom is a car, and I am the engine.
My mom is the cover, and I am the page.
My mom is my heart, and I am her soul.
Michael Sinclair, Grade 3
Public School 114 Ryder Elementary, NY

Flowers

Flowers come in the spring,
They leave in the fall.
They are so nice,
I love them all.
Hayden Taylor, Grade 3
Our Lady of Hope School, NY

Fall

F lowers going down
A ll different colored leaves
L eaves falling
L iving things hibernate
Isabela Placencia, Grade 1
St Agatha School, NY

What Am I?

I am blue.
I am rolling.
Why would I roll?
I am a ball!
Michaela Cosgriff, Grade 1
St. Rose School, CT

Family and Friends

As the dark clouds gather,
As the rain falls down,
I think of family and friends
Who lighten up my day.
Adelle Mitchell, Grade 3
Willow Creek Elementary School, PA

Love Is

Love is friends.
Love is fun.
Love is happy.
Love is feeling!
Carolanne Scinto, Grade 1
St Rose School, CT

Balloons

Pink
Balloons
Popping
Birthdays are fun!
Lily Charles, Grade 1
St Rose School, CT

Pucker Face

Lemon, lemon sweet and sour;
When I tasted you
I want to SCREAM!
Your oval shape looks like a football!
Justyce Moore, Grade 2
Public School 235 Lenox, NY

Spring

In the spring, the flowers blossom.
You can plant, so spring is awesome.
In the spring, I can run all day.
In the spring, it's fun to play.
Antonio Zgombic, Grade 3
Our Lady of Hope School, NY

Who Are You? Who Am I?

Who are you? Who am I?
I don't like you, but I do not know you.
How do I not know you?
I see you every day.
Jordan Smith, Grade 2
Wyoming Valley Montessori School, PA

Blankets

Blankets are cozy
Blankets are warm
Blankets are long

I love my blankets

People need them to be warm
People use them when they are sick
People need blankets when they are cold

I love my blankets

Blankets can be of different texture and color
Blankets feel and remind me of a favorite teddy bear.

I love my blankets

Mandy Lucero, Grade 3
Public School 131, NY

Summer

Whisper, whistle —
I hear the birds chirp.
Splish, splash —
I jump in the pool.
Buzzz, buzzz goes the bee —
I should hurry,
so it doesn't get ME!

Chloë Laudano, Grade 1
Milton Terrace South Elementary School, NY

My Chubby Cat

My
Chubby cat
Is so cute
She is really heavy
And hard to lift up
My puppy always chases her around
She really loves, loves, loves cat treats
She is chubby because she eats a lot
She likes to play with my other cute cat
I love her because she is so cute and chubby

Anneliese Probeck, Grade 2
Wyland Elementary School, PA

It's Life So Live It
When you think school stinks, it's life so live it.
When you don't have a good day, it's life so live it.
When you are sad and think everybody is against you, it's life so live it.
When you close your door and I knock and knock and knock, it's because I love you.
It's life so live it.

Symone Brooks, Grade 3
Brookewood School, MD

Mad
Mad is black.
It tastes like grapefruit.
It smells like a rotten egg.
It feels like a puffed up pufferfish.
It sounds like nails scratching a chalkboard.
Mad is an ogre smiling.

Isaiah McCarthy, Grade 3
Asa C Adams School, ME

Cookies, a Penguin's Tale
Once there was a penguin named Jacob. He and his friends ran a bakery
together. One day they ran out of dough for big cakes. So they made little cakes
instead. When they came out, they did not look like cakes at all. So he named
them cookies. Then he put the cookies on display. A lot of penguins bought them.
Every penguin in Ice Town loved the cookies. The bakery became so popular;
Jacob and his friends needed more help.

Sarah Cridland, Grade 3
Hope Lutheran Christian School, PA

The Snow
Snow falls at night
White, wet, and cold
Twirling around
To the ground

Jonathan Baird, Kindergarten
Mary Burgess Neal Elementary School, MD

Stars
Stars glow in the night.
Stars are pretty in the night.
Stars are fun to see.

Marisa Mycek, Grade 2
Fonda-Fultonville Elementary School, NY

Poems
About anything
Beautiful masterpieces
Think outside the box!
Mary Balagna, Grade 3
Sacred Heart School, CT

Homework
fun to start in school
spelling, reading and language
math done in my room
Nicole Lawton, Grade 3
Sacred Heart School, CT

Snoopy
Charlie Brown's dog friend
funny and energetic
solves any problem
Grace Doyle, Grade 3
Sacred Heart School, CT

Friends
A good friend will
treat you the way you'd like
with joy, no problems
Mundia Njoroge, Grade 3
Sacred Heart School, MA

Tennis
playing with my friends
two people opposite sides
enjoying the court
Jack Adille, Grade 3
Sacred Heart School, CT

Books
Keeping me busy
Perfect to hold in backpacks
Great graphics added
Noah Adam Hayes, Grade 3
Sacred Heart School, CT

Reading
Expressing my voice
Many words change book meanings
A great way to learn
Grace Murphy, Grade 3
Sacred Heart School, CT

The Calm River
The river is deep.
I would like to swim in it.
The river is fast.
Eric Billard, Grade 3
Sacred Heart School, MA

A River
The river streams close.
The river shines in the night.
The river is nice.
Ashley Medeiros, Grade 3
Sacred Heart School, MA

World
In the world there are…
trees, flowers and things special.
And it is all a dream.
Aine Lavin, Grade 3
Sacred Heart School, MA

Winter
Winter is icy.
You can ski on the cold snow.
Animals sleep now.
Marvin Chan, Grade 2
The Fourth Presbyterian School, MD

The Dog Likes the River
There is a river,
The dog is swimming slowly
The river is calm.
Fiona Duggan, Grade 3
Sacred Heart School, MA

Books

Books are the best.
They can help you on a test.

You can read a lot.
Just make sure you don't read in the parking lot.

You can get them anywhere.
Just check in the library over there.

There are many stories in a book.
All you have to do is look.

Alyssa Cole, Grade 3
Ellicott Road Elementary School, NY

My Heart Beat

Bump, bump! goes a heart as it pumps
through the night
Bump bumpety bump goes a heart as you
play in the morning!
Pump pumpity as you go to sleep
Knock knock as people bang on the door
You're very scared
PUMP! PUMP! BUMP! your heart beats fast
as blood flows through your heart
Bump! Bump! your heart is resting again
As I sleep through the night

Madison Hickok, Grade 2
Mayfield Elementary School, NY

Jumping Elephants

One day an elephant jumped into the air
and when he got up the wind swiftly blew away his hair

One day an elephant wanted to go up up up looking like a clown
and when he got up he sank right down

One day an elephant was attached to a fly
he tried but it didn't work to go up into the sky

One day an elephant jumped up into a cloud
and when he got up he was looking very proud

Sophia Griffin, Grade 1
E Ethel Little School, MA

The Sweet Air

The sun is shining on the flowers and on my back
The butterflies are coming out and flying everywhere
I smell the fresh sweet air
I'm playing with my friends
Bees are singing
Branches are shaking
Leaves are whispering
The sun is shining on my back

Gionna Ianne, Grade 2
Helen B Duffield Elementary School, NY

The American Flag

Our flag has changed over
Hundreds of years.
Through lots of work
And lots of tears.
It first had thirteen stars
For the thirteen colonies,
It now has fifty stars
For all fifty States.

Ethan Wayman, Grade 2
Commonwealth Connections Academy, PA

Spring Flower

Snap! Snap! go the flowers as the children pick them
Run, run go the children
The other flowers grew and were picked
All but one
Seasons past but that flower kept
Growing
Until it was six feet tall
Amazing, enormous and stupendous

Cassie Bruse, Grade 2
Mayfield Elementary School, NY

Earth Day

I think it's helpful to pick up garbage
Because littering is a mean thing to do

On Earth Day we remember to treat the world nice
Every day is Earth Day for birds, cats and mice

Bridget Clarry, Grade 1
Our Lady of Mercy Regional School, NY

Spring

S hiny sunshine
P laying on the playground
R eally wet rain
I cy cold ice cream
N ice flowers
G rowing grass

Grace Mina Dugan, Grade 1
Milton Terrace South Elementary School, NY

Energetic

Energetic is bright orange.
It tastes like a bottle of fresh, cold water.
It smells like a daisy picked from the garden.
It's squishy like a tennis ball.
It sounds like someone dribbling a basketball.
Energetic is a fun summer day.

Audrey Smith, Grade 3
Asa C Adams School, ME

Spring Is…

Spring is green and brown like grass and dirt around the pond.
It tastes like strawberry popsicles that Dad brings on fishing trips.
It smells like fishy water.
Spring reminds me of family members fishing together,
And sounds like fish splashing in the water.
Spring feels like the tug of the fishing rod.

Jacob Ruffalo, Grade 2
Curtisville Primary Center, PA

Halloween

Monsters, ghouls, and witches flying
Kids in costumes
And lots of candy too!
Come Halloween you will see me on a broom!

Ashley Jimenez, Grade 3
Public School 115 Alexander Humboldt, NY

The Presidents

Jefferson was nice.
Roosevelt had polio.
Washington was great.

Jackson Thompson, Grade 2
Fonda-Fultonville Elementary School, NY

Fun at the Beach
The beach the beach is so much fun
I play and laugh and run, run, run

A bucket, some water, and sand will do
To make the perfect castle for me and you

A collection of shells is what I need
To make my castle perfect indeed

The beach the beach is so much fun
I love to play in the sun
Alyssa Arocho, Grade 3
Public School 2 Alfred Zimberg, NY

Babies
babies cry
babies laugh
so cute
arms like soft blankets
smooth round heads
ten tiny fingers
ten tiny toes
skin as soft as silk
mouth with no teeth
diapers as stinky as can be
time for a change!
Alessandra Zaffina, Grade 2
Tashua School, CT

Together
'Tis the day,
I am awake.
I am lonely.
My heart aches for you.
How our destiny,
To be together,
May never happen.
But as the sun rises,
My heart lifts up a bit.
If the sun can shine,
We can be together still.
Catelen Wu, Grade 3
Public School 206 Joseph F Lamb, NY

School
School is fun
with all the teachers
so nice and kind
They help us learn
and read and write
all the best teachers
from K to 5
the nicest teachers
in the world
hooray hooray
no one can
be nicer
200 days
of school
calendar math
nothing can
be funner
I like school a lot
don't you
I love school!
School!
Jackson Lapham, Grade 2
Tashua School, CT

The Meow
My cat is meowing.
Meow Meow
She is annoying me.
Meow Meow
I want her to stop.
Meow Meow
I don't want to feed her.
Meow Meow
Or she will be kicked out of the house
Meow Meow
I am on the couch watching TV.
Meow Meow
I'll just go over and feed her.
Meow Meow
Bark!
Now she stops!
Brookelyn Tallman, Grade 3
Colebrook Primary School, NY

Recess Fun
Recess, Recess,
the FUN I love —
We swing on the swings,
and slide on the slide.
You better make sure —
your shoes are tied!

Brennan Halbohm, Grade 1
Milton Terrace South Elementary School, NY

Summertime
Summer is the smell of cherry snow cones.
Summer is the touch of sand.
Summer is seeing the sun.
Summer is tasting cold lemonade.
Summer is hearing seagulls.
Summer makes me happy!

Erica Palmieri, Grade 1
St. Rose School, CT

Colors of the Rainbow
Red is a fire truck speeding down the lane.
Orange is a big beehive with bees in it.
Yellow is a banana ready to be eaten.
Green is tall grass being cut.
Blue is the sky with thousands of clouds.
Purple is my pencil that I'm writing with right now!

Dylan McDermott, Grade 1
St. Rose School, CT

Fall
In the fall, I see scary, Halloween costumes walking up my street.
In the fall, I feel bumpy, orange pumpkins sitting in the pumpkin patch.
In the fall, I taste steamy, hot chocolate warming me up.
In the fall, I smell warm, apple pie baking in the oven.
In the fall, I hear spooky, weird Halloween music playing on my neighbor's porch.
In the fall, I don't hear wild, noisy kids splashing in a pool.

Camryn Mincemoyer, Grade 3
Watsontown Elementary School, PA

Lots of Things
Where the fern grows
Spring goes by quickly, then summer too.
Leaves grow on the trees
Snow is falling
I am so sad.
We are at school
I see spring coming again
I can't wait for summer.
I see the summer.
I see the farm babies are here.
Spring's here, spring's here!
There is a lot to do.

Caroline Cilento, Grade 2
Public School 232 The Walter Ward School, NY

A Forever Friend
A forever friend
Someone who is there for you when you're devastated or gloomy
Someone who shares in your excitement
Someone you can tell your deepest secrets to,
Even the ones they don't want to hear
Someone who will help you when you need a helping hand
Someone who will stand up for you
Someone who will never forget you
Someone who always tells the truth
Someone who shares their toys with you,
Even the fragile ones
A forever friend

Taylor Streeter, Grade 3
Sarah Dyer Barnes School, RI

One Day I Found America
One day I found America
It was one good day for me
But then I felt blue then green
Because there were Indians and pilgrims and black beards too
They told me to go
But I didn't know what to do
So I got in my boat and rowed away
But in my head I thought
America is the home for me

Eric He, Grade 3
Mystic Valley Regional Charter School, MA

Summer

Hello, outdoor family barbeques,
Good-bye to old snowshoes and winter coats,
Hello to fire pits, toasting marshmallows, and eating s'mores,
Good-bye to mountains of snow at the end of my driveway,
Hello, outdoor swimming pools,
Good-bye, TV and sitting inside,
Hello to kite flying at the beach,
And good-bye to sledding down hills!

David Gardiner, Grade 2
St Anna School, MA

Music

Music makes me figure out all the unfigured
Music makes me understand what's happening in life
How I wonder how this happens
But it does
Music talks to me in a language only I can understand
Like I'm from another plant just here to make me shine
How I wonder how this happens
But it does.

Julia Rosen, Grade 3
Park Avenue Elementary School, NY

If the Rain Was Silent

If the rain was silent, would the sun make noise?
If people were quiet, would the whisper have a voice?
If not, would the rain start talking?
If so, would the sun keep walking?
If the world were different, would anything be the same?
Please answer my questions, this is not a game.
Now let me tell you something, this is very confused.
If I were you, I'd say brain work is used.

Natalie Perron, Grade 3
St. Paul's Lutheran School, MD

School

School is the place to learn
You have to go 5 days a week.

Schools are where you get an education.
Schools are where you become your own person.

Tanjim Haque, Grade 3
Public School 40 Samuel Huntington, NY

Rocks/Soldiers

Rocks and soldiers. Soldiers and rocks.
That's what I need to succeed.
Toy soldiers are fun, I make them compete.
Rocks are hard, I found most on the street.
They both can be colorful and cool.
Rocks and soldiers rule!!!

Brian Kenny, Grade 3
St Barnabas Elementary School, NY

Love

Love is in the air —
it's like a butterfly...
I like to think of it,
just fluttering by!
Love is easy to see —
'cause it's in you, and me!

Isabella Todd, Grade 1
Milton Terrace South Elementary School, NY

My Mom

My mom is as good as
the sun shining on her
all day she is nice to me
she is a good mom
she loves me so much
she would like to hug me

Brandon Lopez, Grade 2
Public School 232 The Walter Ward School, NY

Rainbow Colors

Red is fire that is burning high.
Orange is the sun that shines in the sky.
Yellow is the dandelions that come every spring.
Green is the grass that grows so tall.
Blue is the sky that decorates the world.
Purple is the glasses my teacher wears.

Rebecca Walsh, Grade 1
St Rose School, CT

Shapes

There are different kinds of shapes
You see them wherever you go
Like triangles, squares, circles, rectangles, pentagon, octagon, a cube,
And other shapes.

When you eat a pizza, you see a triangle.
A square and cube are like a box.
I circle is round like a ball.
A rectangle is like a long door.
A pentagon is like a house.
An octagon is like a stop sign.
A cone is like the shape of an ice cream cone.
An egg has an oval shape.

You see that they all have different sides.
A triangle has 3 sides, but a square has 4 sides.
A pentagon has 5 sides and a hexagon has 6 sides or angles
But an octagon has 8 sides.
There are different shapes and you can see them everywhere.
Just look around and you will find many shapes.

Derek Chen, Grade 3
Public School 131, NY

Learning in Third Grade

Learning in third grade
Is actually really fun!
It is cool just like second and first
I am learning cool stuff like one plus a ton!
Learning in third grade
Could be really tough
But it does not matter
Because I am learning cool stuff!
If you are in second grade
You will be lucky next year
Do you want to learn about Mexico, Japan?
Maybe in art you will make a Japanese fan?
You will love 3rd grade.
I am telling you now,
It's really fun.
If you don't believe me,
You will find out how.

Caroline Mondiello, Grade 3
Shelter Rock Elementary School, NY

Valentine's Day

Love-filled holiday
It brings my family love.
Long and heart shaped day
Waking me up to see my
Joy-filled awesome family.
Evan Hattenburg, Grade 3
Heron Pond Elementary School, NH

Birds

They tweet and twerp and twirl in the air
They treat their babies with lots of care
Most eggs hatch in spring
All birds are wonderful things
Gabriella Permatteo, Grade 3
Lincoln Street School, MA

Alvin and the Chipmunks

Alvin and the Chipmunks rock
They did a guitar solo
Alvin took off his shirt
The girls went crazy!
Nick Cornay, Grade 3
Milton Fuller Roberts School, MA

Airplane

Flying airplanes in the sky
Making noises as it zooms by
Taking you places day and night
How I love a good flight
Macey Festa, Grade 2
Klein Elementary School, PA

Love

Roses are red violets are blue
When I see you
I think to myself
How much I love you!
Arielle Terranova, Grade 2
Milton Fuller Roberts School, MA

Earth

Earth spins round while we play.
It spins while we peacefully sleep.
Earth never stops spinning.
Thank you earth for all you've done.
Chris Bader, Grade 3
Jeffrey Elementary School, CT

Balloon

Big and bright for me to hold,
At a park or carnival.
Bright colors soaring through the sky,
Like a bird.
Alexa Molinelli, Grade 2
Helen B Duffield Elementary School, NY

Stormy Day

Rain falling
Lighting struck
Giant waves
Struggling outside
Emily Young, Grade 2
Helen B Duffield Elementary School, NY

A Cat

Sometimes crazy
They play with people a lot
They're always happy with you
Smokey!
Jacob Lombardo, Grade 3
Clinton Street Elementary School, NY

Johnny Brown

I know a guy named Johnny Brown
Every day he goes to Brown Town
He always buys the big fat pies
When he goes home he's oversize
Matthew Mosbacher, Grade 2
Klein Elementary School, PA

I Really Want One

I really want one!
Furry and cute
but it might
eat a boot.

I really want one!
If it catches
a stick
it learned a trick.

It can find its way
in the fog.
It's
a dog!
Declan Debold, Grade 2
Pine Tree Elementary School, NY

Spring

Flowers blooming everywhere,
People playing here and there
Buzzing bees flying in the sky
Bringing pollen to flowers
Sun shining in my eyes,
Rain falling from the sky.
Birds come back from the south,
Saying hello instead of goodbye.
The big old tree in my backyard,
Grows new leaves and branches.
The seed I planted grows roots,
And there is no doubt it will sprout.
Summer's coming so I say goodbye,
To spring.
Richard Lee, Grade 3
Shelter Rock Elementary School, NY

Family

Family
Kind, fun
Playing, helping, laughing
Having so much fun
Relatives
Emma Eggleston, Grade 3
Willow Creek Elementary School, PA

A Flower

Green and colorful
Short and thin

When the sun shines I smile
I am happy in the spring

My arms and body dance
When the wind blows

I wear a hat on my head
That sometimes makes people sneeze

Bees like to sit on me
For I am
A flower
Jacqui Clair, Grade 3
Indian Lane Elementary School, PA

Ode to a Poem

A poem can be sad
A poem can be glad
They usually rhyme
But not all of the time

They might use personification
And help your education
If you want to see every style
It would take you a while

My poem is about poems
Because I want you to know 'em
I like to write 'em
I hope you like 'em
Taylor Sorensen, Grade 3
Mary C Howse Elementary School, PA

Flowers

Colorful, pretty
Planting, watering, growing
Coming in the sunlight
Spring
Madison Pazareskis, Grade 3
Lincoln Street School, MA

Nature
Rain comes, then stops
Chirping birds
Joyful nature springs alive.
Charlie Fairfax, Grade 1
Dartmouth Early Learning Center, MA

Wolves
Strong, fast, and deadly
Together, intelligent
Graceful, beautiful
Ben Cohen, Grade 3
Meadow Drive School, NY

Deer
Fast runners — quick — fat
Deer always fight other deer
Deer are animals.
Cody Byrne, Grade 3
Helderberg Christian School, NY

Animals
Fuzzy, cuddly, cute.
Animals are very kind,
Playing in the woods.
Abigail Knowles, Grade 3
Helderberg Christian School, NY

My Mom
My mom is pretty.
My mom is kind and helpful.
I love my mom so much.
Melody Jean Wray, Grade 3
Helderberg Christian School, NY

Kittens
Cute, soft and loving,
Kittens always crawl in balls.
Kittens are cuddly.
Taylor Knowles, Grade 3
Helderberg Christian School, NY

Glue Ball
Glue ball.
First gooey
Then dry.
Bouncy.
Clack.
Clack.
Clickady click.
Click.
It hits the ground.
It snaps in half.
Michael Lancia, Grade 2
Tashua School, CT

105 Cats
Black, white,
up all night
Yellow, brown,
out of town
CRASH! SMASH!
Oh no more!
The lamp just crashed
to
the
floor!
Maile Latham, Grade 2
Primrose School, NY

Doll
Oh little doll,
Pretty like a china doll,
Little eyes staring at me,
Cute little mouth smiling,
Long, black hair
With a red bow,
People on her shirt
Dancing in the night,
Small like my sister,
Loves the color red
Damiya Coleman, Grade 2
John L Edwards School, NY

The Moon

As I look into the night sky
I see something round, shiny,
white and bright,
like a ball rolling through the sky,
leading me everywhere,
shining like a lamp
guiding me like a friend
who knows the way
Sometimes full, sometimes half
or crescent
but always there.

Evangeline Gilmer, Kindergarten
Mary Burgess Neal Elementary School, MD

Spring

In spring it rains,
It rains in the lanes.

In spring people plant flower,
There is a flower in the tower.

In spring there are bugs,
I saw a bug in a mug.

Spring is cold,
I saw a piece of gold.

Matthew Weibel, Grade 3
Susquehanna Community Elementary School, PA

Orange

Orange is sweet and juicy the juiciest ever!!!
Orange is a football speeding through the air for a touchdown.
Orange is my favorite color which makes me feel perfect.
Orange is a great color to have inside you.
Orange smells like orange juice pouring down a waterfall.
Orange tastes like the richest oranges in the world.
Orange sounds like the wind blowing on my face.
Orange looks like a basketball going for a swish three pointer.
Orange feels like a football caught in the end zone.
Orange makes me feel like I will have the best day in the UNIVERSE!!!!!

David J. Stuart, Grade 3
Evergreen Elementary School, PA

I Think About You All the Time

I think about you all the time
Wish you could be here with me
Days are goin' longer now

Can you come set me free?
When you used to hold my hand
And tell me it will be OK

I'll hold on to my feelings
'Til I'm home with you again.

Days turn to weeks
Weeks turn to months
I miss you more and more
I miss you more and more
Mommy, I love you.

Adam Smith, Grade 3
New York Institute for Special Education, NY

Music

Music, music —
I do it at school.
Music, music —
I'm good at it too!
I sing! Sing! Sing!
I am good, and I LOVE it!
Just…sing!

Joseph Poirier, Grade 1
Milton Terrace South Elementary School, NY

Green

Green is a chalk board filled with chalk,
Green is the aura of a filthy sock.
Green is the towering tree,
Green is the nature around me.
Green is the leaves changing color as autumn rains in,
Green is the frog who puts on a shy grin.
Green is the seasons summer and spring,
Green is the color of the little girl's ring.
Green is the freshly made tea,
Green is the ocean, looking right back at me.

Téa Baum, Grade 3
Zervas Elementary School, MA

Shyness

Shyness is a dark, dark red
It tastes like cotton candy stuck in your mouth
It smells like food burning in your kitchen
It reminds me of so many secrets
I hear silent people
Shyness feels like butterflies in your stomach

Elyssa Hulse, Grade 2
Klein Elementary School, PA

Horses

H eartful creatures roaming about
O vercoming their fears without any doubt
R iding the range
S oaring about with
E vergreen grasses and
S oul hearted with you on their back

Lauren Nahrgang, Grade 3
Willow Creek Elementary School, PA

Friend

F riends stick together
R olling in the grass is fun with my friend
I nterested in gymnastics
E ating ice cream
N to bake with
D o pranks on each other

Madison Markelon, Grade 2
Long Meadow Elementary School, CT

Winter

Making snowmen at my house.
Skating at the rink and drinking hot chocolate by the fire.
Playing with my brother in the snow.
Cuddling with my grandpa when he reads me a story.
Petting my grandma's dog watching the snow fall.
Winter is fun!

Ranee Danker, Grade 1
All Saints Catholic Academy, NY

Summer
It is summer, yes it is.
It comes around once a year.
Summer is fun!
Ryan Yager, Grade 2
Helen B Duffield Elementary School, NY

The Jungle
Lots of animals.
A good place for animals.
Snakes hanging from trees.
Michael DeRienzo, Grade 2
Long Meadow Elementary School, CT

Dogs
Dogs are very cute.
Dogs sometimes bite bad people.
Dogs could be playful.
Joshua Joseph, Grade 2
Long Meadow Elementary School, CT

Leaves
Leaves float in the breeze,
after they fall off the trees.
They land so softly.
Shreya Balaji, Grade 2
Cornerstone Academy, MA

Squirrels
They collect acorns,
to store them for the winter.
They climb many trees.
John Houley, Grade 2
Cornerstone Academy, MA

Snow
Snow is white and cold.
You can play in snow and sled.
You can play in snow.
Ryan Furr, Grade 2
Long Meadow Elementary School, CT

Daisies
Daisies bloom in spring
Fields are very colorful
They sway in the breeze.
Vasant Sundaresan, Grade 2
Cornerstone Academy, MA

Blue Jays
They are colorful,
a beautiful shade of blue,
flying gracefully.
Alex Cordova, Grade 3
Cornerstone Academy, MA

Roses
They are very red,
swaying gently in the breeze.
They are pretty too.
Nidhi Ramesh, Grade 2
Cornerstone Academy, MA

Dogs
Some dogs are very big.
Dogs can live in a doghouse.
Some dogs have rabies.
Dylan Rivers, Grade 2
Long Meadow Elementary School, CT

Buds
Quietly on trees,
Buds will turn into flowers.
Flowers are so cool!
Andrew Wickremeratne, Grade 2
Cornerstone Academy, MA

Snow
You can make snow balls
You can play in a snow fort
You can drink hot tea
Henry Mescavage, Grade 2
Long Meadow Elementary School, CT

Puffle

Fluffy, floating, furry hair balls
Float for fun in the wide, black, beautiful galaxy.
Sailing the razor-blue sea.
Scuba diving the deep, dangerous ocean.
Doing a jig in the splashing rain.
But always remember...
That at last they peacefully, always rest.

Aden Clark, Grade 2
Carlyle C Ring Elementary School, NY

Outside Music

I am taking all the sounds from nature and turning it into music.
The wind is blowing,
The water is flowing.
Acorns,
Apples,
Everything is falling.
Everything is chirping and roaring!

Dean Truesdell, Grade 1
Winchester Elementary School, NH

Flowers

Flowers are growing up and leaves are growing too.
The roots are sprouting on the flowers that are just in.
Sprouting into a flower.
The wind is blowing but everything else is silent.
The flowers that are halfway grown are done growing.
The other flowers were halfway done.
Now they were done fast because of the shade and the sun!

Sierra Hines, Grade 1
Wyoming Valley Montessori School, PA

God Bless the USA

I am from wave
I am from the African jungle
I am from the star bright as the light from heaven
I am from the moon shy like the golden angel.
I am from the sun bright like my mom.
I am from the Ziegler School.
That is who I am and I am proud.

Mohammed Kesselly, Grade 3
William Ziegler Elementary School, PA

Friends

You go through good times,
bad times,
great times,
worse times,
perfect times,
the best times,
the worst times,
the normal times,
No matter what you will always have friends,
to help make your times!
Just remember the times...
and you'll be fine!
You help them they help you.
You can even make more!
Some people think that friends are nothing...
but they are wrong!
The nicer you are,
the more you have!
All you need to live is friends!

Tyler Edwards, Grade 3
The Edgartown School, MA

2010 Hockey Olympics

The Olympics are so fun,
The USA almost won.

Watching Crosby score,
Makes my head sore.

Kane is sad,
But they never played bad.

Ryan Miller got a silver medal,
They did not win the gold so they had to settle.

Canada won the game,
But USA will never be the same.

Maybe USA will do even better in four years!

Chandler Kujawa, Grade 3
Ellicott Road Elementary School, NY

Snow Fun

Snow is like a
Winter music
Fluttering a song.

Snowballs
Are fun to make
Every child can
Make one.

It's perfect winter fun
So much to do in the snow.

Snow is a wonderful winter prize.

Zachariah Campbell, Grade 3
Public School 40 Samuel Huntington, NY

Spring Is Here

Spring is coming
the sun is out
kids are playing in the park
Buds blossom
birds are chirping
flowers grow
kids want ice cream
parents are hot
everybody goes outside
but they get too hot
so they take a ride
and open their window
and get some fresh air.

Taylor Rosenblatt, Grade 2
Public School 232 The Walter Ward School, NY

Stars

Stars are big and bright
Stars glitter in the moonlight
Stars are hot and clear
Stars make lots of deer look up
Stars are far away
Stars appear at the end of the day
Stars are one of the mysteries in the universe

Brahm VanAntwerp, Grade 3
Lincoln Street School, MA

The Great Fireworks

I went to see the fireworks at the public park.
Then I heard the fireworks.

BOOM! CRASH! BEEP!

I screamed with surprise
because I didn't realize
fireworks were so cool.

Then the mayor started to speak
but then he just said, "SQUEAK!"
The fireworks started up again.

OOH! AHH! OOH! AHH!

We packed up and started home.
The cars went BEEP!
So I started counting sheep
and soon I was fast asleep.

SNOOOOOZE!

Jennifer Tillman, Grade 3
Emmanuel Baptist Christian Academy, PA

I Have One Teddy

I have one teddy
That is black
And two hats
Orange and blue
I have three apples
Red, yellow, green
And four bats
Wooden, silver,
brown and fat
I have five toys
And six shiny buttons
I see seven boys
They have eight pets
I lost nine shoes
I lost one
Or else I'd have ten.

R.G. Woodwens, Grade 2
Public School 40 Samuel Huntington, NY

The Kitten and the Pug
The puppy pug and the cute kitten
Fought under the table.
Crash! Boom! Thump! Meow! Woof!
They made one last leap
And fell right asleep.
Caitlin Warne, Grade 3
New Freedom Christian School, PA

I Love to Play
I love to play
But I don't like to put my toys away.
I don't care what my mother will say!
My toys are here to stay
But I think I'll put them away.
Wendy Castrejon, Grade 2
Public School 1 The Bergen School, NY

My Special Collection
B eautiful to wear
E asy to sew, glue, and string
A nywhere they are good to wear and go
D ifferent colors are red, white, blue
S imply beautiful
Arianna Verapen, Grade 3
St Barnabas Elementary School, NY

It's Hard to Let Your Mind Free
I'm stuck,
my mind is on vacation,
I don't know what to do,
I should have stayed home today,
and said I have the flu.
Will Lehmann, Grade 3
Thoreau Elementary School, MA

My Fish Lea
She swims
and squirms.
She's Lea.
I love my fish Lea.
She's orange.
Alexis French, Grade 2
Fountaindale Elementary School, MD

Winter Days
Waking up to clouds and rain
Nothing is ever too white or too plain
Snowball fights oh so fun
Building snowmen 'til day is done
Weather that is way too cold
Winter jackets almost sold
Animal tracks that fill our yard
Decorating our holiday card
Snowflakes falling eight by eight
Huge snowstorms that make us late
Sitting inside what a bore
Winter could you stay some more!
Zoe Spitz, Grade 3
Zervas Elementary School, MA

All About Me
I am from my laptop.
I am from my red roses.
I am from my waterbed.
I am from my PSP game.
I am from Xbox 360.
I am from my Mariah Carey.
I am from my WII game.
I am from New Jersey.
I am from my mom and my dad.
I am from my friends.
I am from my teacher.
I am from everybody.
Kyla McLaughlin, Grade 3
William Ziegler Elementary School, PA

The Song of the Bird
The song of the bird
flows like the seas.
Through mountains and hills
and bushes and trees.

So fine and nice.
So great and good.
It's stuck in my head
from morning till bed.
Katherine Burton, Grade 3
Flower Hill School, NY

Seaweed
Swaying at the ocean floor,
All different shades of green.
Fish like to swim about,
Diving in and out.
Seaweed, seaweed, seaweed.

Light green, dark green, brown,
Twisting twirling everywhere,
Round, fat, and tall.
Water waving round and round.
Seaweed, seaweed, seaweed.
Hannah Rose Mikol, Grade 2
Memorial School, NH

Clear
Clear is the vase holding my flower
Clear is the contact in your eyes
Clear is the wind in my hair
Clear is the window on my house
Clear smells like the salt in the sea
Clear tastes like water from the sink
Clear sounds like an ear of corn
Clear looks like plastic
Clear feels like soap in my hand
Clear makes me happy in every way
Clear is the end of my poem
Roland Delage Jr., Grade 3
Lincoln Street School, MA

I Love You a Lot
Sweetarts and candy
I love you a lot!
I'll eat you in spring, when it's real hot!
Daisies and flowers
I love you a lot!
I'll smell you in spring, when it's real hot!
Ocean and sand
I love you a lot!
I'll swim in you and play,
When it turns to spring day!
Hooray!
Mackenzie Condon, Grade 3
The Edgartown School, MA

My Little Brother
My little brother's always fun.
My little brother likes to run.
He likes to play
All the day.
He likes Bob the Builder.
He's my favorite little brother.
Mason Dale, Grade 3
John T Waugh Elementary School, NY

The Red Quilt
A sparkly, red quilt
Lying on the road
Sparkling in the moonlight
Found by a little boy
Reminding him of his mother
And her quilt
Dodge May Doyle, Grade 2
John L Edwards School, NY

Snow
white as the moon
cold as ice cream
soft as a cuddly friend
deep as the day
big as the night
such a beautiful sight
Riley Comparetto, Grade 2
Primrose School, NY

Fairies
Fairies
Are like sunbeams
Dancing
Through the air.
Tessa DeSpagna, Grade 1
St. Rose School, CT

Summertime
Like to pick flowers
Play lots of games with my friends
Like to go swimming
Derek Maringa, Grade 1
St Louis Elementary School, MA

Bubbles

Bubbles
Moving across the light blue sky
Swish — swish!
Pop — pop!
Bubbles like balloons,
They pop when you touch them with something
Oh — no!
Pop — pop!
That's the end of the bubbles and this poem.

Gwenevere Healey, Grade 2
Tashua School, CT

My True Friend Jared

My true friend Jared listens to me
My true friend Jared respects me
My true friend Jared doesn't judge me
My true friend Jared accepts me for who I am
My true friend Jared shares with me
My true friend Jared is someone I can call any time
My true friend Jared helps me when I fall
My true friend Jared tells me the truth
If you were me you would see why he's my best friend

Eric Messier, Grade 3
Sarah Dyer Barnes School, RI

A Piece of Chalk

Chalk is used every day.
It starts out very long.
Each time it is used to write, part of it goes away.
It gets smaller and smaller.
Today my piece of chalk is gone,
but I take another that is taller.

Olivia Anne Sudol, Grade 3
Our Lady of Hope School, NY

Recess

Recess is fun —
Playing games,
Running,
Jumping…
Recess IS fun!

Charles Walsh, Grade 1
Milton Terrace South Elementary School, NY

Blue Jay
Blue and small
Happy and hyper

During spring and summer
I sing opera from the top of a skinny branch

As I get closer and closer to earth
I look for people outside
I dance down to say hi to them

During the winter
I travel south for vacation

For I am...
A blue jay

Bobby Hoffman, Grade 3
Indian Lane Elementary School, PA

Spring
It is spring
flowers growing
kids are yelling in the park
people are passing by
kids are playing
people are talking loud
the ice cream truck is making music
people are playing kick ball in the park
kids are sliding down the slide
people are riding their bike in the bike lane
I hear kids screaming in the park.
People are leaving the park and going home to eat dinner
Trees grow from the ground
people plant flowers in their garden and they smell so beautiful
Spring is beautiful

Nicholas Nocera, Grade 2
Public School 232 The Walter Ward School, NY

Balls
Balls go up balls go down balls go to side to side balls go over your head
balls go over the world balls go over your glasses balls go over your arm
balls go over your leg balls go over everyone.

Patryk Wojcik, Grade 2
Public School 69, NY

Day and Night
Day
Sunny, warm
Playing, jumping, writing
Clouds, blue sky, moon, stars
Hiding, sleeping, dreaming
Dark, cold
Night
Tylanie Benton, Grade 3
Brant Elementary School, NY

Snowman
S nowy night outside.
N obody in sight.
O n the ground the snowman shivers.
W ow — so much snow!
M an, it's like a winter wonderland!
A snowman is waving its hand.
N ow that is amazing.
Nate Stone, Grade 2
DeMello Elementary School, MA

The Ocean
Splish splash
The ocean is mad
Get out of my water
Stop stealing all my fish
Now!
Get out before you wipe me out!
Alex Petion, Grade 2
Buckley Country Day School, NY

My Cat
A colorful puff ball
laying in the sun
her ears the softest
Velvet, when she
walks up the stairs
plunk! plunk!
I love my cat.
Peggy Mothershed, Grade 2
Fountaindale Elementary School, MD

Sun
The Sun
Is
Deep, deep
In the sky
Lighting
Up the world
In the morning
Joshua Lassin, Grade 1
Buckley Country Day School, NY

Winter
I'm gently falling to the ground
I'm squished by feet.
I sink in the snow
I make it wet
The clouds make me fall
I melt when warm
But will come back
Jake Dorn, Grade 3
Colebrook Primary School, NY

Fun at the Beach
Crunchy sand on my feet
Mushy mud near the water
Splash! go the waves
Awk! Awk! scream the annoying gulls
Smack! waves over my head
Kerplunk! I'm in a washing machine
I love the beach!
Jed Orndorff, Grade 2
Covenant Life School, MD

Red
Red is the color of lava.
Red is the color of anger.
It is the color of Lightning McQueen.
Red is a rose.
Red is a tulip.
It is my favorite color!
Do you like red?
Alexander Gohringer, Grade 3
Colebrook Primary School, NY

Courage

Have faith in yourself
No matter what others say
Stand up for what you believe
Even if it's not the way.

Don't let anyone tell you
That your dreams are out of reach,
Because everything is a lesson
Some we learn; some we teach.

So, no matter what color —
No matter how big or how small
Always know in your heart
That together we can do it all.

Taylor Hans, Grade 3
Burgettstown Elementary Center, PA

Refrigerators

You put things
that belong
in there like
milk some are
different than others
some people
hang pictures
on them or
ABC magnets
there are colors
some open straight
and some open
from the middle
they are expensive

Neima Suleiman, Grade 2
Public School 69, NY

Phoenix

Phoenix
Black, fun
Chewing, barking, playing
Has a curly-Q tail
Mutt

Megan Dunkle, Grade 3
Willow Creek Elementary School, PA

Spring

S unny hot
P laying with friends
R unning fast
I t is baseball time
N ice weather
G oing to the park

Alexander Batista, Grade 2
Helen B Duffield Elementary School, NY

Easter

E ggs
A pril
S pring
T oys
E aster
R abbits

A. Roman, Grade 1
St Agatha School, NY

Winter

In winter it's fun,
So I better run
To go out and play
With my new sleigh.
In winter there's snow
So now here I go.

Shannon Hogarty, Grade 3
Penn-Kidder Campus, PA

Hockey

swift, smooth
hitting, skating, falling
leaning over the ice
winter fun

Nathan Czebiniak, Grade 2
Caryl E Adams Primary School, NY

The Big Orange Star

The sun is moving
The sun is high in the sky
Sun is near the Earth

James Canney, Grade 1
St Louis Elementary School, MA

Summer

I see a cool bike and a baseball,
I hear a red dog and kids jumping in the pool,
I taste some hot dogs and water,
I smell a grill and food,
I feel sweaty and hot.

Ethan Beebe, Grade 3
Mary J Tanner School, NY

Thanksgiving

Thanksgiving — I love
That wonderful holiday!
It's happy, it's loving.
That's all you need
For Thanksgiving!

Pedro Echavarria, Grade 3
Public School 115 Alexander Humboldt, NY

Flowers

Flowers blowing in the wind, looking confident.
Petals all different colors, yellow, green, blue, purple.
Marching down the path, very proudly.
Beautifully sitting in the sunlight
Always a colorful shiny flower.

Kyra Arena, Grade 3
Jeffrey Elementary School, CT

Our New Years

I am happy with my family
It is snowing
All the presents have been opened
I see a tree with lots of colors
Happy New Year!

Giambi Cruz, Grade 3
Public School 115 Alexander Humboldt, NY

Rascal and Mom and Dad

We called him Rascal because he is a Rascal
He is black, he is brown
He is a rascal, my rascal.
And my mom loves me and stares me right in the eyes.
And my dad likes some jokes and hangs out with me.

Caleb Thayer, Grade 2
Thatcher Brook Primary School, VT

Giving Thanks
T hankful for everything that I have.
H appy for Thanksgiving feast with family
A great day for giving thanks
N ice day to see your family and play family games.
K itchen goodies everywhere!
S anta arrives to end the Macy's Parade.
G reat food, family time and fun
I t reminds me of a peaceful day.
V ery thankful day.
I ncredible
N ice day for peace.
G reat day to play games.

Anna Dobkowski, Grade 3
St Madeleine Sophie School, NY

What If?
What if
The sky was green
And the grass was blue

what if a dog was blue
And a cat was pink

What if the trees were red and the branches
were orange

What if the world's colors were all mixed up
What if?

Thanasi Pappas, Grade 1
Buckley Country Day School, NY

Birds
Eating worms
Standing alone in the grass
Flying away in the breezy wind
Going through the trees
Making nests
Having their babies
Above the trunk in the branches
Now that they hatched the birds will fly away
Into the tired sunset

Eddie Stepanek, Grade 2
Helen B Duffield Elementary School, NY

Cat and Mouse

A cat chased a mouse.
They raced into a house.
Crash! Clang! Boom!
The cat hit a broom.
The mouse ran into a room.
He hid under a bed.
And wished the cat was dead.
Hissss! Hissss! Hissss! Chomp!
The cat ate the mouse.
It started to really rain.
He had a belly pain.
Pitter-patter, pitter-patter.
Meeeeeoooooowww!

Morgan Koppenhaver, Grade 3
Emmanuel Baptist Christian Academy, PA

Spring Lions

A storm is approaching
like a lion readying to attack.

The thunder filling the sky is a lion's roar.

Lightning sparks and gleams
like the flash of a lion's teeth.

The rain streams quickly across the plains
like a lion thunders over the hills and flats.

When the storm has ended
it's like a lion going back to its den with its catch.

Nathan Fuguet, Grade 3
Mary C. Howse Elementary School, PA

Zoo

Standing on the hard ground
Looking at wild animals
Lions roar
Monkeys screech
Snakes hiss
Elephants stomp
Welcome to the zoo!

Desean Williams, Grade 3
Public School 40 Samuel Huntington, NY

Sunset

See the sun dive down
In a big blast of colors
Darkness is coming
Malcolm McCarvill, Grade 3
Buckley Country Day School, NY

Rainbows

Spring rain brings rainbows
They are very colorful
Arching in the sky
Leanne Schwartz, Grade 3
Brant Elementary School, NY

Spring

Flowers are blooming
Birds are flying by my house
Butterflies glide by
Clay Scanlan, Grade 3
Brant Elementary School, NY

Car

My Dad's silver car
is like a rocket ship
blasting off on the road.
Aidan Gordon, Grade 2
Avery School, MA

Rain

Rain is water
Rain is cold
Rain drips and drops from the sky.
Marco Pisano, Grade 2
Avery School, MA

Bees

Bees buzzing around
Pollinating the flowers
Flying to their hive
Terrence Haring, Grade 3
Brant Elementary School, NY

School Outfit

Looking in my wardrobe
For a fantastic outfit for school
Know you're somewhere
Come on!
Come out!
Maybe you
Never, never!
Not for school
How about you?
I think you're perfect!
Francesca Gentile, Grade 2
Avery School, MA

I Want a Dog

I want a dog
I want a dog
Why can't Mom get me a dog?
Dogs are so cute
Dogs are so loving
If I had a dog
I would play
With it
I want a dog
Why can't my mom get me a dog?
Julia Gulbransen, Grade 1
Buckley Country Day School, NY

Steam Engine

A convoy of trucks,
But powered by steam,
A man turning with gears,
A man working with heat,
The rhythm of darkness,
It feeds upon that,
Moving,
Spilling out voices of smoke,
The monster of power,
Made for a task.
Thomas Mowen, Grade 3
St Bernard's School, NY

About Me
I am from a barrette box.
I am from red roses.
I am from a dining room table.
I am from my mother, Nathelle.
I am from a wise man who hears one word
      and understands two.
I am from lettuce and tomato salads.
I am from a picture of me.
I am from New Jersey.
I am from troublemakers.
I am from Beyonce.
I am from a pizza party.

Nathelle Downes, Grade 3
William Ziegler Elementary School, PA

Green
Green is the color of a Celtic hat
Green is the color of a leprechaun's clothes
Green is the color of a four-leaf clover
Green is the color of my eyes
Green smells like grass
Green tastes like a sweet green apple
Green sounds like crickets
Green looks like Luna moths
Green feels soft and gentle
Green makes me giggle
Green is my favorite color

Niall Cremin, Grade 3
Lincoln Street School, MA

My Naughty Feet
My feet are very naughty that's what everyone said.
Those feet make me do bad things like jump on my bed.
On Sunday I kicked my brother in the shin.
On Monday I stepped on a pin.
On Tuesday I lost the running race.
On Wednesday my feet were so excited I couldn't tie my lace.
On Thursday my feet knocked over my experiment.
On Friday a ball I kicked crashed into our car and it got a big dent.
On Saturday I fell and skinned my knee.
Now those feet are naughty, why won't they let me be?

Anusha Chinthalapale, Grade 3
William B Gibbs Jr Elementary School, MD

Glitter Ball

Round
Round
Up and down
Bounce
Bounce
High and low
Where'd it go?!

Caden Rose, Grade 2
Fountaindale Elementary School, MD

Fun in All Seasons

Winter
Cold, snowy
Rolling in snow, making snowmen, skiing
Seasons both full of fun
Sweating, jump roping, swimming
Hot, sunny
Summer

Stephanie Eckl, Grade 2
St. Madeleine Sophie School, NY

Piano

Piano, piano
Your keys of ivory
Are your teeth
The ebony keys
Are the gaps or
Spaces between
The teeth

Entonia Jones, Grade 2
Tashua School, CT

Friends

Good friends, bad ones,
Short friends, tall ones
Old friends, young ones,
Happy friends, sad ones,
Nice friends, mean ones,
All friends are here and there,
Friends are everywhere.

Jessica Chau, Grade 2
Helen B Duffield Elementary School, NY

Monsters Monsters

Monsters, monsters
In your house
Running all about
Monsters, monsters
In your house
Come on let's chase them all
Out!

Abriana Austin, Grade 3
Public School 114 Ryder Elementary, NY

Mookie Willson

Mookie Willson
Played center field for
the New York Mets
Always smiling when running
Faster than the speed of lightning
If only I were him
I would be the best Met of all time.

Kieran Kelly, Grade 3
Our Lady of Hope School, NY

I Did Not Eat Your Ice Cream

I did not eat your ice cream,
I did not stuff your lunch box
with rubber bands and rocks.
I did not hide your sweater,
I did not dent your bike.
It must have been my sister,
'cause we look a lot alike.

Brianna Sacchetti, Grade 2
Public School 69, NY

Free-for-All

Running
so fast
can't stop
almost done
the race is finally
finished
I win!

Tess Dougall, Grade 2
Tashua School, CT

Oh, Soccer Ball
Oh, soccer ball,
Why do you get kicked?
Does it hurt?
Devin Bauer, Grade 3
John T Waugh Elementary School, NY

Stuffed Dolphins
My little dolphins:
They are nice, and cool.
Blue, pink, white.
Nick Lombardo, Grade 3
John T Waugh Elementary School, NY

Ethan
Ethan is silly.
I love him so much:
Cutey, stinky, fun!
Victoria Stack, Grade 3
John T Waugh Elementary School, NY

Mr. Leprechaun
Oh, Mr. Leprechaun,
Let me have your gold!
I'll steal it!
Jack Perry, Grade 3
John T Waugh Elementary School, NY

Alien!
Oh, evil alien,
Don't destroy our Earth! Please!
I need it!
Shane Stout, Grade 3
John T Waugh Elementary School, NY

Nasty Bee
You little bee,
You stung Mom, Dad, me!
That really hurt!
Trinity DelValle, Grade 3
John T Waugh Elementary School, NY

Spring
Spring gives many birds.
Also flowers and green plants.
Butterflies soar high.
Isabella Azzolino, Grade 2
Killingly Memorial School, CT

Spring Leaves
The long skinny leaves.
They are really big and green.
I love those trees.
Beau Fortier, Grade 2
Killingly Memorial School, CT

Trees
Trees better not die,
Or the big earth will get sick.
Then people will weep.
Jiamin Li, Grade 2
Killingly Memorial School, CT

Birds
I saw small blue eggs
In a tidy, brown, warm nest
Then there were babies.
Kelly Weiner, Grade 2
Killingly Memorial School, CT

On Dad's Birthday
On Dad's birthday,
Randi says Daddy needs cake!
Funny! So yummy!
Jade Haskins, Grade 3
John T Waugh Elementary School, NY

My Annoying Brother
My annoying brother:
He never stops talking today,
Second after second.
Jordan Butterfield, Grade 3
John T Waugh Elementary School, NY

Spring

Spring brings flowers,
for many hours.

April brings rainbows,
it is always a great show.

May is cool,
too cool for the pool.

June is my birthday,
It is a fun day.

Spring and summer are seasons,
Spring I do a lot of sneezing.

Payton Rhone, Grade 3
Susquehanna Community Elementary School, PA

Spring

All kids have fun in spring,
and all day long the wind chimes ring.

It is getting close to summertime,
I whine to my parents at supper time.

The wind sings in my ears,
my eyes water, but it's not tears.

The sun glistened on the lake,
we all jumped in and so did our dog Jake.

From April, May, and June we will all go outside,
but since last summer I miss the ocean tide.

Kaylee Landry, Grade 3
Susquehanna Community Elementary School, PA

Peace

Peace is like sitting around outside on the porch
Peace looks like people playing around
It sounds like the wind blowing and
It can be Heaven but,
Peace is always fun.

Nontsikelelo Mathwasa, Grade 3
Coram Elementary School, NY

Earth Day
We shouldn't cut down trees
Because they make the air we breathe clean

It takes a year to grow a tree
Chopping them down is mean

Joslyn Lessard, Grade 1
Our Lady of Mercy Regional School, NY

Winter
Winter pops out with
Snow, snowflakes
And it is turning cold
When it is blowing cold
Leaves start to clear out.

Stephanie Graves, Grade 2
Public School 40 Samuel Huntington, NY

Dogs
Big golden furry
wet tongue licking
chewing bones
chasing cats
I love dogs!

Mackenzie Day-Budd, Kindergarten
Mary Burgess Neal Elementary School, MD

Peace
Peace is the crickets being quiet at night,
my brother chewing with his mouth closed,
Cammi's dog not barking and jumping,
my brother not yelling at me,
and quietness on the whole Earth all day and all night.

Jeyda Crubbrest, Grade 2
Wells Central School, NY

Summer
I see green leafed trees and colorful flowers,
I hear birds chirping and dogs barking,
I taste cool refreshing water and cold frozen ice pops,
I smell fresh air and beautiful scented flowers,
I feel scratches from sharp prickled bushes and rough tree bark.

Benjamin McHugh, Grade 3
Mary J Tanner School, NY

Roller Coasters

Roller coasters
Go slowly up
Up
Up
The hills

And then
You fall down
Down
Down

Then you go up
In a hurry

It feels like you
Touch the sky!
Anthony Dorazio, Grade 1
St Rose School, CT

7 Kittens

There were 7 kittens
sleeping in their cozy bed.
The first kitten woke up and
rolled on the second.
The second got mad and
hissed at the third.
The third was angry and
pounded on the fourth.
The fourth turned red and
scratched the fifth.
The fifth started whining
and jumped on the sixth.
The sixth started crying
and woke up the seventh
The seventh started sighing
because he felt like he was dying.
Kerrianne Koenig, Grade 3
Our Lady of Hope School, NY

My Teacher

My teacher is cool.
My teacher can never be fooled
My teacher can be mean
My teacher makes us work hard
My teacher shows us right from wrong.
My teacher…
Karen Aragon, Grade 3
Public School 131, NY

Dogs and Cats

Dogs
Silky fur, athletic
Chew toy, dog food, fluffy, sneaky
Purring, sleeping, relaxing
Cuddly, clawing
Cats
Madison May, Grade 2
Klein Elementary School, PA

People

People running as fast as lightning
People running as slow as a turtle
People listening to music
People talking to other people
People walking
People racing
People humming
People singing
People hugging and people smiling
Different kinds of people
People doing these things and more!
Evelea Prescott, Grade 3
Public School 114 Ryder Elementary, NY

I Cry

When my brother hits me,
I cry.
When he hits me
in the face,
I cry
because it hurts.
I cry
He calls me a baby,
I cry
because he hurts my feelings.
I cry.
Kevin Rauccio, Grade 2
Tashua School, CT

City/Countryside
City
Noisy, busy
Talking, honking, running
Traffic, els, pigs, horses,
Farming, plowing, planting
Quiet, green
Countryside
Steven Wilkinson, Grade 2
Helen B Duffield Elementary School, NY

What I Collect
Baseball cards, baseball cards.
Some are old and some are new.
Yankee cards are best, Red Sox just a few.
I collect from all teams and states.
Derek Jeter cards are highest in the rates.
Some cost a lot and some were free.
But all of them are special to me.
Lucca Egiziaco, Grade 3
St Barnabas Elementary School, NY

Bees
Bee stung me ouch ouch ouch
then more come I yell aaaaaa
Boo
hoo
hoo
I dash inside
as fast as I can
Christian vanZyl, Grade 2
Tashua School, CT

Playing Through the Year
Winter
Cold, chilly
Snowing, ice skating, snowboarding
Both seasons are for play
Sweating, swimming, fishing
Hot, sunny
Summer
Lucas Mitchell, Grade 2
St. Madeleine Sophie School, NY

$100 Dollar Bills
$100 dollar bills
Are really green
And look like
Green grass.

They look
Really shiny.
Hunter Smith, Grade 1
St Rose School, CT

Rainy Day
Lightning strikes
Trees dancing
Wet ground
Playground still
Birds hiding
Puddles deep
Animals creep
Kaylee DiSalvo, Grade 2
Helen B Duffield Elementary School, NY

Cat and Dog
Cat
Furry, cute
Loving, sleeping, purring
Both are nice pets.
Barking, running, licking
Fast, friendly
Dog
Victoria Lindman, Grade 2
St. Madeleine Sophie School, NY

City/Countryside
City
Noisy, busy
Running, shopping, talking
Planetarium, els, cows, pigs
Planting, plowing, raking
Green, quiet
Countryside
Aiden Philippe, Grade 2
Helen B Duffield Elementary School, NY

What Is Beautiful to Me
Above, above,
The sun is shining in the sky
Below, below,
Snakes shimmering in the grass
In the mountains, the mountains,
Goats eating the glistening, tall grass
In the ocean, the ocean,
Shiny fish swimming in the water
Here ends my song,
The beautiful world.
Courtney Browne, Grade 2
John L Edwards School, NY

What Is Beautiful to Me
Above, above,
A butterfly soars over my head
Below, below,
A ladybug searching for food
In the mountains, the mountains,
A little boy praying to the sky
In the ocean, the ocean,
A clownfish shimmering in the moonlight
Here ends my song,
The beautiful world.
Natasha Smith, Grade 2
John L Edwards School, NY

What Is Beautiful to Me
Above, above,
A plane flying in the sky
Below, below,
A car driving on the road
In the mountains, the mountains
Hikers climb up the cold, snowy rocks
In the ocean, the ocean,
The clownfish swim slowly
Here ends my song,
The beautiful world.
Michael Lonigro, Grade 2
John L Edwards School, NY

Sleepover
When I got there
They were outside
Carelessly playing
Throwing pine cones
Up and down
Then hula hoops swing
Blue and pink
Now it's time for bed
I sleep in Sanoa's room
All pink but she loves blue
Cherise Birchwood, Grade 3
Public School 114 Ryder Elementary, NY

Ice Cream
I scream
You scream
We hear the truck
Run, run
Run to the truck
I get chocolate
you get an ice pop
lick, lick
yummy, yummy
It's all gone
Hannah Brownstein, Grade 2
Primrose School, NY

Twister
gray
a natural
disaster
a heavy wind
a
VERY
destructive
thing
that is what a
TWISTER is!!!
Alec Varma, Grade 2
Primrose School, NY

It's All About Me
My name is Sarah I am 6 years old
I like to play in the snow and I get very cold.
My eyes are brown my hair is long
I'm known as me and I like to sing songs.

Sarah O'Donnell, Grade 1
St Joan of Arc School, PA

The Hat and a Bunny
I see a hat.
It looks very funny.
It looks like a bat.
And it's on a bunny.

Justin Ruiz, Grade 2
Public School 205 Alexander Graham Bell, NY

Dogs
Dogs come in different sizes and shapes.
Dogs are lovable and funny.
It doesn't matter how dogs look as long as you have a friend.
Dogs are loyal and truthful, they're always good and sweet.

Zariah David, Grade 3
Public School 114 Ryder Elementary, NY

Stars
Stars are great and cool.
Stars are awesome at night time.
Stars are really bright.

Julianna Hickey, Grade 2
Fonda-Fultonville Elementary School, NY

Star Wars
Star Wars is so cool.
I love Star Wars so so much.
Star Wars is a game.

Kameron Fitzpatrick, Grade 2
Fonda-Fultonville Elementary School, NY

Squirrels
He is a grey squirrel.
Chester is two years old now.
Chester is my pet.

Emma Agnes, Grade 2
Fonda-Fultonville Elementary School, NY

Spring

Spring is good,
You wear a hood.
Spring is fun,
I see the sun.
Spring is warm,
Frogs have a good form.
Spring has green grass,
The mower will make a pass.
Spring has trees,
There are bees.
In spring you catch fish,
Fish gave a wish.
Spring has turtles,
Turtles jump over hurdles.
Spring has rain,
Horses have a mane.
You can run,
I'm still not done.
Spring is decent,
Flowers have a good scent.

Garrison Kiernan, Grade 3
Susquehanna Community Elementary School, PA

Too Many Cookies

Too many cookies are sitting on the plate.
Chocolate mint and chocolate chip are just a few I ate.
I'm feeling sick, but they're too yummy.
Now they're filling up my tummy.

Which one should I have now?
Vanilla, strawberry or one shaped like a cow?
Ohhh, I don't feel so good,
But I must have another. I could. I should.

I'm dead. They're almost gone.
And I didn't leave any for my brother, John.
I'm going to get in trouble, but now it's too late.
Just because I ate and ate.

Even though it's so much fun,
I think it's time to be done.

Kayla Sickler, Grade 3
Heron Pond Elementary School, NH

Spring

In Spring it is a pain,
Because all it does is rain!

In Spring I might get new shoes.
I can easily count by twos.

In Spring it's not very warm.
If you see a bee, hope it's not in a swarm.

In Spring the raindrops are clear.
I wish it didn't rain all year.

In Spring you can fish.
When you have an eyelash on your finger you make a wish.

Tommy Laudico, Grade 3
Ellicott Road Elementary School, NY

Chrysanthemum

C oncentrate on a chrysanthemum beauty.
H appy to be admired by all people.
R esting so very peacefully.
Y ellow is the color of chrysanthemums.
S pring is when you're born
A ll people love chrysanthemum.
N ever forget a chrysanthemum.
T aking everyone's breath away who looks at you.
H aving the time of your life.
E verybody picks you in the spring.
M aking everyone's day so bright.
U nique beauty is you.
M ay you shine in the sun.

Anastasia Meltzer, Grade 2
Long Meadow Elementary School, CT

Peace

Peace is reading on a very snowy day,
Maggy is sleeping on me or sleeping in her cage,
I am in my mom's room watching TV,
my classmates are working hard,
and I am reading quietly in school.

Macayla Courtney, Grade 2
Wells Central School, NY

My Little Pup
I have a little puppy
he is so cute
loving
and he gives
lots of
kisses
this is my
dog my
dog Bear.
Rebecca Margolnick, Grade 2
Tashua School, CT

Bouncy Ball
Bounce
bounce
bounce
goes the bouncy ball
up and down
down and up
bounce
bounce
bounce it's fun!
Meghan Cody, Grade 2
Tashua School, CT

Bubble
Up and down
high to the sky it goes
then before your eyes
here comes the bubble
dropping from the sky.
Westley Lyon, Grade 2
Fountaindale Elementary School, MD

Rainbow
Red balloon
Orange shirt
Yellow sun
Leprechaun
Blue sky
Purple trash can
Travis Gause, Kindergarten
Robert M Hughes School, MA

My Best Friends
My best friends play with me
when I'm alone.
My best friends cheer me up
when I'm hurt.
My best friends are always by my side
when I need them.
My best friends are
active listeners.
My best friends, Lenny and Nathan
Richard Beliveau, Grade 3
Sarah Dyer Barnes School, RI

Summer
Summer is warm,
Summer is nice.
The leaves blow,
Not once but twice.
Summer is a season
When flowers bloom.
Well, who am I
I am Haley.
I love the butterfly.
Haley Kuehner, Grade 2
William Penn Elementary School, PA

About Eamon O'Reilly
Eamon O'Reilly
For singing and drumming
Rapidly drumming bongos
as good as a great drummer
If only I was him
Jack Roche, Grade 3
Our Lady of Hope School, NY

Wish Wash
Wish, Wash.
I hear love in the sky,
But suddenly I hear nothing.
and I feel empty inside.
My love went away,
Wish, Wash.
Dylan Meltzer, Grade 3
Willits Elementary School, NY

Earth Day

Earth day has come again
A tree makes a difference
Recycling helps the earth
Trees give off oxygen
Help make the earth a better place
Don't litter
Any trash might trash the earth
You, everybody has to help out
Caleb Zhang, Grade 3
Shady Grove Elementary School, PA

Daffodil

The daffodil's head
Is like
The sunshine.

It lives
In a
Playful
Garden.
Abigail Markey, Grade 1
St Rose School, CT

Toys

Toys are so fun
you can fun.

Toys are so cool,
but then run to school!

But don't bring a toy, bring a book
and have a look.
Pharoah Glenn, Grade 1
Park Avenue School, NY

Chucka Chucka Chuchu

chucka chucka chuchu here
it comes
the train is smoking
like an erupted
bomb
move move it's gonna hit
you chuck chucka chuchu
here it comes
Keneil Desir, Grade 3
Public School 114 Ryder Elementary, NY

Angelica

A lways promises good things
N ice girl
G ood person
E njoys eating ice cream
L ikes kittens and puppies
I mportant to mom and dad
C heerful
A ble to do anything
Angelica Uzar, Grade 3
Penn-Kidder Campus, PA

Cookies

Cookies you smell so good
When you come out
of the hot oven
So crispy
So delicious
With chocolate chips
Inside
You taste sooo good!
Isabela Yoguez, Grade 2
Tashua School, CT

Cheetahs

Wild Cats
Faster than I
Eating meat all the time
Running fast to catch his dinner
Cheetahs
Joshua Lisiecki, Grade 3
Clinton Street Elementary School, NY

Puppy

Puppy
Ordinary, gold
Running, playful
Soft, fat, bundle of fun, cute, white
Foxy
Autym Tomaszewski, Grade 3
Clinton Street Elementary School, NY

I Can Count

I can count by twos
Mittens, gloves, and shoes
I can count by fives
I do it all the time
Fingers, nickels, toes
I can count by tens
Fingers, toes, and dimes.

Basint Eltaiar, Grade 2
Public School 40 Samuel Huntington, NY

Listen to Summer

Splish, splash in the lake —
Whooshy, washy in the pond.
Whooooo, whoooooo sings the wind.
Tweet, tweet goes the bird.
Crunch, crunch snaps a twig.
There are lots of sounds of summer.
Do you hear them?

Gabriel Larocque, Grade 1
Milton Terrace South Elementary School, NY

Christmas

I love Christmas
Because I can play in the snow
I can see lighted trees too
Everybody is happy too
We celebrate the birth of Jesus
We prepare for a party
Merry Christmas

Nayeli Aquino, Grade 3
Public School 115 Alexander Humboldt, NY

Earth

A big circle —
where people live.
Floating in space —
away from the sun.
Lots of water —
covers the Earth.
Some land too!

Eric Hodnett, Grade 1
Milton Terrace South Elementary School, NY

Swimming

Swimming
Wet, fun, liquid
Racing, diving, jumping
A lot of fun in deep water
Warm
Paulo Manalo, Grade 3
St Clement Mary Hofbauer School, MD

Friendship

My friends and I are like race cars,
Racing on a track,
Speeding up together,
Slowing down together,
We don't care who wins.
Jack Wolin, Grade 3
Meadow Drive School, NY

Soccer

Soccer
Big, grassy field
Kicking, blocking, dribbling
Fun, cool, crowded, good times, real blast
Cool sport
Julia Conner, Grade 3
St Clement Mary Hofbauer School, MD

The Sound of Rain

Rain brings happiness to flowers.
The rain makes me sad.
I like to hear the pitter patter of rain.
I like to jump in the puddles.
April showers bring May flowers.
Skylar Erna, Grade 2
The Tobin School, MA

Buddy

Buddy
crazy, kind
runs, jumps, sits
He is my friend
Labrador
Declan Hannigan, Grade 2
Long Meadow Elementary School, CT

Derek Jeter

Derek Jeter
For the win and team
Rapidly hitting
Hitting more than other players
If only I could play like him!
Matthew Kyle Stabiner, Grade 3
Our Lady of Hope School, NY

Darien's New Song

Christmas is almost here
Time for toys and time for cake
I can't wait 'til it is here
Hurry Christmas very fasssst
Yah!!!
Darien Goosen, Grade 3
Milton Fuller Roberts School, MA

Dyane Jonson

Dyane Jonson
Running and scoring
Always playing basketball
Faster than lightning
I wish I was him
Stephanie Nicole Filip, Grade 3
Our Lady of Hope School, NY

Spring

Spring time
Kids are jumping and cheering
Flowers are blooming
The sun is shining
Pollen is in the air and everywhere.
Ashley Tobin, Grade 3
Our Lady of Hope School, NY

Barack Obama

Barack OBAMA
Takes care of America
He always works
Always helps people
If only I were him!
Antonino Gagliardo, Grade 3
Our Lady of Hope School, NY

My Bike
Shiny pink metal
Strings blowing in the wind
Fast as a motorcycle
Smooth bumpy rough
Racing with friends

Kaitlyn Sayers, Kindergarten
Mary Burgess Neal Elementary School, MD

Candy in My Dreams
A world of candy in my
Dreams, where castles are made of gumdrops
And Hershey Chocolate Bars
Where everything is made of candy and people like to sing
The world of candy you've never seen before except for me in my dreams

Maryam Choudhury, Grade 1
John F Kennedy Elementary School, CT

Football
Running, throwing
Blocking, tackling
Fast as a corvette
Coaches helping
Touchdown!

Michael Hellwig-Lemons, Kindergarten
Mary Burgess Neal Elementary School, MD

Hurricanes
Hurricanes blow houses away.
The wind is strong, and —
The wind is fierce!
Trees fall to the ground,
There's craziness all around!

Jovie Acacio, Grade 1
Milton Terrace South Elementary School, NY

The Little Fish
Glub! Glub! the little fish swims in the deep blue sea
Splish! Splash! the tiny fish likes to wiggle his tail
Snore, snore the little fish dreams
through the night

Jacob Cullen, Grade 2
Mayfield Elementary School, NY

The Bus

Get Up! Get Up!
You'll miss the bus!
Come on! Come on!
Hurry up! Hurry up!
Run out the door!
Oh no, mom has to drive me!

Faith Gold, Grade 2
Primrose School, NY

Freedom

Now in the sunlight
It sets them free
Shining on their souls
In the afternoon
They were sad and hurt
Now they're free

Andrew Seawright Jr., Grade 2
John L Edwards School, NY

Orca Whales

killing other whales
in the big, blue Arctic Ocean
quiet at night time
quietly catching predators
swimming up close to the beach
teeth for eating fish

Cosmo Signorile, Grade 2
Primrose School, NY

Fly Baby Bird Fly

Fly baby bird fly,
Don't cry
Just try
Fly high in the sky.

Viridiana Cerero, Grade 2
Public School 1 The Bergen School, NY

Sunshine

I like the fresh air
Spring mornings are beautiful
Flowers are pretty

Georginna Nganga, Grade 1
St Louis Elementary School, MA

Water Music

Water is rain
and raindrops glisten.
Teardrops fall off the leaves
in the trees.
Everywhere is water.
Rain's name is water.

Charie Cohen, Grade 3
Jeffrey Elementary School, CT

Popcorn

Pop! Pop!
in the microwave
lots of butter and salt
so yummy...so good
Pop! Pop!
in the microwave

Peter MacNeil, Grade 2
Primrose School, NY

What Is Fall?

Fall is the smell of apple pie.
Fall is the touch of grass.
Fall is seeing leaves fall.
Fall is tasting the apples.
Fall is hearing the wind.
Fall makes me happy!

Perry Ghosh, Grade 1
St Rose School, CT

Time to Go to Bed

Mom says it's time to go to bed.
But I would rather play instead.
I'll watch TV I'll eat a snack
Mom says no and that's that!

Jiovanni Garcia, Grade 2
Public School 1 The Bergen School, NY

River

River blue and fun,
Shiny, cool, deep, and pretty
Awesome as the wind.

Shreya Voruganty, Grade 3
Sacred Heart School, MA

Spring

A flower,
takes an hour.

When I wish on a fish,
I get my dish.

When seasons come,
people start to hum.

When it's my birthday,
it's on a Thursday.

There are lots of bugs,
under my rugs.

Brooke Conklin, Grade 3
Susquehanna Community Elementary School, PA

How School Is Fun

How school is fun, oh how, it is
I don't even know if I can list all of these things!

Like writing, math, reading and science,
oh how they all go together!
How school is fun it really is all the work,
work, work it is so much fun so everyone should think!
How school is fun it really, really is
What this poem is all about is how school is fun! Nah!
How school is so, so, so much fun and the
big helper whose name is Mrs. Smith!

Riley Gallagher and Liliana Hosefros, Grade 2
Thatcher Brook Primary School, VT

I Am a Girl

I am a girl who is creative.
I am a girl who loves to read.
I am a girl who has over fifty best friends because I can't decide.
I am a girl who wants peace on Earth.
I am a girl named Katie Wolf.

Katie Wolf, Grade 3
Como Park Elementary School, NY

Earth

God is our savior
I know of good behavior.
I recycle, and I reuse.
I watch out for the rest.
This I think is best.
When I go outside,
I feel a breeze,
It smells so fresh and clean,
flowers, grass, and everything in between.

Ryan Waski, Grade 3
Our Lady of Mercy Regional School, NY

My Spa Day

I went to the spa
the outside
looked like a box
and you know
I had a lot of fun
I smelled something good
and heard water drops
and I remember tasting the ice cream
and I will always think about it.

Nia Yhun, Grade 3
Public School 114 Ryder Elementary, NY

Recycle Your Trash

God made the world
for everyone. I pick up trash and
find more then none. I recycle the
trash and it's a great big bash. After
I'm done, I go around the neighborhood
and find more trash in a flash.
When I'm finished, I get out posters
and walk around the neighborhood and
say "recycle trash and have a blast!"

Blaise Clarry, Grade 3
Our Lady of Mercy Regional School, NY

Babe Ruth

B abe Ruths are awesome
A nd special just for the crowd
B abe you're good
E xcellent taste for candy

R eally good
U p at the top
T he crunch is good for its job
H e likes the candy, the crowd does too.

Matt Joyce, Grade 3
Sacred Heart School, MA

Hunter

Something big
Something black
Something playful
It is my dog,
HUNTER.

Grayson Cuneo, Grade 1
Buckley Country Day School, NY

Bird

Hey bird
Sing me a song
Make sure it's good
Or
I won't wake up!

Matthew Sampson, Grade 2
Avery School, MA

Fish

big blue and black fish
very very hungry fish
will eat other fish
gulp…

gone!

Ian Selby, Grade 2
Fountaindale Elementary School, MD

Fatty

Fat cat
brown and black
sneaking in my door
get out get out
I push him out
then I close the door

Terryk Lesko, Grade 2
Fountaindale Elementary School, MD

I'm a Little Circle

I'm a little circle
In the shape of a head
I'm a little circle
The shape of the rug
By your bed
I'm a little circle
I look like the number zero
I'm a little circle
I look like the letter O
I'm a little circle
Round as can be
In the shape of a ball
Bouncing down the hall.

Semone Persaud, Grade 2
Public School 40 Samuel Huntington, NY

My Mom

My mom loves me
I love her
My mom takes care of me
I take care of her
My mom is the best woman
And very nice and special to me
My mom helps me
I help her
My mom hugs me and says goodnight
I hug her and say goodnight
My mom does what she needs
To do for me
I do what I need to do for her

Krista Browne, Grade 3
Public School 232 The Walter Ward School, NY

Finger Piano

Oh finger piano,
You look like a coconut carved
With bumps on your back,
Sounding like a lullaby,
Reminding me of
A Midsummer Night's Dream,
Do you have a long memory of African music?

Mason Grey, Grade 2
John L Edwards School, NY

Winter

I see snow and leaves falling down,
I hear wind blowing and my yelling when I'm going down a hill,
I taste hot cocoa when I drink it in the house and watery snowflakes,
I feel cold when I go outside and then warm when I go inside next to the fireplace,
I smell chicken and stuffing.

Britney Betit, Grade 3
Mary J Tanner School, NY

Land in the Sand

Once there was a leprechaun named Land,
Who lived in Ireland in the sand,
One night he ate corned beef,
And lost all of his teeth,
Then started a band named "Grand."

Mark Leonardi, Grade 3
St Rose School, CT

Rover on Saint Patrick's Day

There once was a leprechaun named Rover,
He wanted to find a four leaf clover,
He looked outside for days,
He circled through fields like a maze,
And instead he found his friend Grover.

Grace Wagnblas, Grade 3
St. Rose School, CT

Grace

There once was a leprechaun named Grace,
Who started to win every race.
She said, "O, GOLLY!"
And screamed with jolly,
And some people said "pick up the pace!"

Catherine Herrick, Grade 3
St Rose School, CT

Mandy the Leprechaun

There once was a leprechaun named Mandy.
His teeth were rotten from cotton candy.
He brushed and brushed.
He was in a big rush.
Now his teeth are so scary.

Catherine DiMaria, Grade 3
St Rose School, CT

Starburst

S tarbursts are chewy and yummy.
T hey soothe the tummy.
A ll the fruity squares I will never share.
R aspberry, strawberry, cherry make me merry.
B ursting blueberry I shall savor.
U nwrap one and see.
R ainbow colors with fruity flavor.
S omebody else will share.
T ry one if you dare.

Jonathan Knowles, Grade 3
Sacred Heart School, MA

Spring Days

Spring flowers are beautiful,
and leaves are growing on trees.
Birds are flying so so high,
and then comes out the bees.
The grass is growing high,
and the rain is coming down.
The clouds are coming with the rain,
and the rain touches my head before it touches
the ground.

Nicole Werner, Grade 3
Our Lady of Hope School, NY

Autumn

Autumn is red, orange, yellow, brown, and green.
It tastes like hot apple pie with apple cider, and vanilla ice cream.
It sounds like kids walking through crunchy leaves.
It smells like freshly ground cinnamon.
It looks like oranges, apples, and pumpkins.
It makes me feel warm.

Dorian Philpot, Grade 3
Evergreen Elementary School, PA

Who Is He?

He helps me with my math.
He takes me dirt bike riding and snowboarding.
He helped me drop in on the half-pipe.
He sometimes plays football on Sunday.
My amazing dad.

Michael Tullo, Grade 3
Meadow Drive School, NY

Charly
C oolest dog
H e's brown
A wesome
R unner
L over of food
Y elp
Ryan Krauss, Grade 2
Primrose School, NY

The Library
Books waiting.
Librarian helping.
People reading.
Children shouting.
Adults shhhh!
Everyone whispers.
Samuel Godino, Grade 1
St Rose School, CT

Game Time
Coaches teaching.
Boys playing.
People watching.
Parents clapping.
Friends cheering.
Winners hugging.
Joseph DiMaria, Grade 1
St Rose School, CT

Fall
The leaves are falling off the trees.
The wind is blowing there's a breeze.
The air is getting very cool.
Don't get sick and don't miss school.
Evelyn Ramos, Grade 2
Public School 1 The Bergen School, NY

In March
Spring brings cheerful days,
with lots of pretty flowers.
School is ending soon.
Audrey Richdale, Grade 3
Willow Creek Elementary School, PA

Green Dollars
When I dream
Of dollars

They are
Green birds
Flapping their wings
In
The
Wind!
Rosie Simms, Grade 1
St Rose School, CT

The Rain
The rain
Is like
God loving
Jesus.

By crying
His tears
Come down
To Earth.
Katerina Crowe, Grade 1
St Rose School, CT

Summer
The birds are chirping,
The flowers are blooming,
The earth is coming to life.
The sun is shining,
The butterflies are flying,
The kids are out of school,
The animals wake up
From their deep winter sleep.
Margaret Walting, Grade 2
Wyoming Valley Montessori School, PA

Small Seed, Big Oak
I was a small seed,
I grew taller and taller,
I am a big oak.
David Yan, Grade 3
Sacred Heart School, MA

The Sky

The sky is big.
The sky is blue.
Isn't all of this true?
I like the sky, don't you?

Some clouds are gray.
Some clouds are white.
Aren't I right?
I like the sky don't you?
The sun shines through no matter the day.
Even if the clouds are gray.
And when it snows or rains.
I like the sky, don't you?

The sky is a beautiful thing.
You can look up at it and enjoy the scene.
Watch the birds fly back and forth
Watch the clouds move round and round.
I like the sky, don't you?

Anastasia Dye, Grade 2
Public School 235 Lenox, NY

Sleepover at Nana's House

I'm looking at the rain out the screen in my nana's front door.
A car rides by.
It makes a giant splash.
Thunder sounds like boulders from the sky.
The lightning lights up the sky white
And it sounds like TZZZT!
I put my hands outside to feel the raindrops.
They are warm on my hands.
It feels like my hands are buzzing.
The breeze blows on my face.
The rain puddles look like a giant river.
The rain is making a lot of noise.
I wish I could go outside.
I'd examine the rain.
I'm sitting on a chair with my nana talking about making good memories
And eating ice cream with chocolate syrup.
It is sweet.

Benjamin Kam, Grade 2
Willits Elementary School, NY

Mrs. Sun
The sun shines on the grass
Glowing everywhere you walk
Like it's following you wherever you go
Like a little brother or sister
Why can't it change colors?
Why can't we just go in the sky and say "hi" to Mrs. Sun?

Madison Cisco, Grade 3
Como Park Elementary School, NY

Summer
Summer pops in with
The cool sun and people
Having fun is what it's all about
So be happy because it will be long
Until it comes again
Have your fun and it's done.

Tameia Tripp, Grade 2
Public School 40 Samuel Huntington, NY

Cats
Some cats have spots.
Some cats have stripes.
Some cats purr.
Some cats fight.
My cat plays.
My cat loves me.

Jocelyn Quinones, Kindergarten
Mary Burgess Neal Elementary School, MD

Camping
The fire is crackling sparks fly out like bullets
We roast marshmallows nice and crisp
We take a nighttime walk
Then we go to sleep and the lights go out

Lucas Schepp, Grade 3
Colebrook Primary School, NY

Numbers Are Fun!
Numbers are fun
Numbers are important
Numbers help us count.

Brandon Sharrow, Kindergarten
Mary Burgess Neal Elementary School, MD

I See a Rainbow

Red is a juicy apple.
Orange is a tiny goldfish.
Yellow is some yummy honey.
Green is the tall trees.
Blue is the endless ocean.
Purple is the color of a flowering bush.

Jacob Anthony, Grade 1
St Rose School, CT

Spring

Spring is so beautiful
Spring is warm
Spring is happy to me

But most of all
Spring is the most fun!

Emma Walsh, Grade 1
St Rose School, CT

Raindrop

A raindrop
Is like
an angelfish
Swimming in
Your
Eyes.

Cameron Reichenbach, Grade 1
St Rose School, CT

Spring

Hello bunny,
I think you're fuzzy,
You're so funny,
I love you bunny.

Emily Henriquez, Grade 1
Park Avenue School, NY

Fall

Colors everywhere
Birds and geese coming and going
Apples are juicy

Robbie Elliston, Grade 3
Southold Elementary School, NY

I Really Don't Like Poetry

I really don't like poetry
It's extremely hard to write
My neighbors think it's really fun
But I'd rather say GOODNIGHT

I really don't like poetry
Alliteration's stinky
Haikus, similes and limericks
Are more than I can THINKY

I really don't like poetry
Creating can be so hard
Alas my feeble attempts fall
In the poetry JUNKYARD

I really don't like poetry
It is very, very rough
I wish it could just go away
For now I have had ENOUGH!

Olivia Schanbacher, Grade 3
Edgewood Elementary School, PA

Sleepy!

Hiding from my mom
Under the covers

"Gentiana, wake up for school."
"No! No way!"

My body is weak
My eyes are closed
I roll over

"Gentiana, wake up for school!"
"No! No way!"

She tickles me and tugs my shirt
Grabs my feet and pulls me out of bed.

I slowly begin to wake up.
Sleepy!

Gentiana Ismaili, Grade 3
Meeting House Hill School, CT

Colors

Colors are pretty
Colors are the earth

Colors are
On
Me.

Colors are
everywhere.

All colors are
different
like
people!
Megan Seman, Grade 1
St Rose School, CT

A True Friend

Is someone that
shares SECRETS with you

Is someone that plays
with you if you are alone

Is someone that shares
toys with you

Is someone that listens
to you when you speak

That's who a true friend
really is.
Nathan Kaye, Grade 3
Sarah Dyer Barnes School, RI

Hockey

Hockey
Rushing, skating
Scoring, passing, shooting
My favorite coach is Linda
Winning
Madeline McCartan, Grade 3
Clinton Street Elementary School, NY

Ice Cream

I cy
C hocolate
E xtra large

C herry dip
R eally good
E xtraordinary
A ppetite
M ost delicious
Andrew DeOliveira, Grade 3
The Edgartown School, MA

My Best Friend

My Best Friend
doesn't judge me
My Best Friend
is an active listener
My Best Friend
lets me join in on games
My Best Friend
cheers me up when I am sad
My Best Friend
Deltta Daigle, Grade 3
Sarah Dyer Barnes School, RI

The Sad Good-bye

Yesterday
I started to cry
My mom was leaving
It was a sad
good-bye
Julia Manuali, Grade 1
Buckley Country Day School, NY

Winter

Winter is white.
It tastes like hot chocolate.
It sounds like people skiing.
It smells like snow.
It looks like snowball fights.
It makes me feel excited.
Gabrielle Timoteo, Grade 3
Evergreen Elementary School, PA

In the Pool

A nice and splashy place to hide
A very fine type of tide
What a wonderful place to dive
In the pool

I touch the bottom nice and blue
On the raft, my sailing crew
I'm the captain sailing the blue
In the pool

Oh, no! A shark is very near
I see its fin, so that's my fear
Quick! Skedaddle! Here it comes
In the pool

But wait! Is that really a shark
Coming to get me in the dark?
No! It's mom swimming with me
In the pool

Mia Gianacopoulos, Grade 3
Craneville Elementary School, MA

My Desk Is a Mess

M y desk is a mess.
Y ou could tell if you saw it.

D o you know how it got this way?
E lephants ran through it.
S kunks sprayed it.
K angaroos jumped in it.

I really don't know.
S issy said I should clean it.

A great idea!

M aybe I should.
E xcept the parts that stink!
S issy said she'll tell the teacher if I don't.
S o I cleaned my messy desk.

Kaelyn McClain, Grade 2
Central Elementary School, PA

Art

Fantastic
Crayons
Tape
Paint
Scissors
Glue
Markers too
Art is fun

Jianna Rose Ruggiero, Grade 1
Buckley Country Day School, NY

Spring

Spring, spring
oh dear spring
flowers, birds all come out
cherry blossoms, magnolias
starting to bloom
caterpillars turning into
butterflies too
I LOVE SPRING!

Nina Kellner, Grade 1
Buckley Country Day School, NY

Ladybugs

L ovely ladybugs
A beautiful sight
D andy bugs
Y oung and old
B est of the rest
U nder a tree
G ood luck
S o great

Molly Stefl, Grade 2
Central Elementary School, PA

Kittens

Kittens
Sleepy, playful
Scratching, biting, chewing
They eat everything that they see
Tabbies

Victoria Hock, Grade 3
Clinton Street Elementary School, NY

Wishing

W ant to happen
I know I can do it
S o if I believe I succeed
H ave to try you know you'll make it
I n trust of yourself you can
N o backing down
G o and try

Anna Nitardy, Grade 3
The Edgartown School, MA

City/Countryside

City
Busy, noisy
Talking, walking, running
Skyscrapers, museums, farms, silos
Plowing, harvesting, farming
Quiet, green
Countryside

Giavani Martens, Grade 2
Helen B Duffield Elementary School, NY

Cheetah

C ubs
H unt
E ats gazelles
E xotic
T ense
A ctive
H ind legs are strong

Camden Emery, Grade 3
The Edgartown School, MA

Snowflakes

White and fluffy they fall
each in their own shape
landing on people's tongues
such a refreshing taste
letting kids play
I see snowmen everywhere
Oh how I love snowflakes

Tara Henry, Grade 3
Jeffrey Elementary School, CT

Mom

Mom, Mom
You make
me so
happy with
your
big
SMILE.

Joshua David, Grade 2
Pine Tree Elementary School, NY

The Pretty Flowers

My flowers
Are so pretty.
They are
So cool
And awesome.
They stand
Like a statue.

Luke Braun, Grade 1
St Rose School, CT

City/Countryside

City
Noisy, busy
Talking, walking, running
Traffic, sidewalks, farms, silos
Plowing, farming, raking
Quiet, green
Countryside

Julian Falletta, Grade 2
Helen B Duffield Elementary School, NY

Cheese

Cheese
Is a box
With giant
Holes
That have nests
That have birds
In it.

Peyton McKenzie, Grade 1
St Rose School, CT

Spring

Every spring we rain coming down,
we have a school-is-out countdown.

We see trees growing,
and our lawn we are a mowing.

The sun is very bright,
in our sight.

Some people go to get flowers,
they need rain showers.

Many people have birthdays in spring,
some might get a ring.

Michael Braun, Grade 3
Susquehanna Community Elementary School, PA

Spring

I like this season,
for a special reason.

When I am in the sun,
I usually have a lot of fun.

I would rather be giving hugs,
then be getting bitten by bugs.

I like to wish,
my wish is usually just catching a fish.

When I go hiking in the gentle breeze,
I usually start to wheeze.

C.J. Stone, Grade 3
Susquehanna Community Elementary School, PA

Morning

It is sunrise right now.
I see black birds flying though the pink and red sky.
Look! The sun is rising!
Now look! The people are waking up singing,
"Morning! Morning! Morning! Morning!"

Brianna Skinner, Grade 3
Carlyle C Ring Elementary School, NY

Ginger Pancakes

G inger is my second favorite
I s very yummy in my tummy
N o, give me more
G et me more
E xcited for more
R umbling tummy over here

P an is getting rusty
A nd I am getting full
N eed more
C ake, I mean pancakes are yummy
A nd more ginger this time
K eep on cooking
E xtra ginger please
S o tasty

Grace Gambardello, Grade 3
Sacred Heart School, MA

Rainbow Cookies

Squishy
Soft
Pink
Green
Blue
Rainbow
Black or brown
Chocolate
Not crunchy
Chewy
Good
Chocolate raspberry
Delicious
Mouthwatering
Homemade cookies are the best!

Megan O'Connor, Grade 2
Helen B Duffield Elementary School, NY

The Moon

Silver and gray
Bold and reflecting

I light up the dark
With my brightness

Never lonely
I travel all over the world

If you are lucky
I will smile when you see me
In the darkness of the night sky

For I am
The moon

Margaret Howe-Consiglio, Grade 3
Indian Lane Elementary School, PA

Me

When I'm by myself
and I close my eyes,
I'm a cat
I'm a puppy in a hat
I'm a bunny that is funny
I'm not sad when it is sunny.
I'm a cute dog
I'm a log
I'm a funny silly ball
I'm a girl that is tall.
I'm whatever I want to be
And anything I care to be.
When I close my eyes,
What I care to be
Is me.

Chelsea Ouellette, Grade 3
Van Buren Elementary School, ME

Super Winter

Winter — very cold.
Bears hibernate in winter.
Winter is super.

D. Gray, Grade 2
The Fourth Presbyterian School, MD

Spring Came

Spring is here right now.
We can see red roses bloom.
Spring is beautiful.

Natalia Gonzalez, Grade 2
The Fourth Presbyterian School, MD

Love

Sunset in the night
Shining upon a star,
Making the tight sky
Fly upon the floor.

The butterfly in the sky
Wants love and peace,
Gliding through the air
Like a ballerina's grace.

The love come pouring
Out of the sky like a rainbow.
Peeking through the clouds
After a storm.

Sunset in the night
Shining upon a star,
Making the tight sky
Fly upon the floor.
Kevanna Babyak, Grade 2
Carlyle C Ring Elementary School, NY

Dive in the Deep Sea

Dive in the deep sea,
   dive,
      dive,
         dive.
Don't go without me,
   don't,
      don't,
         don't!
Shadows lurk around corner and edge —
Seaweed shaped like a garden hedge.
Down we go onto a ledge.
We explore coral shaped like a hen
Then it's back up to the surface again!
Down,
   down,
      down,
to the bottom floor.
Let's go have fun and explore!
Olivia L. Neale, Grade 3
Farmingville Elementary School, CT

My Cousin Brendan

He's fun to play with
We go outside
Sledding or
Two hand touch
Vacations
Outer Banks
Going to the movie theater
And amusement park
And boogie boarding

He loves me,
Car racing,
Pasta,
The New York Giants,
And football

He gives me something he makes
Every time we see each other

I love him
Ryan Grimaldi, Grade 3
Meeting House Hill School, CT

Rain

It was bright
and shining
'til
   the storm clouds
      rolled in
so I got
my raincoat
to enjoy it.
Kept on raining 'til
I was
soaking wet.
Now the fun
is over.
I go back inside
'til more
rain
comes.
Caitlin Schleimer, Grade 3
Buckley Country Day School, NY

Presidents

Presidents, Presidents there are so many,
Presidents, Presidents one is on the penny,
Presidents, Presidents how would you like
to know how many,
Forty-four Presidents in a line but their
names do not rhyme,
Do you know about any that rhyme,
The Presidents are very nice men to
the end, again, and, again.

Sarah Holland, Grade 3
St Maria Goretti School, PA

I Like to Count to Ten

I like to count to ten
I can count by ones
I can also count by twos
Two, four
I can count some more
Six, eight
I cannot wait
Ten
I am all done.

Jazmin Williams, Grade 2
Public School 40 Samuel Huntington, NY

Roses

Roses, roses so bright and red
Bathing in the sun's warmth
Looking so beautiful
But don't touch!
She'll prick you with her
Thorny thorns.

Zhanna Cruz, Grade 3
Public School 40 Samuel Huntington, NY

Friends

The color of friendship is like light red
The taste of friendship is like sweet sugar
The smell of friendship is like a blooming flower
The sight of friendship is like a sunset
The sound of friendship is like two friends laughing

Amber Shaffer, Grade 2
Klein Elementary School, PA

The Marshmallow Snowman

Mom says: "Go to sleep,"
but instead I lie in bed
pretending...

that the snowflakes
were marshmallows.
They smelled sweet like candy.
They fell all around
and my face
was a big smile.
I put my tongue out
to catch marshmallows.

I made a marshmallow snowman.
It felt soft
like a nice, warm blanket.
Its eyes were raisins.
Its hands were "churros."
I made a marshmallow snowman
and I ate him.

Mallelys Reyes, Grade 3
Number 2 School, NY

Storms

Storms
Are
Like Jesus
Crying.

Lightning
Is like
A horse
Slashing
Its hooves
On a rock.

Thunder
Is like
Rocks
Hitting against
Each other.

Alyse Adamcheck, Grade 1
St Rose School, CT

Numbers

Here we go, 1, 2, 3, I love you,
Do you love me too? 4, 5, 6
In a line, count with me,
here comes 7, 8, 9
With me count 10, 11, 12
7 X 7 is forty nine.
13, 14, 15 come to me
Let's go to the park. If you come with me.
we will count more
16, 17, 18, 19, you counted, you see
That makes 20 and you did it with ME!

Grace Blosky, Grade 3
St Maria Goretti School, PA

My Aunt

My aunt is very special to me.
She is very pretty and kind.
She is always helping those who need her.
She has fair skin like a caramel.
She has long black hair.

My aunt is a funny character.
She's always telling jokes
And making everyone laugh
She is my special aunt.
I love my aunt and she is just like me.

Rahena Bhuiyan, Grade 3
Public School 131, NY

Red

Red is the color of an apple.
Red is a marker.
Red is a crayon.
Red is a strawberry.
Red smells like a rose.
Red tastes like cherry Kool-Aid.
Red sounds like a volcano erupting.
Red looks like a fire.
Red feels like an apple.
Red makes me happy.
Red is my favorite color.

Bennett Martinko, Grade 3
Evergreen Elementary School, PA

My Heart

My heart
is like popping popcorn
a kangaroo bouncing
bounce bounce
rainbow shining
pots of gold
shooting stars shining so bright up so high
twinkling lights
razzling and dazzling

Tiago Frazao, Grade 2
Tashua School, CT

A True Friend

A true friend
Never interrupts you when
You're speaking to them
Makes you happy when you're feeling blue
A true friend plays with you
When you have nothing to do
Someone who takes care of you when you're sick
Never tries to change you for who you are
I feel ecstatic to have a friend like Kyra

Aaliyah Leonardo, Grade 3
Sarah Dyer Barnes School, RI

I Am...

I am a smart and athletic girl.
I wonder how to get into the Olympics.
I hear my mind inferring about the book I'm reading.
I see Shawn Johnson in my class doing flips.
I want a gymnastics bar.
I am a smart and athletic girl.

Jessica Clark, Grade 3
Como Park Elementary School, NY

Racing

Diving, splashing
Fast as a flying bug
Wet as rain
Racing heart
Winning

Laura Vance, Kindergarten
Mary Burgess Neal Elementary School, MD

Waves

I like you waves
when you splash in my face
I go under water
into the big blue sea
when I swim
on top of you
back to shore
I go on my towel
and watch you swoosh through
the
wide blue ocean.

Joanna Pirog, Grade 2
Tashua School, CT

Springtime

Flowers blooming
Grass growing green
The sun peeking out
Birds chirping, singing a song
Warm air wrapped around you
Smell the fresh air
Trees tall and healthy
Everyone is happy,
Wearing smiles on their faces
See all the vivid colors…
Spring Has Sprung!!

Nancy Beinlich, Grade 3
William Penn Elementary School, PA

The Numbers on the Clock

Tick tock
Tick tock
goes the hands
on the clock
around like you're running
around and around
has numbers like you're counting
on the grid
Tick tock
Tick tock
Ring!

Shawn Abraham, Grade 2
Public School 69, NY

Mud

Mud on the floor
I'm scared I might fall
I should be clean
Not dirt at all
I took a chance
And what do you know
I got some mud
Stuck on my big toe
I took another step
I slipped and fell
I heard people moving
I hope they won't tell
My face is red
I'm embarrassed now
I wish I was home
Sleeping in my bed
Mud is slippery
As you can see
It's as slippery
As can be

Cameron Fillion, Grade 2
Memorial School, NH

Hail

White and icy
Hard and cold

I jump from the sky
Looking forward to
Cold and icy weather

I stare at the city lights
As I fall fast
Screaming and yelling

I dance in the air
And whisper to my friends
Saying good-bye
As I get closer to the ground

For I am hail

Brendon Stocku, Grade 3
Indian Lane Elementary School, PA

2010 Olympics

Skaters are sliding,
while Shaun White is gliding.

Goalies are diving,
between periods they are hiding.

There go bobsledders,
while I'm wearing my sweater.

People are shivering,
while I'm quivering.
John Connors, Grade 3
Ellicott Road Elementary School, NY

I Used to Be

I used to be little
But now I'm big.

I used to have blonde hair
But now I have brown hair.

I used to like cats
But now I like dogs.

I used to like cinnamon candy
But now I like cinnamon gum.
Lauren Dawicki, Grade 1
Maureen M Welch Elementary School, PA

Hair Cut

We sit in the kitchen
And I start to listen

I listen to the buzzer's buzzing sound
It looks like my hair is on the ground

My hair is gone
So I sing a sad song

Me and my hair used to have so much fun
But now our fun is done
David Lemaire, Grade 3
Craneville School, MA

Flower

I'm a flower
As
I sway
in the
cold
shivering
in
the
ice   in
the
middle
of a
hill
lying on the
ground
dead
killed
forever
in my
flower
pot
Sirena Winakor, Grade 3
Buckley Country Day School, NY

A Lion

Loud and mean
Fast and proud

I yell and scream
While my prey runs away

I smile as I listen
To the beautiful waterfall
That crashes into the lake

But where I live
I mostly look forward to
Finding wild animals
And hunting them down

For I am a lion
Allison Kirchoff, Grade 3
Indian Lane Elementary School, PA

A Crystal
Shiny and beautiful
Clear and heavenly

I will make your dreams come true
I am the perfect thing for you

When lost in a cave
I might turn on the bright light

Do not abuse me because you will be cursed
And if you destroy me I will be reborn

For I am a crystal

Alexander James Cheasty, Grade 3
Indian Lane Elementary School, PA

Happy Spring
Bugs waking
Trees waving hello and goodbye
Beautiful sky
Butterflies flying
Shining down below
People are tanning at the beach
The trees are not waving goodbye and hello
Now I can play two seasons in a row
I don't need to wear a jacket
Trees are still
I can climb them
That's my story about the best spring ever
And it's all 100% true

Angelo Molinelli, Grade 2
Helen B Duffield Elementary School, NY

Church
Singing
And praise dancing
For the Lord
Banging drums
Piano playing
Singing
In the house of the Lord.

Lakeima Williams, Grade 3
Public School 40 Samuel Huntington, NY

Rainy Day

Rainy
Rainy
Rainy day
I feel so lonely walking alone
Drip drop like a tear
From a cloud
The wind plays that sad sound
With a quiet beat
Yellow coats
Yellow hats
Black boots
And umbrellas
Ready to get wet
Quietly walking and pretending
I'm on an adventure in an ocean
In a puddle
Splish splash
The mud on my shoes
First wet then dry
Mom calls me inside
When I walk in I feel warm and clean
Bree Crum-Hieftje, Grade 3
Simon Lake School, CT

On the Go...

I get up
I get down
I get dressed
I lay down
I get back up
I tie my shoes
I brush my teeth
I eat breakfast
I do my hair
I get in the car
I drive to the bus stop
I find a seat
We get to school
I do my agenda
I do my morning work
I do my journal
I do science
I do math
We go home
I eat dinner
I go to bed!
Matthew Scudero, Grade 2
Helen B Duffield Elementary School, NY

The Ocean

Blue and moist
Massive and foamy

When I get mad
I crash my arms
Against the ground and roar

Sometimes when I cry
I squirt white, foamy bubbles all over
It looks like raining marshmallows

I open my doors to other creatures
That tell me they are thankful I'm here
Because I give them life

For I am the ocean
Makayla Doran, Grade 3
Indian Lane Elementary School, PA

Emerson

A big brother.
Hilarious as a baseball player,
That does the cha-cha slide as he
Scores his home run.

Cracks me up,
And soothes
Me,
Like your favorite blanket
Tickling against your cheek.

Behind his clean old glasses,
Lay a pair of kind brown eyes.

That's what makes him
My big brother.
Aeven O'Donnell, Grade 2
Buckley Country Day School, NY

First Frost

Today we had first frost. I wonder how cold it was. I hope it snows tomorrow because I want to play in the snow. The snow feels so cold inside my body when it falls to the ground. It makes me feel like sprinkles. When I fall to the ground I love to make snow angels all day long. But when it is time to go in I have to say good-bye. When I come inside I have lots of hot chocolate. I lay in my bed with a smile on my face. Then we had a storm come and hid underneath my covers. It seemed like the wind was angry. I don't know why but it does not seem good. I hope tomorrow will be a better day!

Katharine Barrett, Grade 3
Jeffrey Elementary School, CT

Robbie Frasca

Robbie
Energetic, smart, Steelers fan
Son of Bob and Holly
Lover of Snood, Steelers, and snow
Who feels that Steelers are awesome, summer is great, and cars are great
Who fears fire, wasps, and bees
Who would like to see New York, Japan, and Italy
Frasca

Robbie Frasca, Grade 2
Klein Elementary School, PA

Art Class

Paints are flying
Paintbrushes are diving into big buckets of watercolor
Markers are swaying through the air
My teacher says, "Come on, just a little more than that."
I dip my paintbrush in a big bucket of blue paint
The paint splatters on the paper
The bell goes ring, ring, ring
We all run out in a rush

Carolyn Tierney, Grade 2
Memorial School, NH

The Shore

Swish the water hits the shore
As clouds come rushing to the sandy beach
Rocks are covered
By drops of water
As a black storm cloud moves in

Madison Boswell, Grade 2
Mayfield Elementary School, NY

My Collection

I have a collection of animal pencil toppers
They are
tiny
squishy
squeezable
colorful
funky
mushy
enjoyable
Those are my pencil toppers,
they are the collection I like the best.
I even think they bring me
good luck on my test.

John O'Connor, Grade 3
St Barnabas Elementary School, NY

Trees

What do you need to live?
You need trees.

Trees do
a lot for us.
They give us clean air.
They give us shade.
They give birds a home.

They give us tasty berries, cherries and such.

We need to save
the Earth's trees!

Maya Neckles, Grade 2
Buckley Country Day School, NY

Candy

Candy, candy
Sweet and syrupy
Taste so yummy in my tummy
Sweet, sweet candy
It melts in your mouth
Like it fell from heaven
All you want to say is Mmmm

Kianna Paul, Grade 3
Public School 40 Samuel Huntington, NY

School

Pencils, reading, learning.
Writing, science, spelling, lunch and recess.
Snack and superstar and extra recess
Technology, problem solving and a party.
But my favorite thing about school...
is when we go home.

Grace Mensi, Grade 2
Primrose School, NY

Wind

Wind blowing, whispering to me
Nice to me
Cooling me off from the nice, hot, spring day
It feels nice on me from the hot day
But sun, sun, sun,
That's what it's cooling me off from

Riley McDonnell, Grade 2
Helen B Duffield Elementary School, NY

Agreeable

Agreeable is a nice light pink.
It tastes like cherry ice cream.
It has the beautiful scent of a red rose.
It feels like freshly cut grass underneath your feet.
It sounds like blue birds chirping.
It is a warm and sunny summer day.

Anna Fergusson, Grade 3
Asa C Adams School, ME

Tacos

Some like tacos with cheese, lettuce and tomatoes.
Not me, I like tacos with meat.
Some like soft tacos and some like crunchy tacos.
Tacos are delicious...CRUNCH!

Jacob Tyler Carr, Grade 3
Colebrook Primary School, NY

Baseball Cards

Baseball cards are fun.
Baseball cards are hard to find.
Baseball cards are rare.

Jake Bowles, Grade 2
Fonda-Fultonville Elementary School, NY

City/Countryside
City
Noisy, busy
Shopping, walking, talking
Sidewalks, subways, silos, farms
Planting, raking, farming
Green, quiet
Countryside
Emily Pfeuffer, Grade 2
Helen B Duffield Elementary School, NY

The Rose
Swish! Swish! of a flower in the wind
Red and pink are the colors of a rose
So beautiful in the summer
Brown and dead in the fall
Not looking the same
But in the spring will bloom
Looking gorgeous once again
Kayla Smith, Grade 2
Mayfield Elementary School, NY

The Mango Tree
I was drinking
A mango smoothie
I was reading a
Book about a
Mango tree
I was sleeping under
The mango tree
Nicole Rozanski, Grade 3
Ridgeway Elementary School, MD

Perspective Depends
The branch is tree
The clouds are sky
The water is ocean
The grass is leaves
The ground is space
Opposites depend on our eyes
The universe
Joshua Broderick-Phillips, Grade 3
Thoreau Elementary School, MA

The Sun and the Moon
Sun
Hot, big
Heating, burning, blinding
The Earth needs the sun and the moon
Orbiting, shining, shimmering
Craters, silver
Moon
Cayla Anderson, Grade 3
St. Madeleine Sophie School, NY

Rain
Rain
dripping down
pouring drizzling
rain shower
like
little gum drops
falling down.
Natalia Markowski, Grade 2
Tashua School, CT

Kitten to Cat
Kitten
Little, small
Falling, hearing, scratching
Grows bigger and bigger
Eating, running, caring
Cute, big
Cat
Abigail Hamilton, Grade 2
St. Madeleine Sophie School, NY

Tasha Jumps
Tasha, the happy horse,
Was a beautiful horse.
She loved to run a course.
Whoosh! Bang!
Tasha jumped.
Tasha landed.
Wow!
Lillian Troyer, Grade 3
New Freedom Christian School, PA

The Owl
An owl hoo's hoo hoo
Echoing through the night.
Cold air *narrows down to the owl*
The owl's wings shiver as
the night passes by
He *flies* high in the sky
The owl *flies* back
While there's still dim light.
Savannah Willette, Grade 2
Memorial School, NH

The Pencil
The wooden, pointy pencil.
Helps me write
my words.
It's very like a cylinder,
bumpy around the edges
Tap-Tap-Tap!
scratch-scratch-scratch!
and sometimes it is quiet.
Madison Villines, Grade 2
Fountaindale Elementary School, MD

Baseball
B aseball is fun to play.
A udiences are big fans of baseball.
S ounds are made by baseball fans.
E verybody likes baseball.
B aseball players hit the ball.
A ll players run the bases.
L ights are in a stadium.
L ines are on a baseball field.
Dion Zhuta, Grade 2
Long Meadow Elementary School, CT

Monday Morning
Mom wakes me up
Dressed up
I eat breakfast
Crunch, crunch, crunch!
I put on shoes and coat
I go to the bus stop
Thumb wars with my brother
I go to school
Talha Ali, Grade 2
Helen B Duffield Elementary School, NY

Rose
Red
beautiful red
smells good
when I plant it
the wind blows
the smell goes
in my nose
it smells good
Rachel Mease, Grade 2
Fountaindale Elementary School, MD

About Me
Goes bowling,
Plays computer,
Bakes cookies,
Runs laps,
Plays DSI,
Does homework,
That's me!
Justin Miele
Justin Miele, Grade 2
Helen B Duffield Elementary School, NY

A Dog
A dog
Barks at people
barking, running, playing
loving, playful, caring, awesome
Casey
Rachel Castello, Grade 3
Clinton Street Elementary School, NY

Hockey
Hockey
goalie players
skating scoring cheering
skating back and forth on the ice
The fall
Jesse Pfeiffer, Grade 3
Clinton Street Elementary School, NY

Soup

I love soup!
I slurp it up.
Sometimes I use a spoon.
Sometimes I don't.
Soup is really great!
No matter what type I'll eat it up.
Tomato soup is good.
But chicken is better!
I like noodle too!
But the very best is homemade.
Raven May McCormack, Grade 3
The Edgartown School, MA

Spring Is Here

Spring is here!
It's that time that
flowers bloom
Roses, Tulips, Daisies
birds fly so, so high in
the sky
children play outside with
their kites
The rain makes flowers
very, very tall
Dana Cerillo, Grade 3
Our Lady of Hope School, NY

The Beach

Little grains of sand
crawling on my hand
the turquoise tides
come over my feet
the waves crash
the sea flows silent
people talk, the castles stand
the sun peers over the water
as if it was in it at sunset
the moon then shows silent over the water
Gracie Dougherty, Grade 2
Sabold Elementary School, PA

September

Sometimes I play.
Even if I can't stay.
Playing is fun won't you stay?
Time to go,

Every day at the mall.
Monday is the right day to go to the mall.
Because we like to eat something small.
Even if I can't eat at all.
Red and golden leaves fall.
Nicole Pawling, Grade 3
St Maria Goretti School, PA

Reach!

REACH! Now swing! NO! Not with
that hand!
Starting over, once again
REACH!
ten hours later…
Starting over
REACH! Now swing. Yes! Now
again finally! Want to try again?
good…
Now…REACH!
Emma Duggan, Grade 3
Thoreau Elementary School, MA

Moon

Mom says: "Go to sleep,"
but instead I lie in bed,
pretending…

The moon is the light.
It's bright in my room.

It makes me feel like
I am alive…
like I am shining.
Eileen Brizuela, Grade 3
Number 2 School, NY

Spring
Blooming flowers,
Raining showers.
Days are warming,
Bees are swarming.
Trees are growing,
No more snowing!
Birds sing,
I love spring!
Gianna DiJohn, Grade 3
Evergreen Elementary School, PA

NBA 2K10
Dwight Howard made a hoop
Michael Jordan made an Alleyoop
Dwayne Wade did a Slam Dunk
A 3 pointer LeBron James sunk
Paul Pierce made a Buzzer Beater
Chris Paul is the best feeder
The NBA is really cool
Watch it don't be a fool.
Joey Lovetro, Grade 3
Colebrook Primary School, NY

Chickarees
Chickarees hurrying and scurrying,
Late for lunch
At squirrel's oak tree,
Trying to be as quick as chickaree
Out comes the squirrel,
Gray tail swishing
Swish, swish, swish,
Acorn and tea to share
Lili Barglowska, Grade 2
John L Edwards School, NY

Hungry
I'm so hungry
"Mom, I am hungry!"
I hear my belly. Is that normal?
Feel like I am dying.
Belly getting louder
More and more hungry
Food, food, food
It's my best friend
Kerrigan Quinn, Grade 3
Meeting House Hill School, CT

Birds
I saw a robin pecking at the ground
Then there were two robins
One was looking at me
My loud noise scared them away
There were no more birds
At recess I heard chirping
Looked up
I saw that same robin looking back at me
Augusto Rodriguez, Grade 2
Helen B Duffield Elementary School, NY

Stapler
like
a croc
snapping
its jaws
then leaving
a surprise
on the
paper
Charlie Kane, Grade 2
Fountaindale Elementary School, MD

Summer
Summer
so very hot
swimming in a cool pool
playing outside with my friends
No school
Zachary Loucks, Grade 3
Clinton Street Elementary School, NY

Hockey
Hockey
shot, score, puck, net,
slap shot, wrist shot, rush puck,
coach yells, penalty, switch the lines,
Sabers.
Thomas Leatherbarrow, Grade 3
Clinton Street Elementary School, NY

I Wish I Was the Earth

I wish I was the Earth,
A big part of the universe.
My favorite colors are blue and green.
Rotating, big mountains, oceans in between.
I would see stars,
Like the Big Dipper.
I would see clouds on me.
I would see the sun's light in front of me.
I would always look at the
planets, Jupiter, Pluto, Mars, Saturn
and the moon.
I would feel earthquakes.
Rockets would look like shooting stars.
I would see all the countries.
The planets would be my classmates
The sun would be my teacher.

Chris Atkinson, Grade 3
Our Lady of Mercy Regional School, NY

Fall

Crunch! Crunch!
The leaves crunch!
Whoosh, whoosh says the wind.
Clink, Clank go the pebbles on the ground.
Drip, drop sings the rain.
Boo! Boo!
There goes a ghost!

Mila Jones, Grade 1
Milton Terrace South Elementary School, NY

Dolphins

Dolphins
Are very
Very, very shy
They're scared you will
Hurt them so they don't
Let you ride them. They eat
A lot of fish. They eat whatever fish
They want. They stay under water for a while
When they run out of breath they go to
The top of the water and squirt out some water.

Ashlyn Pfeuffer, Grade 2
Wyland Elementary School, PA

Writing

We all love writing!
Read, then write.
I love writing stories.
Tell people about writing.
I do not hate writing.
Need to practice.
Get a good grade for writing.

Arianna Zaccour, Grade 3
Colebrook Primary School, NY

Flower Garden

The beautiful blues and the radiant reds
Of the floral flower garden.
The lovely lilies and the precious poppies
You could just snooze in the blues
Of the radiant reds and the yelling yellows
The lovely lilies and the precious poppies
Of the wonderful flower garden.

Grace Gerhauser, Grade 3
Edgewood Elementary School, PA

Valeria

Valeria is yellow.
She smells like roses.
She sounds like daisies.
She tastes like vanilla.
She feels chubby.
She looks like the brightest star.
I love my baby sister, Valeria.

Nicholas Leonard, Grade 3
Evergreen Elementary School, PA

Dinosaurs/Dragons

Dinosaurs
Dead, extinct
Roam, walk, eat
Teeth, claws, wings, fire
Flying, biting, snoring
Creature, scales
Dragons

Alec Epstein, Grade 3
Edgewood Elementary School, PA

My Grandma and Me

My grandma's a bottle
and I'm the water inside.

My grandma's a lunch box
and I'm the snack inside.

My grandma's a wallet
and I'm the money inside.

My grandma's some water
and I'm the fruit coloring put inside.

My grandma's a pencil
and I'm the eraser.

My grandma's a folder
and I'm paper inside.

My grandma's her
and I'm me.

Aaron DeCourte, Grade 3
Public School 114 Ryder Elementary, NY

A True Friend

A true friend is someone who
you can share your toys with.
A true friend is someone who
can accept you for who you are.
A true friend is someone who
can tell the truth to you.
A true friend is someone who
listens when you have something to say.
A true friend is someone who
sees you for who you really are.
A true friend is someone who
makes you feel better when you are
gloomy or devastated.
And my true friend is Luis Medrano
and no matter what he will
always be my true friend.

Zachary Zambarano, Grade 3
Sarah Dyer Barnes School, RI

Nurse Sharks

N urse sharks are gentle.
U nlike other sharks they can pump water over their gills.
R un when a nurse shark bites you.
S quid can blind them.
E ats crabs and small boney fish.

S ome can have up to 3,000 teeth.
H armless if you don't bug it.
A favorite food is seal.
R apid.
K rill is mm good.

Sean Hegarty, Grade 3
The Edgartown School, MA

The Earth Is God's Gift

God made people happy by giving them Earth,
it is the extraordinary place of our birth.

We have to take care to keep the Earth clean,
so we can see the beautiful colors of blue and green.

In the clear sky you can see the stars blooming bright,
it is an unforgettable sight.

This gift of our Earth is so great,
so let's do all we can before it's too late.

Karina Ellis, Grade 3
Our Lady of Mercy Regional School, NY

Nature

Nature lets people and animals stay alive
The water that nature gives us lets the water animals dive.

Sounds of nature makes plants feel alive
When you see buzzing bees on the hives.

Now you see what many things nature can do
And plants from nature can cure a flu.

Nature oh nature many things you can do
Nature oh nature many things it can do for you!

Melody Anthony, Grade 3
Public School 131, NY

Leaf

Leaf, you're so pretty
with all those bright colors
green, orange, yellow, red
all mixed together
you look so
pretty under water
you shine like a
spider's web.

Avery Rice, Grade 2
Tashua School, CT

The Sun

The sun is yellow
The sun is high up in the sky
The sun is near other planets in space
It brightens our lives
It warms our bodies
It helps the plants and animals survive
Without the sun everything would be dark
The sun is very important for all of us

Anayeli Vazquez, Grade 3
Public School 131, NY

Hearts

Hearts, hearts, in the sky
Hearts, hearts, way up high
They go away when you're mad.
They come back when you're sad
Hearts are red, sometimes pink.
When you're mad they will shrink.
Hearts, hearts, in the sky.
Hearts, hearts, way up high.

Marleena Detweiler, Grade 3
St Maria Goretti School, PA

Hamster

Hamster
tan with red eyes
she sleeps most of the day
happy whenever I come home
snuggles

Nathan Cooperdock, Grade 3
Clinton Street Elementary School, NY

Soccer

I like soccer
Yes I do
Kick the ball
And maybe score

Dodge opponents
Charging at you
Make a move
And pass quickly

Now you're free
Get ready
Receive the pass
Shoot, score, you won

Avery Hudson, Grade 2
Memorial School, NH

Reading with Dad

Sweet sounds
coming from his lips

The words from a
wonderful book
whisper to me

Every night
as I am falling asleep
I dream of the book
and wonder what's
going to happen next.

Elizabeth Durham, Grade 2
Fountaindale Elementary School, MD

Puppy

Puppy
Cute, fluffy
Fetching, chewing, barking
Puppies love to play fetch in the park.
Dog

Lindsey Turner, Grade 2
Wyland Elementary School, PA

My Best Friend Lexus

My best friend Lexus
That special friend
who I can tell my
deepest secrets to
That special friend
who never leaves me
out when I'm alone
That special friend
who never likes to
lie to me when we talk
That special friend
who never judges me
about who I am
My best friend Lexus
          Brittany Mollicone, Grade 3
          Sarah Dyer Barnes School, RI

Ice Skating

Ice skating, ice skating
Very very fun
Be careful!
To hold on tight
Tie your laces
And
You'll do just right
Very very great
I know it's hard to stop
Oh my gosh
You know what it is
It's ice skating
Whoa it's so fun
Come join before it's done!
          Ayanna Agarrat, Grade 3
          Public School 114 Ryder Elementary, NY

My Friend Is a True Friend

My friend is a true friend
whose there for me when I need them.
My friend is a true friend
who likes to share a friendship.
My friend is a true friend
who accepts you for you.
My friend is a true friend
who likes to hear what you say.
My friend is a true friend
who shares secrets with you.
My friend is a true friend
who loves to see you happy.
My friend is a true friend like Shania.
My friend is a true friend
          Amber Scoco, Grade 3
          Sarah Dyer Barnes School, RI

Spring

I am waiting
I am waiting
I am waiting for
beautiful spring to come.

I am waiting
I am waiting
I am waiting to play
outside with my best friends.

I am waiting
I am waiting
I am waiting for
the smelling flowers to bloom.
          Rahul Raja, Grade 2
          Pine Tree Elementary School, NY

Peace

Peace is quiet,
my sister being nice,
my mom cooking,
playing calmly,
and me sleeping.
          Tyler Flynn, Grade 2
          Wells Central School, NY

Love

Love is like blood that
Pumps through my body
Every second of every day.
Love flows through me…
Always!
          Rebecca Pietrafesa, Grade 3
          A.P. Willits Elementary School, NY

Spring

In the spring we go outdoors,
It is better than indoors.

Spring is a beautiful season,
The sun is the reason.

In spring the sun is very bright,
It's very bright later at night.

In spring the bugs really bother us,
Even on the bus.

Cameron Wasko, Grade 3
Susquehanna Community Elementary School, PA

Summer Lions

The sun is warming the Earth,
like the lion's warmth of adrenaline chasing down its prey.

The thunder is a raging roar of lions,
trying to fight over a female.

Rain is the shaking sweat of the lion.

Their manes flapping in the wind while running,
are the cool breezes of the end of summer.

Siddharth Chenrayan, Grade 3
Mary C Howse Elementary School, PA

Feelings

Mad feels as red as fire
Sad feels as blue as the ocean
Scared feels as black as a blackout
Lonely feels as gray as a cloudy day
Shy feels as gold as glitter
Angry feels as orange as an orange
Happy feels as yellow as a lemon
Silly feels as pink as bubblegum
Hurt feels as green as grass
Excited feels as purple as the purple in the rainbow
Grumpy feels as brown as a log

Vincent Geiger, Grade 1
Buckley Country Day School, NY

Fire

Orange and red
Hot and dangerous

When I get tired
I turn out my light
As I prepare for the long long night

I am very happy when I am alive
Because I love to help and love to destroy

I am feared by many when I breathe my hot breath
I can also destroy any building or house

For I am fire

Billy Huggett, Grade 3
Indian Lane Elementary School, PA

Beauty Is…

Waking up with a smile,
that lasts the whole day
The confidence to be yourself,
and not change in any way
To be an individual
and persevere to succeed
To be smart, strong, and honest,
without any fear
To be kind, caring, and giving,
to those that you meet
These lessons my Mom has taught me,
show compassion and be sweet.
Beauty is from within, and only by showing that,
will Beauty show on the outside.

Michelle Husslein, Grade 3
Mount Pleasant Elementary School, NY

Peace

Peace is when my brothers are not at my mom's house being loud,
my mom, my baby brother, and I playing on a sunny day,
people not picking on me or other people,
no one talking or making a sound,
and walking with my mom and baby brother on a sunny day.

Camryn Brenan, Grade 2
Wells Central School, NY

The Stars

Yellow and white
Little and bright

I will reach out with my little hands
And hug you in your sleep

I will look over you at night
I will be your guardian

I look like I have been
Sunbathing at the beach

For I am the stars
Aurora Difranco, Grade 3
Indian Lane Elementary School, PA

Spring

Flowers, flowers
Here and there

Flowers, flowers
There and here

Flowers, flowers
Blue and yellow

Flowers, flowers
Purple and pink

Flowers are everywhere!
Bryan Nam, Grade 1
Corl Street Elementary School, PA

Ocean

Dad says: "Go to sleep,"
but instead I lie in bed
pretending...

my bathtub
is the ocean.
I swim around
in the deep water.

The water is like
the breeze outside.
It makes me
shiver.
Brenda Martinez, Grade 3
Number 2 School, NY

A Pebble

Small and dirty
Smooth and flat

When night falls I am lonely and sad
I am nowhere to be found

When summer comes around
I look forward to skipping with my friends

When the sun is up in the sky
I love to dance as the water moves me

For I am a pebble
Sean McGroary, Grade 3
Indian Lane Elementary School, PA

Rain Drops

Dropping from the sky
on a spring night
making lots of puddles
on the ground
making lots of mud too
so wet and muddy
I think I'll go inside!!!
Sarah Murphy, Grade 2
Primrose School, NY

Hockey Star

Edward is my name
like my dad's it is the same
hockey is my game
fans will shout my name
mad skills will bring me fame
this is what I claim
Edward is my name
Edward Clark, Grade 1
St Joan of Arc School, PA

Jake

There once was a fellow named Jake
He liked to swim in a lake
One day he jumped in
And saw a big fin
And that was the end of young Jake.

> *Michael Daddona, Grade 3*
> *Southold Elementary School, NY*

Man from Space

There once was a man from space,
Who ran a very good race.
He came in first
And died of thirst.
Now he is in last place.

> *Liam Redmond, Grade 1*
> *Mater Christi School, VT*

My Dog

B est bud to me,
R aces me down the yard,
U sed to follow me,
N o one can stop him,
O h, you are my best friend!

> *Salvatore Prestigiacomo, Grade 2*
> *Helen B Duffield Elementary School, NY*

I See a Hippo

Hippo
high, low
walking on ground
peeking from the mud
Cool!

> *Meghan Chipman, Grade 1*
> *St Rose School, CT*

Fall

Watch the leaves fall from branches.
Flowers losing petals.
Acorns dropping from trees.
Listen to the sound of crunchy red leaves.
Everything so colorful!

> *Ally Appel, Grade 3*
> *John Ward Elementary School, MA*

Spring

Spring sings the king
rings the castle bell to
tell the people come out!
He shouts winter is done!
Time for fun

> *Travis Wright, Grade 1*
> *Park Avenue School, NY*

Bunny

Bunny
Furry fluffy
Hops, nips, sleeps
They are so cute.
Cage

> *Lou Johnston, Grade 2*
> *The Fourth Presbyterian School, MD*

Hats

I have a hat on my head.
My hat is a Mets hat.
My hat is a baseball hat.
My hat keeps the sun out of my face.
I like my hat.

> *Liam Trears, Grade 3*
> *Our Lady of Hope School, NY*

Fall Is Coming

Fall is really here!
I can feel the chilly air.
The leaves are falling everywhere.
The football championship is very near.
I love fall!

> *Van Karsten, Grade 3*
> *Southold Elementary School, NY*

I Love You

I love you the pinkest...
I love you more than the pink roses
I love you more than the pink dress
The touch of a pink teddy bear
The taste of pink lemonade juice

> *Ashley Lang, Grade 3*
> *Southold Elementary School, NY*

School

S mart students
C omputer class
H ome schooled
O pen doors
O rganized desk
L ittle children
Cheyenne Celletti, Grade 3
Milton Fuller Roberts School, MA

The Wire

I thought
that a
wire was
a snake
that could
ZAP things.
Shalor McKee, Grade 2
Avery School, MA

Friends

My friends and I are like trees,
Growing tall into the air.
We have the same trunk.
Our branches grow out in
different directions,
But we are always together.
Sean Hembach, Grade 3
Meadow Drive School, NY

Clocks

C locks tell time.
L ots of parts.
O range clocks are cool.
C locks can be digital.
K eep clocks as decoration.
S ome clocks ring when it is 12:00
Isabella Mariani, Grade 2
Long Meadow Elementary School, CT

Rainbow

Red roses
Orange crayon
Yellow leaf
Leprechaun
Blue bird
Purple folder
Ileiny Lacen, Kindergarten
Robert M Hughes School, MA

Teacher

Mrs. Sharon
EEEEEK!
Red hair
Freckled skin
Brown eyes
Fast walker.
Cameron McMaster, Grade 3
Milton Fuller Roberts School, MA

Balloon

My balloon is bright red.
It has a long swirly string.
It is very fat and round.
It flies high.
Christopher Jablonski, Grade 2
Helen B Duffield Elementary School, NY

Summer

Hot, fun
Swimming, sweating, playing
It's a hot day
Season
Nermine Dani, Grade 2
Long Meadow Elementary School, CT

Spring

I love rain puddles,
because you can jump in them.
Then, you make a splash!
Yannick Ashton DeBarros, Grade 2
The Fourth Presbyterian School, MD

Spring

Birds chirping in nests.
Rainbows after the rain.
Cherry blossoms bloom.
Megan Wormald, Grade 2
The Fourth Presbyterian School, MD

The Tiger
Silently, silently, the tiger stalks his prey
He watches the antelope that he's about to slay

His paws are so silent, they never make a sound
He crouches so low, he's nearly part of the ground

The antelope senses danger and starts to run
But the tiger does too, and now here comes the fun

The antelope starts going as fast as he can
It's like lightning! Whoosh! That's how fast he ran

"Oh no!" thinks the tiger. "My prey got away!"
"I'll have to try again some other day."

Paige Looney, Grade 3
Craneville School, MA

Sea
Wonders of the ocean world,
It is a land which into man can be hurled.
Wonders, wonders of the sea,
I can hear them calling me.
Whales, sharks, dolphins dance,
Truckfish, coral, otters prance.
Swimming wonders, what a sight,
Beauty, beauty, day or night.
The sea is a wonder to us.
There's a whale as long as a bus!
The sea is something for which we should care.
It is really quite rare.
So please, take care of the sea.
It's quite important to you and me.

Heather Parkin, Grade 3
Woodlin Elementary School, MD

Winter Wonders
Ice skates gliding on the pond,
while sounds of people slipping and falling on the ground.
Snow is drifting. People are lifting each other's spirits.
As we had our outfits on with all of the knits,
we went home to have some fresh hot soup.

Anna Duquette, Grade 3
Craneville School, MA

Dogs

Dogs, dogs, I love dogs!
If I had a dog she would be a golden retriever.
She would sniff, jump and bark,
Be loved, be brave, roll over.

Dogs, dogs, I love dogs.
I can't stand it that I don't have a golden retriever!
She would jog, hunt, and howl,
Have puppies, sleep with me, love me the best,
Go wherever I go.

Dogs, dogs, I love dogs!
If I had a dog she would be a golden retriever.

Jalyss Nichols, Grade 2
Carlyle C Ring Elementary School, NY

Summer Lions

The air gets cool.

Lightning gets ready to revolt,
like a pack of lions ready to attack.

The shine of the yellow coats and shrewd claws
is the moon glistening in the night sky.

The lion's boisterous roars,
are only the blaring winds howling.

When the lightning stops,
the lion retreats to its den.

Aditya Deshmukh, Grade 3
Mary C Howse Elementary School, PA

Game Stop

In the store breathing really hard
In and out I puffed
Like a human
Jumping up and down
People shopping
Making Game Stop
Come alive!!!

Omaree Williams, Grade 3
Public School 40 Samuel Huntington, NY

My Mother's a Mother

My Mother's a mother
She's honest and true
And if I'm stuck
She helps get me through
She takes me out shopping
And makes me dinner
And if I had to rate her
She'd sure be a winner
Whenever I'm scared
Or have some big fears
Instead of my mother,
Super Mom appears
When there's a bump in the road, she flattens it
When there's a hill to climb, she gets out my gear
She helps me get confident without a doubt
And helps me overcome my fears
All I can say now is "thank you" Mom
For bringing me into this world with no trouble
And now I admit it, I say it's true
Boy do I owe you double!

Rose Kohler, Grade 3
Stall Brook School, MA

Spring

Some are evil, some are kind.
I think in my mind.

Pretty flowers come to mind every day,
Stars are very bright.

The Easter bunny is nice and kind,
When we have an easter hunt eggs are hard to find.

My mom and dad start to plant,
I see ants.

Andrea's Birthday is April 2, 2001.
Spring is done.

Pretty colors come out in the spring,
The birds sing.

Angela Bianco, Grade 3
Susquehanna Community Elementary School, PA

Pears

Pears are so sweet.
I like to eat.
If it could smile, I would smile too.
They're so crunchy and green like grass,
It is fun to share with my class.
Rebecca Whittam, Grade 3
St Maria Goretti School, PA

Zig-Zag

Up and down and all around
Point in every corner
Wavy, straight, easy to concentrate.
Once you get a paper.
Draw and make a person great!
Molly Nero, Grade 3
Heron Pond Elementary School, NH

Dots and Spots

Dots and spots everywhere.
On the ground and in my hair!
Dots with spots, spots with dots!
Dots and spots are meant to share!
Dots and spots everywhere!
Madison Uth, Grade 3
St Maria Goretti School, PA

Easter Is Fun

Easter is special.
A bunny brings a basket.
Candy is so sweet.
Hunting Easter eggs is so much fun.
I like finding the big blue ones.
Alexis Harris, Grade 3
Penn-Kidder Campus, PA

Cereal

Milky, yummy, sweet,
Crunchy, cold, tasty, tender,
Succulent, flaky,
Savory, delicious meal,
Letting me have even more.
Drew Johnson, Grade 3
Heron Pond Elementary School, NH

Easter

Do you like candy?
It is a good tasty treat.
Candy is so sweet.
I feel like I'm in heaven,
When I eat a piece of it.
Shantel Nicholas, Grade 3
Penn-Kidder Campus, PA

Bikes

B ikes get your legs moving
I like to ride bikes
K ids love bikes
E very tire has air
S ometimes bikes have pegs
Anish Patel, Grade 2
Long Meadow Elementary School, CT

My Sister

My sister is the best.
She aces every test.
I love her so dear.
She always brings me cheer.
But sometimes she's a pest.
Stefanos Kosmidis Jaramillo, Grade 3
Public School 2 Alfred Zimberg, NY

Fish

Here I see a tiger, into the water he goes
Looking for a fish
With his large nose.
He throws his fish up in the air,
Into a rose.
Katie Shambaugh, Grade 3
Somerset Elementary School, MD

School

School is great school is good!
We're learning everything we should.
Social studies, science, math,
Music, gym, reading art,
I think we will be very smart!
Ada Onofre, Grade 3
Public School 1 The Bergen School, NY

Hair

Hair can be any color.
Black, brown, yellow, or blonde.
Don't matter if you're old or young.
It just matters if you have hair.
Your hair can wave in the air and fly.
You can feel your hair soft and smooth if you wash it.

Nikkita Louis, Grade 3
Public School 114 Ryder Elementary, NY

The Ocean of Maine

Splash! the waves crash onto the beach
Timber! yells a guy on the sandy beach
While a dark brown tree falls to the ground
Crash! a huge tsunami wave hits the coast of Maine
Earthquake shocks rumble through the ocean!
Look as cars and waves crash into buildings!

Shawn Allen, Grade 2
Mayfield Elementary School, NY

What Is Black

Black is the night.
Black is the road.
Black is an owl hooting
Black is a toad jumping log to log
Black is a thunder storm on a very dark night
Black is a taste of being out of sight

Gerald Drumgoole, Grade 3
Colebrook Primary School, NY

Spooky Night

In the night, people say the night's a fright.
Bushes rustle, people silently bustle.
Owls hoot, looters loot.
Mice scuttle, cats rumble.
A deathly silence.
That's why people say the night's a fright.

Shidong Xu, Grade 3
The Tobin School, MA

Niagara Falls

Fog is spreading
Beauty is arriving
The legend is watching you
Rain coats wearing
All the tourists watching its beauty
You have to see it for yourself
You could smell nature
The water beast is inside
Good bye Niagara Falls
You have a noble heart
Sreedatta Kaligotla, Grade 2
Helen B Duffield Elementary School, NY

Canada

I used to live in Canada
For about 5 years

The winters were cold
But summers were hot
And beaches were cold
But mountains were not

I used to live in Canada
But now I do not!
Syeda Mahnoor Zainab, Grade 3
Public School 131, NY

The Lemon

The lemon
Is as
Yellow
As the sun!

It is so
Bright it
Seems
Bigger
Than me!
Logan McAloon, Grade 1
St Rose School, CT

Spring Is Like My Baby Sister

Spring is like my baby sister.
Sometimes she cries just like
spring can bring a lot of rain
When I see her she makes me
feel good inside like a warm
day under the sun
They're full of life and joy
They're soft and sweet
Everyone loves to have them around
That is spring to me.
Evan Karagiannis, Grade 3
Public School 2 Alfred Zimberg, NY

A True Friend

A true friend is
someone who is nice to you
A true friend does not
say mean words to you
A true friend is a good listener
A true friend calls you when you
are sad or sick
A true friend makes you
laugh when you are down
That is a true friend
Joshua Remington, Grade 3
Sarah Dyer Barnes School, RI

Candy

To me
Candy is like
Paper
In my mouth.

I don't like chocolate
I don't like lollipops
I don't like caramel

It all tastes so bad!
Nina Furrier, Grade 1
St Rose School, CT

I Am
I am a squirrel who has never had a peanut.
I wonder if I like peanuts.
I hear squirrels chewing on peanuts.
I see squirrels looking for peanuts.
I want to taste one.
I am a squirrel who has never had a peanut.
Brittany Martin, Grade 3
Como Park Elementary School, NY

Music & Things
There's music in an alien
There's music in a dog
There's music in people
I can't wait to see everyone again.

So, I wish everyone nothing but a GREAT day!
Joshua Rainone, Grade 2
Milton Fuller Roberts School, MA

Summer Fun
Splish, splash —
The kids are in the pool…
Squirt those kids!
Buzz, buzz —
The bees go by.
I love Summer!
Sydney LaVoy, Grade 1
Milton Terrace South Elementary School, NY

Differences
All around the world people are different
Sharing their cultures on their mountains,
On their islands, in their deserts.
Around the world we celebrate our differences.
John Fitzpatrick, Grade 2
Dartmouth Early Learning Center, MA

Dogs
I like dogs a lot.
Dogs like to play all day long.
My dog's name is Max.
Giuliana Capparello, Grade 2
Fonda-Fultonville Elementary School, NY

The Seven Dogs

There were seven dogs
Chewing a bone
The first one felt tired
and went to sleep.
The second one kept barking
The third one chased a cat
The fourth one rolled over onto another dog
The fifth one wanted his owner
The sixth one still chewing a bone
And the seventh one
Was still alone

Lea Frawley, Grade 3
Our Lady of Hope School, NY

I Am an Alien

Aliens are green
they are yucky
they have 16 eyes
he has really long
arms and little toes
they have red eyes
and no teeth!
And they have really
cool gadgets and
a big ship and
they are big.

Cody Camilo, Grade 2
Public School 232 The Walter Ward School, NY

Blue

Blue is the color of the sky.
Blue is the color of foamy waves, washing up on shore.
Blue is the color of sweet blueberry popsicles.
Blue is the color of party balloons.
Blue tastes like freshly washed blueberries.
Blue smells like soap in the bathroom.
Blue sounds like rain falling to the ground.
Blue looks like a pair of jeans.
Blue feels like a leather jacket.
Blue makes me sad.
Blue is my favorite color.

Joshua Bolan, Grade 3
Evergreen Elementary School, PA

Spring

Spring's coming, spring's coming!
Are you happy that spring's coming?
I see people riding their bikes
Do you see what I see what I see?
Birds, squirrels and bears come out from their homes
Spring's coming, spring's coming!
Are you happy?
Do you see what I see?
People are walking
Do you see the sun shining?
Everyone is out!
Do you see what I see?

Michelle Mitchell, Grade 2
Public School 232 The Walter Ward School, NY

The Happiest Spring!

Beautiful sunshine,
school passes by.
Right out in the yard,
little birds would fly!
There might be some rain,
but that doesn't matter.
Spring excites my brain,
I cannot wait for spring to
come! We do work in the sun,
spring is tomorrow!
I'm having so much fun,
with the best teacher Blum!!!

Altay Ozkan, Grade 2
Public School 232 The Walter Ward School, NY

Monica

Monica
Funny, active, caring, smart
Sister of Richard and Cameron
Lover of summer vacation, stuffed animals, and sunny days
Who feels that school is too long, McDonald's should be less expensive,
And bee stings should be less painful
Who fears fire, ghosts, and animals dying
Who would like to see the Amazon, Africa, and Oklahoma
Burke

Monica Burke, Grade 2
Klein Elementary School, PA

All About Spring

The spring is here, the winter is gone,
I can finally run barefoot on the lawn.

The air is warm and my clothes get lighter,
it seems the sun shines even brighter.

The flowers start growing out of the ground,
and you also hear the bird's singing sound.

I'm looking forward to go to the park with my friend,
I want to stay the whole day to the end.

I can hear the buzzing bees,
and see new leaves sprouting on the trees.

I can't wait for the butterflies to come out,
that's the time I can drink from the playground's water fountain spout.

Spring is here, summer is coming soon,
now I'm imagining what I could do in the hot time by looking at the moon.

Taina Padilla, Grade 3
Public School 105 Senator Abraham Bernstein, NY

Spring

Spring is fun,
Spring is fun in the sun.

In spring you can feel the gentle breeze,
In the spring I sneeze.

In spring you see the pretty rainbow,
I like to play with yo-yo's.

The flowers start to bud,
There is a lot of mud.

My birthday is in Spring,
It is a big thing.

I like to go hiking,
You start biking.

Andrea Westbrook, Grade 3
Susquehanna Community Elementary School, PA

Buds
Buds
Red, small
Growing, opening, sprouting
Leaves can be small.
Leaves
Hannah Buhl, Grade 3
Chestnut Street Elementary School, PA

Forest Fog
Fluffy clouds surround me
As cool, moist air
Tricks my eyes
Blurry trees dance
In misty gray fog
Nashwan Habboosh, Grade 1
Dartmouth Early Learning Center, MA

Twilight a Hamster
Hamster
Fat, sweetheart
Eating, squeaking, sleeping
Loves sunflower seeds
Hamster
Breanna Fasanella, Grade 3
Evergreen Elementary School, PA

Books
B ooks take us away
O pen our imagination
O ffer inspiration
K nowledge grows inside us
S weeping us to different places.
Quinlan Roscoe, Grade 1
Dartmouth Early Learning Center, MA

My Teacher
Mrs. B.
Smart and kind
Teaching, working, and grading
Queen of The Bee Team
Teacher
Morgan Gonyer, Grade 3
Evergreen Elementary School, PA

A Bird's Song
Walking through the forest
I hear the tweet of a bird
Singing its own song.
Sitting down
I fall asleep to that beautiful music
Mirelle Hadley, Grade 2
Dartmouth Early Learning Center, MA

Baseball
Baseball
Fun and active
Hitting, catching, throwing
A fun sport
Wiffle ball
Connor McShea, Grade 3
Evergreen Elementary School, PA

School
School
learning, teaching
time to go to my class
I love school and my new teacher
classes
Katherine Klein, Grade 3
Clinton Street Elementary School, NY

Daisy
Flower
Small, colorful
Planting, growing, blooming
They are very colorful.
Daisy
Alex Rezzelle, Grade 3
Chestnut Street Elementary School, PA

Ice Cream
Ice Cream
Cone with 3 scoops
Greeny, Orangey ice cream
just came out and I ate them all
yummy
Tyler Arndt, Grade 3
Clinton Street Elementary School, NY

Arctic Fox
Is an omnivore
Fur is a blanket of snow
Lives on the tundra
Noah Levine, Grade 2
The Burnham Elementary School, CT

Waves
Sandy is the shore
as the waves crash into it.
Out to sea it goes.
Kamari Holder, Grade 2
Simpson-Waverly School, CT

Penguins
Black and white feathers
Bird of different sizes
Eats fish, krill, and squid
Annika Vikstrom, Grade 2
The Burnham Elementary School, CT

A Walk in the Woods
Walking in the woods
a snake twisting and swirling
winding through the grass
Micah Duncan, Grade 2
Simpson-Waverly School, CT

Spring
The yellow sun shines
Flowers begin to blossom
Butterflies fly high
Olivia Seger, Grade 3
The Burnham Elementary School, CT

Fierce
The fierce tornado
moves fast and furiously
through the dusty town.
Justin Vega, Grade 2
Simpson-Waverly School, CT

The Monkey
Monkey with a shoe
Swinging on a big long vine
Eats the large laces
Ethan Southard, Grade 3
The Burnham Elementary School, CT

Shark
The shark swims quickly
zigzagging through the green sea
chasing his dinner
Keith Williams, Grade 2
Simpson-Waverly School, CT

The Mystery Owl
It has orange claws
Big bold yellow and black eyes
It can turn its head
Kaitlin Stumpf, Grade 3
The Burnham Elementary School, CT

Sharks
There are many sharks
In the ocean deep and big.
All sharks have sharp teeth.
Owen Breisch, Grade 3
Willow Creek Elementary School, PA

6 Hours of Awesome School
Exciting schoolwork
Adventurous days at school
Heartwarming homework
R. Kyle Monaghan, Grade 3
The Burnham Elementary School, CT

The Sun
So bright as the stars
Very hot as daylight
So yellow!
Anesha Sandiford, Grade 2
Public School 235 Lenox, NY

Colorful Leaves
I jump in colorful leaves
I hear crunch, crunch everywhere
The leaves come down
It is fall
Everybody eats turkey
They come from the trees
They hit my face
They change colors

Miguelangel Grullon, Grade 3
Public School 115 Alexander Humboldt, NY

A Special Woman in My Life
The special woman in my life is amazing!
She dances and prances and laughs with me.
She's perfect on the inside and special on the outside!
She is the woman I want to be with.
She is the bright light in my heart.
My special woman is enthusiastic
and buys me scholastic books.
My special woman is…my mom.

Tatiana Gallego, Grade 3
Public School 232 The Walter Ward School, NY

A True Friend
A true friend would call you every day
A true friend would share their stuff with you
A true friend would tell you the truth
A true friend would stand up for you
Someone you can tell your secrets to
A true friend would help you get off the ground
A true friend would play with you every day
A true friend

Michael Sabatini, Grade 3
Sarah Dyer Barnes School, RI

At Home
Ride, ride on my bike.
Weeee, goes me!

Run, run with my friends.
Yay! We all say!

Ryan Ditoro, Grade 1
Milton Terrace South Elementary School, NY

Jennifer the Singer
Dad says, "Go to sleep,"
but instead I lie in bed
pretending...

I am a singer.
My music is like singing birds.
When I sing
it makes me feel proud.
All my fans are calling me
and I like that.

They say, "She is the best singer ever."
I feel like
I want to meet them
but I can't.
People keep calling me.

I hear my fans.
They say, "I want to meet her."
All my fans are calling me
and I like that.
Jennifer Reyes, Grade 3
Number 2 School, NY

A Feather
Feather
as soft
as a pillow
as fluffy
as a cloud
a grassy pattern
brown as
tree bark
fading
into white
it fans me
and falls
peacefully
down
to the
ground.
Juliette Doyle, Grade 2
Tashua School, CT

Cactus
Cactus'
Spikes
Are as
Sharp
As a sword.

When I touch it
I feel like 100 knives
Are
Striking
Me!
Zachary Reilly, Grade 1
St Rose School, CT

Tanner
He lies asleep
As I watch TV
I make a move
Tanner looks up at me.
He's orange and white
With a tiger stripe
Running down his tail.
Tanner is my cat
And that is that
I sure love him.
Tanner
Rachel Weiss, Grade 3
Meeting House Hill School, CT

Scissors
Snapping
Like an alligator
Gulping like a fish
Two swords
That go snip snap clack
Pointy
At
The
End
Of
Its tip!
Jennifer Kang, Grade 2
Fountaindale Elementary School, MD

Hares

Bunnies, Bunnies, Bunnies
white, brown, black Bunnies
big, small, little Bunnies
hopping, eating, drinking Bunnies
laying, playing, jumping Bunnies
Bunnies, Bunnies, Bunnies
Natalie Martino, Grade 3
Our Lady of Hope School, NY

Love

Love is a light red color
It tastes like ice cream on a summer day
It smells like a rose
It looks like a beautiful beach
It sounds like laughing
Love makes me feel like hugging
Jack Murphy, Grade 2
Klein Elementary School, PA

Spring

S now melting
P eople walking outside in rain clothes
R ainy
I ce melting
N o snow
G rass growing
Devon Bright, Grade 3
Chestnut Street Elementary School, PA

Clouds

White and fluffy floating in the sky.
It's flying high like a butterfly.
Oh, how I wish I could fly like you.
If I could fly I would come too.
Autumn Sheldon, Grade 3
Craneville School, MA

The Flower

I like the flowers
I like the sun in the spring time
It is hot in spring
Johnson Peow, Grade 1
St Louis Elementary School, MA

Spring

S trawberries start growing
P laying on the playground
R olling in grass
I rises bloom
N ests are being built
G rass gets greener
Kristen Zilkofski, Grade 3
Chestnut Street Elementary School, PA

Spring

S prouts come out
P eople playing in puddles
R ainbows
I ndigo skies
N ew grass growing
G ardens
Raisa Wright, Grade 3
Chestnut Street Elementary School, PA

Spring

S now melting
P retty flowers
R ainy
I nsects coming out to feed
N ice weather
G reen grass
Alysha Biel, Grade 3
Chestnut Street Elementary School, PA

Giving Five

It is nice to give five
When somebody is live
You give it to the teacher
So you do not sit on the bleacher.
Cameron Robertson, Grade 3
Heron Pond Elementary School, NH

Fantastic Flowers

I love the flowers
Spring, the best season ever!
I really love spring.
Julia Smith, Grade 1
St Louis Elementary School, MA

Easter

Eggs are scattered all around
People dressed up
Going to church
Dyeing eggs
Chocolate bunnies
Easter egg hunts
Kids are so happy for Easter
Taylor Albert, Grade 3
Meeting House Hill School, CT

Flowers

Blue and pink and green
Orange to yellow
Tulips and daffodils
Red, white with pink
Bees playing in the flowers
Butterflies drinking juice
Flowers are beautiful
Angelina Caltabiano, Grade 2
Helen B Duffield Elementary School, NY

A Special Friend

A special friend
would share their problems with you
A special friend
would make you feel better
A special friend
is an active listener
A special friend
Marissa Betters, Grade 3
Sarah Dyer Barnes School, RI

A Mess

That room is a mess!
There's a dress in the corner.
A shoe on the floor,
Skis on the TV next to me.
Who's room is this?
No, it's not mine,
or, is it? It is!
Lily Rouleau, Grade 2
Memorial School, NH

Library

The library
is so much fun.
Place to visit
Choosing books
So many! Which one?
It is so hard to choose
fiction or nonfiction?
Because you don't know
what you can get
there are so many
good books to get.
Mikey Rotondo, Grade 2
Tashua School, CT

Exploding Volcano

Splash! a volcano just burst splattering
lava through the air!
Bright orange and red
Oh! it scares me
SAVE ME somebody!
I'm melting so fast!
Oh no save me!
HELP!
I don't want to melt
HELP!
I'm only eight years old!
Haleigh Warner, Grade 2
Mayfield Elementary School, NY

All About Me

I am from lots of books.
I am from swivel chairs.
I am from Wawa.
I am from Aunt Qun.
I am from "Go Green."
I am from cherries.
I am from Buddha.
I am from China.
I am from Wildwood Beach.
I am from the Jonas Brothers.
Crystal Fung, Grade 3
William Ziegler Elementary School, PA

Spring

The flowers are blooming,
the skies are booming.

The birds are singing,
there is lots of ringing.

The bunnies are hopping,
there is a lot of bopping.

It's time to go fishing,
there will be a lot of wishing.

The sun will shine,
the butterflies are mine.

The gardeners are gardening and planting,
and spring buds are sprouting.

It's time to go hiking,
it's time to go biking.

Lia Heath, Grade 3
Susquehanna Community Elementary School, PA

Spring Time

Springtime is really fun.
It brings out joy for everyone.

Every kid searching for Easter eggs.
Running and running with their legs.

Every kid on the block.
Shopping and getting new Easter socks.

Springtime treats are everywhere.
Sometimes moms are curling their hair.

Shopping for new Easter time stuff.
Sometimes for parents is really tough.

Hope you like this springtime poem.
Grab all your friends I hope you'll show 'em!

Raelyn Sepull, Grade 3
Ellicott Road Elementary School, NY

Cars

In my dream
I dream of cars...zooming fast.
Some are old and some are new,
Some are even clever too!
Saving gas and using batteries
As they whizz by.
Some are red
Some are blue
Some are purple too!
Green cars are green for the energy they save.
They come in purple
And are faster than my turtle.
My dream is over...
My cars are gone...
Now it is dawn!

Anthony McKenzie, Grade 2
The Delphi Academy, MA

My Best Friend

Brittany
My best friend Brittany always is my partner
My best friend
always tells me the truth
My best friend makes
me feel better when I am gloomy
My best friend
listens to me when I talk
My best friend always
plays with me at recess
My best friend
doesn't lie to me
My special friend will always
be my friend
My best friend Brittany

Lexus Madirira, Grade 3
Sarah Dyer Barnes School, RI

Jamaica, Jamaica

What a wonderful phrase
A good place to be
Jamaica, Jamaica

Keyona Quashie, Grade 3
Public School 40 Samuel Huntington, NY

Baseball

Baseball is brown and white.
It tastes like mud.
It sounds like bang!
It smells like victory.
It looks like fans going wild.
It makes me feel proud.
Stephen Bafaloukos, Grade 3
Evergreen Elementary School, PA

Spring

S parrows are singing
P lanting flowers all over
R obins are chirping
I t is getting warmer
N o more snow
G rass is green again
Mara Nicklas, Grade 3
Chestnut Street Elementary School, PA

Spring

S pring showers
P eaceful birds
R unning rabbits
I nsects getting food
N ice green grass
G ardens big and small
Paige Niklas, Grade 3
Chestnut Street Elementary School, PA

Sunset

How, howl the wind is blowing
As the sun goes down
And the sky turns colorful in the night
It is as pretty as the glittering light
Gracie Fonda, Grade 2
Mayfield Elementary School, NY

Spring

Spring is cool at night
Spring is fun and it's hot out
I have the best time.
Patrick Kelly, Grade 3
Our Lady of Hope School, NY

Oh, Little Star

Oh, little star!
Your light fills me with glee!
Your flashing light
Is like a far away helicopter
How I wish I could feel,
Your warmness and love.
Your greatest gift,
From high above.
Oh little star,
I can visualize your smell,
As good as a cake,
For how the joyfulness you make,
Chad Chasteau, Grade 3
Public School 114 Ryder Elementary, NY

Orange Flower

Orange crown,
Fire blaster,
Bee attracter,
Yellow sticks popping up.
A nice hat for a bunny,
Curls up,
To protect a dragon fly,
Looks like corn,
Underneath spikes,
My favorite,
Bye flower
It is winter now!
Jared Heller, Grade 3
The Tobin School, MA

Snake

Hiss! Hiss! the slithering, scaly snake
Sneaking by and rattling his tail
A mouth with scary fangs
Blood red eyes
Aagghhh!
It jumped and bit me
My arm beats red with poison
Scratch scratch
Itching itching my arm!
Sean Walker, Grade 2
Mayfield Elementary School, NY

Reuse
R ecycle
E arth
U sers
S top pollution
E arth needs cleaning
Jordon Sampson, Grade 2
Public School 235 Lenox, NY

Me
Pretty and nice,
Kind and dancy,
Beautiful and fancy,
Lovely and friendly,
That's all about me!
Alyssa Brandl, Grade 2
Helen B Duffield Elementary School, NY

The Green Mean Bean Machine
I once met a guy who was green
Although he was very mean,
He did love a bean,
Not the ones that are green,
When he gets sick, he does not turn green.
Thomas Luciano, Grade 3
St Rose School, CT

A Cat's Best Friend
I once met a cat who had a pet leaf,
And he really liked roast beef,
And the leaf's name was Pete,
He had a favorite seat,
Pete always wanted to be called chief.
Carolyn O'Keefe, Grade 3
St Rose School, CT

A Bunny Named Jill
There once was a bunny named Jill,
Sold to a girl against her will.
With fur delicate as crystal,
She was the girl's cutie angel.
But Jill missed her home, her Brazil.
Dana Chiueh, Grade 3
Setauket Elementary School, NY

Fireflies
Fireflies
so up high
like a bolt of lightning
Fireflies, fireflies
like a little light bulb
so tiny
so cute
Fireflies, fireflies
I love fireflies
Anaya Jacob, Grade 3
Public School 114 Ryder Elementary, NY

Bug Bites
B ug bites on my hand look
U gly. Annoying bugs bite
G iant holes on my hand.

B ugs bite and my hand
I tches.
T errible bug bites make
E verything itch, so I
S cream and scurry.
Brenda Hwang, Grade 3
Willow Creek Elementary School, PA

Michael Phelps
Michael Phelps
Swimming for the medals and trophies
Rapidly swimming
Faster than a cheetah
If only I were him!
Owen McClean, Grade 3
Our Lady of Hope School, NY

Hyper
Hyper is bright red.
It tastes like cinnamon.
It smells like chocolate cake.
It feels like metal.
It sounds like a squirrel.
Hyper is an energetic person.
Nathan Manaker, Grade 3
Asa C Adams School, ME

If I Could Be A Chameleon

If I could be a chameleon, I would hide and not be seen.
If I was a chameleon, I could only be seen with a keen eye.
I would change from pink to purple, or blue to green, or red to any hue.
I would leap from branch to branch, in a giant heap,
I would stick my tongue out for flies and munch them down to bits.
I would make my eye go round and round and look for astounding bugs.
My predators, I don't know what they are,
But with no predators, I will go far.

Sam Goodpaster, Grade 2
Wyland Elementary School, PA

Seven Lions Fighting

Seven lions were fighting and they were biting.
The first one said, "Ow that hurt!"
The second one said, "I'm telling!"
The third one said, "Please don't tell!"
The fourth one said, "I want Daddy!"
The fifth one said, "Stop, stop. Please STOP!"
The sixth one started to cry.
The seventh one said, "I'm leaving good bye!"

Kristian Vik, Grade 3
Our Lady of Hope School, NY

Summer

Summer walks by
With a shine of the sun,
All kids splash in the sea
And have fun
Playing in the park
On a hot, warm day
Kids getting ready to play
They run outside yelling "yeah!"

Denym Hills, Grade 2
Public School 40 Samuel Huntington, NY

The Sun

The sun is hot
it makes us happy
The sun is bright
it makes things grow
and melts all the snow.

Melanie Rodriguez, Kindergarten
Mary Burgess Neal Elementary School, MD

Pretty Pretty Petals

As the winter end its chill
from the ground come the daffodils
Here come the bright carnations
back from taking their winter vacation

The brightly colored daisies
sway in the air so crazy
The sunflowers are so tall
just before winter they will fall

Ruby red rose buds
closed so tight
but when they pop —
what a sight!

Amanda Hally, Grade 3
Edgewood Elementary School, PA

Grindstone Island

Grindstone is our summer home
It's a lot of fun up there
We get to do so many things
Except cut each other's hair

We like to go swimming,
We jump on the water trampoline,
But when it comes to Marco Polo
I am the St. Lawrence River Queen

My best friends there are special
Their names are Anna, Lily, and Paige
They are all so much fun
Even though they aren't my exact age

Cara Fisher, Grade 3
Edgewood Elementary School, PA

Bearded Dragon

Black and green
Spiky and hunter

I relax on a piece of wood
Where there is moss
And a moist environment

My skin is rough
My body is green and black

I feel happy when I am near others
I eat meal worms and crickets

For I am a Bearded Dragon

Adam Gramo, Grade 3
Indian Lane Elementary School, PA

The Sun

Yellow and bold
Shining and hot

When you touch me
You burn in the bright light

If you smile at me
I will smile back

My job is to shine in the day
Making the world warm

For I am
The sun

Eric Voorhees, Grade 3
Indian Lane Elementary School, PA

Leprechaun

I once found a leprechaun in the woods.
All of this friends had green hoods.
He bought one at the store.
Then he wanted one more —
That funny leprechaun in the woods.

Emma Goodpaster, Grade 2
Wyland Elementary School, PA

Peace

Peace is no one hurting anyone else,
quiet,
peace between other countries,
peace between my mom and dad,
and the sound of my niece sleeping.

Makayla Scott, Grade 2
Wells Central School, NY

Ladybugs

L adybugs give good luck
A nd some ladybugs are red
D on't fly away, ladybug
Y ou know that all ladybugs are not the same
B eautiful ladybugs
U nder the leaf is a ladybug
G reat creatures
S mall ladybugs

Isabella Scuteri, Grade 2
Tremont Elementary School, NY

St. Patrick's Day

Green, green everywhere
Let's hear it for St. Patrick's Day
Lots of clover cake
With green sprinkles and sparkles
Let's have lots of fun, for it's Green Day
Green day is not only for leprechauns
But all kinds of kids all over the world
I love St. Patrick's Day!

Allan Dilone, Grade 3
Public School 115 Alexander Humboldt, NY

Money Is Math

Money is math
Pennies, nickels, dimes
I count these all the time
Quarters, half a dollar
I spend these at the store
Dollars, fives and tens
I like to count money
Again and again.

Ryan Birch, Grade 2
Public School 40 Samuel Huntington, NY

Spring

Spring, spring,
I know it's spring…
The flowers are blooming,
the grass is growing.
It's definitely SPRING!

Lauren Conneally, Grade 1
Milton Terrace South Elementary School, NY

I Can Show Twelve

I can show twelve
In different ways I can add ten and two
Or 11 + 1
I can use different
Combinations
Like 4 and 8
I can add the numbers
Three and nine
I can show twelve
Using 7+5
I show twelve
With double six.

Hassan Simmons, Grade 2
Public School 40 Samuel Huntington, NY

The Beautiful Beach

Once I went to the beach and the things that I saw!
I couldn't forget that no not all year long!
Pretty white shells and other colors too!
So many things I saw there, the view!
The ocean it shined like the sweet summer sun.
I love the beach. It's so much fun!
The little clouds there they sway in the soft breeze.
The colors are beautiful not to mention the trees.
The beach is the prettiest place I've ever been.
That is what I have to say and again...
I love the beach there's lots of space to run.
I love the beach because it's so much fun!

Madison Conlin, Grade 3
Rose M Gaffney School, ME

Wind

In the summer when you blow through the trees, you whistle like a sad lonely soul, whistling a sad tune longing for love.

In the garden I think of you of how you talk to the flowers to help them grow, you are like a whirlwind happily wanting to be free just like me.

I love your lullabies singing me to sleep all through the night. You signal us when the rain is coming. Then you blow harder and make our wind chimes ring, then I wake up to you, and I feel happy, you are just like me.

Morgan Felty, Grade 3
Forge Road Elementary School, PA

Loving a Big Round Thing
I love a thing
a round thing
that we all see every day.
I know you love it
Your family
Your friends
Even you are in it
One third of it
Is covered with forests
It has so much air in it
I love it
I love it in here
It's wonderful
So wonderful but...
It is getting polluted
By who?
By humans!
And this thing is
Planet Earth.
Alyssa Kamara, Grade 2
Pine Tree Elementary School, NY

Anna Banana
I have a friend
Her name is Anna
Anna Banana
To be precise!

She loves bananas
Anything with bananas
Banana pie
Banana bread
Banana milkshakes
Banana cake
And lots more!

One day
Anna ate too much
And got a tummy ache
Now if Anna hears the word banana
She will go bananas!
Victoria Salerno, Grade 3
Meeting House Hill School, CT

The New Season Is Coming
The new season is coming
Yes, it's coming, it is summer

The sun is rising and school is out
Water parks are opening, with no doubt

Kids are happy
Because, winter is gone

The circus is in town
Bathing suits we wear, without a care

We miss summer, but we don't care
Because, it is just around the corner.
Jaden Adams, Grade 3
William Penn Elementary School, PA

Bugzy
Bugzy is a dog of fight
I can compare him to a night

He howls and growls
and barks and scowls

He is nice and friendly
but not too friendly

Oh Bugzy, oh Bugzy
your teeth are too long

Just don't bite anyone
you're way too strong
Joseph Yusufov, Grade 2
Public School 69, NY

Softball
Softball
different colors
throw the ball very hard
one of my favorite hobbies
Softball
Camilla Cretacci, Grade 3
Clinton Street Elementary School, NY

My Best Friend

My best friends are always there for me
They will share the happy moments of my life with me
They will always make me feel included in anything
They will always cheer me up when
I'm devastated or gloomy
They will always treat me with respect
They will always defend me when I'm getting picked on
No matter what
We can always count on each other
My best friends Nathan, Eric and Brandon
I'll never forget them

Lenny Breit, Grade 3
Sarah Dyer Barnes School, RI

What a True Friend Would Do For You

A friend is a friend until the very end.
A true friend would listen to you
even if he doesn't want to.
A true friend would play with you any time of day.
A true friend would stay with you until the very end.
A true friend would let you call him
any time of day to ask a question.
A true friend is someone who respects you.
A true friend accepts you for who you are
and doesn't try to change you.
A friend is a friend until the very end.

Jared Andrade, Grade 3
Sarah Dyer Barnes School, RI

Spring

Spring.
The weekend of winter.
The non purposeful death of snowmen, and the children's hunt for the remaining
body parts.
The rebirth of grass.
Mother Nature yawns as the trees sway back and forth, and she slowly takes off the
blanket of white.
As that happens, the snow says goodbye and slowly melts away.
Mother Nature gets up and wakes up her children.
As they eat breakfast, the sun gets used to the Earth again and isn't shy anymore.
The leaves open their doors, and they wake up the flowers as spring begins.

Gabriel Petit, Grade 3
Como Park Elementary School, NY

America

A wesome places
M arvelous schools
E njoy America
R emember America is great
I love America
C ommunities in America
A merica is a great place to live in
Christiana Stiber, Grade 2
Long Meadow Elementary School, CT

Books

When a book's
Page gets turned
It sounds
Like a breezy
Wind floating
In the baby blue sky
Books are great!
Anna Wilder, Grade 2
Tashua School, CT

The Horse

I have a horse
He goes Click, Clunk!
All the time.
I like to take my horse
To the race course.
I took the horse to the stable
And put on the saddle.
Steven Caldwell, Grade 3
New Freedom Christian School, PA

A Friend

A friend is a good active listener
A friend makes me laugh a lot
A friend helps me when I'm mad
A friend sticks up for me
When a bully bullies me
A friend shares anything with me
That is a friend
Jonathan Ayer, Grade 3
Sarah Dyer Barnes School, RI

Spring Is Coming

Sunny day nice
Air shiny sun
Spring waking
Bugs wake up
Battle bees
I love spring
I love spring!
Matthew Sullivan, Grade 2
Helen B Duffield Elementary School, NY

A Poem About Me

Bakes cookies,
Chats a lot,
Energetic girl,
Blue eyes,
Likes dancing,
That's me!
Leah Wright.
Leah Wright, Grade 2
Helen B Duffield Elementary School, NY

Resources We Need

Water
Cool, cold
Swimming, cooling, drinking
They are both resources we need.
Burning, warming, flaming
Hot, red
Fire
Mackenzie Sausville, Grade 3
St Madeleine Sophie School, NY

Parades

Parades
Loud, slow
Twirling, whirling, driving
Candy, floats, clowns, drums
Marching, listening, watching
Crowded, bright
Show
Kathryn Ferencsik, Grade 3
Lincoln Street School, MA

Ready to Play

I play baseball outside
catching, batting, pitching
Get a cap also a glove to go
On the field.
That's when I have fun.

Franco Morena, Grade 3
Our Lady of Hope School, NY

Hockey Time!

Players exercise.
Pucks slide.
Sticks break.
Net swishes.
Ice flies.

Sean Thies, Grade 1
St Rose School, CT

Brownies

Brownies are squishy
Squishy as can be
It tastes good
With some sugar
Gooey chocolatey

Katie Johnson, Grade 2
Tashua School, CT

Month

M onths are part of the year.
O ctober is a month.
N ovember is a month.
T here are many months.
H ave twelve months.

Seong Min Oh, Grade 2
Long Meadow Elementary School, CT

If I Were a Clock

If I were a clock
I'd tell time
I'd move my hands
I'd tick tock
If I were a clock

Joseph Doherty, Grade 1
St Rose School, CT

Easter

Do you like Easter?
I like to look at tulips.
Bunnies in the sun.
Bunnies in candy baskets.
Spring is my favorite season.

Makenzie Baird, Grade 3
Penn-Kidder Campus, PA

Grover and His Friends

There once was a clover named Grover,
His sister's name was Rover,
He had a dog named Macy,
And a cat named Lacey,
One night he got run over.

Anna Johnston, Grade 3
St Rose School, CT

Spring Time

The sun is shining.
Birds are chirping
The bees are buzzing.
Flowers are blooming
It's a spring day.

Ava Battaglia, Grade 3
Our Lady of Hope School, NY

Parties

Fun, awesome parties
Birthday, anniversary
Buying cool presents
Inviting you to our party
A really good time with friends

Jenna Mealey, Grade 3
Heron Pond Elementary School, NH

The Little Green Guy

Once I saw a leprechaun named Joe,
He was very, very slow,
He had a green beard,
I thought that was weird,
And then he ran away with the dough.

Gavin Connors, Grade 3
St Rose School, CT

Spring

When spring is here I'm going to the DQ.
I'm going to my cousin's house!
I'm going to jump on their trampoline.
I might fall but I don't care
I just get up again and jump
with my brother this time.

Andres Garcia, Grade 3
The Edgartown School, MA

Gentle Rain

As the rains shimmy down to the ground.
I hear…
The pitter patter on the window.
I hear…
Sweet sounds of angels singing
Sweet sounds of gentle rain.

Madison Bartone, Grade 3
Lincoln Elementary School, PA

Garden

G rowing plants
A corns on trees
R efreshing feelings
D elicious vegetables to harvest too
E dible plants and
N ature all around you

Warner Hess, Grade 3
The Edgartown School, MA

Spring Is Here!

Red
Swedish fish
Rita's opens
Spring is here!

Gianni Miliziano, Grade 1
Maureen M Welch Elementary School, PA

School Lunch

The school lunch is really great!
I can hardly wait to eat the lunch,
Munch, munch.

Luis Ramos, Grade 2
Public School 1 The Bergen School, NY

My Baseball

I hit it
I catch it
I throw it
It's my baseball
I cry when I lose it
My baseball

Brandon Ellsworth Anderson, Grade 1
Buckley Country Day School, NY

Spring

S weet smell of flowers
P laying outside for more hours
R ain showers
I nteresting powers
N eighbors, outdoor showers
G rass grows and tastes sour

Michael O'Brien, Grade 3
The Edgartown School, MA

Jaguar

J umpy
A mazing
G nawing
U nbelievably good climber
A nd very scary
R oar

Michael Courtney, Grade 3
The Edgartown School, MA

Cooking

I have a mom named Brooke
She really likes to try to cook
One time a ham she baked turned black
So now I'm eating a very crunchy snack

Hannah Benes, Grade 2
Klein Elementary School, PA

Winter

Birds fly south this time.
My birthday is in winter.
Cardinals staying here.

Christopher Brubaker, Grade 2
The Fourth Presbyterian School, MD

Playing Soccer
Kicking the ball.
Making a goal!
Running the field.
Winning a game!
Friends helping friends.
Soccer is great!
Brendan Morrissey, Grade 1
St Rose School, CT

Carnival
Clowns juggling.
Music playing.
Rides spinning.
Children smiling.
Food cooking.
People looking.
Gabrielle Kerekes, Grade 1
St Rose School, CT

Mom
Mom makes me
happy, smile
proud, smile
excited, smile
My mom is
very nice.
Hassan Larhrissi, Grade 2
Pine Tree Elementary School, NY

The Tallest Tree
The tree with a buzz of a bee,
So great, so tall
It's tallest of all
I love my tree.
Kaleigh Gibson, Grade 3
Ridgeway Elementary School, MD

The Tree
I will see the flower
When it comes off of the branch
Then the apple grows!
Jean Lussier, Grade 1
St Louis Elementary School, MA

Flower Petal
The flower petal
Is as soft
As laughter.

The pollen
Is God's light!
Nicole Kolitsas, Grade 1
St Rose School, CT

Soccer Game
Friends cheering
Crowd sitting
Players running
Feet kicking
Ball rolling
Goalie blocking!
Torin Kearney, Grade 1
St Rose School, CT

Home
Dad cooks.
Mom cleans.
Brother plays.
Sister sleeps.
Cat meows.
Fish swims.
Richard Bomely, Grade 1
St. Rose School, CT

Little Chick
Little yellow ball
Tweet, tweet
Peep, peep
It's a chick!
Dylan Nytko, Grade 2
Pine Tree Elementary School, NY

When Does Spring Come?
I smell the flower
Do you think she will like it?
I picked it for Mom.
Julia Gately, Grade 1
St Louis Elementary School, MA

Moving West

Moving west is so much fun!
Traveling all day protected from the hot, hot sun.
I rest in my wagon all day long.
I hear the birds sweet song.
We travel all season long
after we make a home we will be healthy and strong.

Drew Webster, Grade 3
The Tobin School, MA

Spring

S un shines very bright.
P retty green grass grows.
R oses are growing.
I go to the park.
N o more winter.
G rass grows very high from the rain.

Irma Cirikovic, Grade 3
Public School 105 Senator Abraham Bernstein, NY

Cat and Mom

My mom is watching my cat
She wanted to go to the beach
The cat is nice to me
He always eats paper
He is a fat cat
Mom and cat play together.

Mesiah Brown, Grade 2
Public School 40 Samuel Huntington, NY

Rain

Rain is special in so many ways
You can run, dance, and even play in the rain
You can hop, skip and jump
You can slide or even roll around in the rain.
But I would rather watch it fall from the sky
Inside with my cat Joey.

Baylee Backiel, Grade 1
The Tobin School, MA

Owls

Talons
Are sharp,
The wings are
Sharply
Cutting the wind
On its journey
To find mice
To give to the
Babies.

Naomi Nishimura, Grade 2
Buckley Country Day School, NY

Playing Outside

I play outside...
Jump, jump, on my trampoline
Bouncing like a bouncy ball.
Bump, bump on my swing
Flying like a bird.
Ring, ring, on my bicycle bell
Like a warning bell on a fire truck
Run, run, my brother chasing me
Like a tiger chasing a bird.

Kenny Miller, Grade 2
Carlyle C Ring Elementary School, NY

Winter

Winter
Snowy trees
Snowmen and snowballs
It is Jesus' birthday
Happiness

Meaghan Kienzle, Grade 1
All Saints Catholic Academy, NY

Apple Tree

Apple tree, oh apple tree
What a joy you are to me
Smile like a star!!
Apple red,
Apple green,
So pretty.

Katey Osz, Grade 3
Ridgeway Elementary School, MD

Ice Cream

Ice cream, ice cream,
Yummy, but cold.
I'll even eat it
When I'm old.

Ice cream, ice cream,
Yummy bubble gum
That's my favorite,
Do you want some?

Ice cream, ice cream,
Yummy in a cone,
I like it better
Than a dog likes a bone.

Ice cream, ice cream,
Yummy, but cold.
I'll even eat it
When I'm old.

Abigail LaBoy, Grade 2
Carlyle C Ring Elementary School, NY

A Cloud

White and moist
Puffy and gray

I walked across the sky
As the wind blew me

When the sky turns pitch black
My body shrivels up and disappears

I watch the passengers
As the planes travel through me

As I stretch out
The sun warms me
I look forward to summer

For I am
A cloud

Sophia Tumolo, Grade 3
Indian Lane Elementary School, PA

Friends
Jack, Christian, Robert
Together we are Cub Scouts
Best buds forever!
Jonathan Foster, Grade 3
Sacred Heart School, CT

Funny Dog
Two funny dogs run
Stinky shoes getting chewed up
Toilet bowl drinkers
Timothy Murphy, Grade 3
The Burnham Elementary School, CT

Bethlehem
Buildings everywhere
Town where Jesus was born.
Nativity Church
Christian Esposito, Grade 3
Sacred Heart School, CT

Spring
Flowers start to bloom
Sun hanging in the spring sky
People plant flowers
Ellie Schmus, Grade 3
The Burnham Elementary School, CT

Reading
Shelves are filled with books.
Words are flowing in my mind.
Makes me stretch my brain.
Robert Ventura, Jr., Grade 3
Sacred Heart School, CT

Winter Is Fun
Building a snowman
Sledding is fun in winter
Snow is white and cold
Frances Dwyer, Grade 3
The Burnham Elementary School, CT

Wrist Watch
Gears make a small clock.
I use math when I read it.
Mini time machine.
Alex Grandolfi, Grade 3
Sacred Heart School, CT

Spring Is Starting
Warm weather begins
Bees fly around town all day
Birds move into trees
Henry McKenney, Grade 3
The Burnham Elementary School, CT

Birds
Uniquely colored
Flapping their wings in the sky
Delightful to watch
Elizabeth Fountaine, Grade 3
Sacred Heart School, CT

My Cat
She loves to snuggle.
Her name is Tinkerbella.
She plays with flashlights.
Jessamyn Allen, Grade 3
Sacred Heart School, CT

Instruments
Some big, others small
From clarinets to tubas
Music talks to me!
Joshua Terry, Grade 3
Sacred Heart School, CT

Sister
Awesome, loving friend
Always there for me
I'm glad I have Kate.
Hannah Schmidt, Grade 3
Sacred Heart School, CT

Saber Tooth Cat

Sometimes moving slowly
Sometimes moving fast
First stalking, then charging
Their teeth are their weapons
The Saber tooth cat
Vicious predator!

Travis Nevins, Grade 3
Dartmouth Early Learning Center, MA

Easter

E gg coloring
A pril time
S howers
T reats in baskets
E veryone playing outside
R abbits' footprints everywhere

Christopher Carbuccia, Grade 3
St Agatha School, NY

Nature

Flowers blooming here and there
Sunshine shining everywhere
Buzzing bees fly in the air
Butterflies flutter here and there
Flowers are looking right at me
Saying please leave me be

Allison K. Lane, Grade 3
Shelter Rock Elementary School, NY

A Poem About Me

Goes bowling,
Reads books,
Writes stories,
Bakes cookies,
Watches TV,
That's me!

Rose Dolderer, Grade 2
Helen B Duffield Elementary School, NY

Deer

Deer,
fast runners
In a blink
of an eye,
they are
gone!

Lauren Malatesta, Grade 2
Tashua School, CT

Spring

S pring is here
P retty flowers blooming
R abbits hiding eggs
I hunt for eggs
N obody at home
G reen grass

Stephanie Neri, Grade 3
St Agatha School, NY

Trampoline

turn, wam
jumping, hopping, flying
bounce up and down
get down

Alexis Nicholson, Grade 2
Caryl E Adams Primary School, NY

Basketball

fast, quick
running, shooting, stumbling
shoot a three pointer
slam dunk

Kody Walker, Grade 2
Caryl E Adams Primary School, NY

Spring Time

Flowers and Butterflies
Growing, Flying, Playing
Bloom

Holly Doherty, Grade 3
Our Lady of Hope School, NY

Summer

Sun is very bright
I like to pick strawberries
Grass is very green

Samuel Francis, Grade 1
St Louis Elementary School, MA

My Dancing Pencil
My pencil is funny when she dances.
She is funny when she prances.

When she prances, she looks like a horse.
She looks like a horse when she is dancing her course.

After she dances her course, she is very happy.
When she is finished she says to the other dancers, "make it snappy."

She was in the newspaper for winning the dancing race.
She had a great dancing pace.

When she saw her self in the newspaper, she danced for joy.
Then she said, "I'm in the newspaper, oh boy!"

She got so excited she leaped off the cliff.
When she landed in the alligator pond, she was scared stiff.

She was never seen again.
Men tried to find her but they only found a pen.

Caroline Fischer, Grade 2
Infant Jesus School, NH

Staircase
I am a flight of stairs.
I love when the mall is closed,
when no high heels are squishing me.
Inside of me is hard marble.
I am the color
of speckled eggs.
I make the sound
of an old door.
I dream of me squishing humans
instead of them squashing me.
Wouldn't I look nice in high heels?
I wish I could walk.
I fear this year's 24-hour sale.
At night I talk to the attic staircase
and she gloats about how nobody walks on her.
P.S. The next time you go to the mall,
please take the elevator.

Emma Markus, Grade 3
Pine Crest Elementary School, MD

Spiders
S pinnerets produce silk
P eople think spiders are useful
I nsects are their food
D angerous arachnids
E nemies to insects
R eproduce venom
Cory Roberts, Grade 3
St Clement Mary Hofbauer School, MD

Summer
S hort pants
U se water to drink
M y family goes on vacation
M y family goes to the beach
E veryone goes to the pool
R ainbows
Hannah Hinds, Grade 1
St Agatha School, NY

My Dog
My dog is very sweet,
My dog is very furry,
My dog is not very neat,
My dog is not very purry,
My dog sure likes to eat,
And she is in a hurry.
Allison Gilles, Grade 3
Heron Pond Elementary School, NH

Easter
E aster candy
A pril
S pring
T oys
E gg hunting
R ainbow
Margie Pineda, Grade 1
St Agatha School, NY

What Is Blue?
Blue is the color of the afternoon sky.
Blue is the color of when you're sad.
Blue is the color of a blue t-shirt.
Blue is the color of the blue ocean.
Blue is the color of a dark blue sky
Blue can be as dark as a dark night.
Mikayla Coffie, Grade 3
Colebrook Primary School, NY

Spiders
S queezes silk from its spinnerets
P rotects its web
I nsects are dinner, lunch, and breakfast
D oes fear birds, snakes, wasps, and frogs
E ight legs
R epels on drag line
Gregory Walker, Jr., Grade 3
St Clement Mary Hofbauer School, MD

Soccer
fast, run
falling, kicking, moving
goaling with a ball
making points
Hailey Smith, Grade 2
Caryl E Adams Primary School, NY

Snow Boarding
downhill, straight
jumping, balancing, grinding
lock your feet in the board
snow riding
Michael Krom, Grade 2
Caryl E Adams Primary School, NY

Spring
I like Spring's flowers
My mom loves to grow flowers
In Spring flowers bloom
Ryan Delarosa, Grade 3
Our Lady of Hope School, NY

What I Like in Spring
I will fly a kite
I love riding my cool bike
I like the fresh air
Andrew Almeida, Grade 1
St Louis Elementary School, MA

My Dream
My dream
Floating on the clouds
Climbing up the high mountains
Looking at the stars
Sydney Slattery, Grade 3
Colebrook Primary School, NY

Four-Wheeling
fast, crazy
zooming, crashing, slipping
stop really fast
mud riding
Garrett Monk, Grade 2
Caryl E Adams Primary School, NY

Puppy
Puppy
Black and white
Sleeping, swimming, dancing
I am very happy with her Dog
Amanda Fenger, Grade 3
Clinton Street Elementary School, NY

Four-Wheeling
bumpy, ride
steering, booming, zooming
use the steering wheel
driving around
Kaylee Moshier, Grade 2
Caryl E Adams Primary School, NY

Cat
I have a cat named Binx
He loves to sleep on laps
He opens his eyes and winks
His favorite things are naps
Sydney Andrews, Grade 3
Craneville School, MA

Sledding
slip, slide
zipping, turning, zooming
sliding down a hill
tobogganing
Liam Lynch, Grade 2
Caryl E Adams Primary School, NY

Food Chain
Quietly stalking its prey
Tiny mouse scampers away
Asian Leopard Cat pounces
Happy cat, dead mouse!
Jonathan Rocha, Grade 1
Dartmouth Early Learning Center, MA

Mattress Surfing
fast, fun
blasting, bumping, sliding
ride in circles
slippery, flipping
William Geiger, Grade 2
Caryl E Adams Primary School, NY

Sledding
swift, slide
smashing, sliding, spinning
walk up the hill
down hill
Aaliyah Taylor, Grade 2
Caryl E Adams Primary School, NY

The Flu
The flu, the flu
What to do?
Hachoo, hachoo
I hope it's not the flu!
Brayan Cuautle, Grade 2
Public School 1 The Bergen School, NY

My Teachers

I love all of my teachers
I love them very much

Even though they are strict
I don't mind a bit
I love hard stuff and
Eager to learn new things

If I have too much work,
I will try my best to finish it all and
Make my teacher proud of me.

I try my best to get all
the best teachers in every grade.

I love any strict teacher
I know they mean well to help all the students
I love any strict teacher
I love all my teachers very dearly

Teachers are the best!

Nayeli Perez, Grade 3
Public School 131, NY

Days in Season

The blooming flowers, the brown dirt
Everything here smells like dessert.
Robins chirping, days are burping.
Playground we play around you,
That is exactly why you grew.
It's not smoky, it's not poky,
It is a fantastic day of nature.
Great, great, great.
Great sweet, cherries, plums, licorice smelling day.
It's spring, it's spring, don't be gray.
Why do you have to be about this size?
Get up sleepyhead, it's time to exercise!
Come outside, blue sky sunny.
Let's get to the rhythm.
We have one things to make and send —
We only have to say "The End!"

Alec Arza, Grade 2
Helen B Duffield Elementary School, NY

Spring

Spring is nice.
It is fun.
You can plant rice.
And play in the sun.

Walter Hwang, Grade 2
Public School 205 Alexander Graham Bell, NY

Evil Ice Cream Sandwich

I am being chased by a giant ice cream sandwich
It might eat me
What if I want to eat him
Aah, he's chasing me

Nicolas Paredes, Grade 2
Rye Country Day School, NY

Pancakes

Pancakes lay in front of me, they look very yummy.
I reach out to grab some, but a cat tried to catch them.
How they fling in the air.
Landing left. Landing right. Basically landing everywhere.

Madeleine Di Antonio, Grade 3
St Maria Goretti School, PA

Summer

Summer has come. Kids are happy.
There goes SPLASH! Splash again.
Sprinklers on, water balloons thrown.
Shirts soaked. Sun is out.

Timothy Lee, Grade 2
Public School 205 Alexander Graham Bell, NY

Piñata

Candy falling like the snow
Tumbling everywhere
Creating a wonderful land
Of sweet sweet candy!

Taliya Furs, Grade 3
Public School 40 Samuel Huntington, NY

Bakugan

I like Bakugan.
I collect Bakugan cards.
Serpenoid is cool.

Gabriel Mormile, Grade 2
Fonda-Fultonville Elementary School, NY

Watermelon

Crunchy, messy,
Dripping, sweet, yummy, seedy,
You can buy it at a store for a nice low price.

Matthew Brown, Grade 2
Helen B Duffield Elementary School, NY

Sunrise

The sun rises, looking like it came out of the earth.
The sky is a blaze of pink and blue,
The night silently slips away, leaving no trace.

Luke Higgins, Grade 2
Dartmouth Early Learning Center, MA

Peace

Everyone has to have peace or else they will fight a lot. If the world had peace,
there would not be any war. I love peace I have a lot of it in my heart. Peace
brings happiness to the world and me.

Maria Tand, Grade 3
Lincoln Street School, MA

Piano

The keys sparkle in the light
Makes a beautiful noise in the room
Sounds like a symphony orchestra in the house

Drew White, Kindergarten
Jacksonville Elementary School, MD

New York City

The city is big.
My dad likes New York City.
Brooklyn is my home.

Stella Williams, Grade 2
Fonda-Fultonville Elementary School, NY

Black

Black is the color of the sky at night.
Black is the color of the road.
Black is a panther running by.
Black smells like smoke coming out of a train.
Black tastes like burnt toast.
Black sounds like thunder.
Black looks like a tire.
Black feels like burnt rubber on a hot day.
Black makes me feel mad.
Black is the color of my shirt.

Felicia Forsythe, Grade 3
Evergreen Elementary School, PA

Red

Red is lava inside a volcano.
Red is as powerful as magma.
Red is Mario battling Bowser.
Red is anger in my veins.
Red smells like burnt toast.
Red tastes like spicy hot chicken wings with hot peppers.
Red sounds like the lava dripping in a volcano.
Red looks like blood out of a man's body.
Red feels like HOT HOT HOT!
Red makes me burn in flames on a hot summer day.

Ethan Gallagher, Grade 3
Evergreen Elementary School, PA

Green

Green
Green is the world beneath me.
Green is my favorite color.
Green is March in all.
Green is help to the earth.
Green smells like a fresh new day.
Green tastes like sweet, happy dreams.
Green sounds like recycling.
Green looks like spring sprouting a new season.
Green makes me feel so proud.

Jessica Eskander, Grade 3
Evergreen Elementary School, PA

New Years

People screaming
Kids running around
I smell rice, chicken,
And beans
4, 3, 2, 1
Happy New Year
We all hug each other
And start dancing
Then the kids go watch TV
In another room

Ashley Rodriguez, Grade 3
Public School 115 Alexander Humboldt, NY

I Love Spring!!

In spring
Flowers bloom in a rainbow of colors.
The sun shines down on blue sky days.
But sometimes it hides
And the rain rains.
Birds sing, fly and play.
They land in trees with bright green leaves.
I play in the pool and sometimes at the beach.
I play on water slides and in the sprinkler
While the sun warms me.

Morgan Britt-Webb, Grade 3
John Ward Elementary School, MA

Rain Forest Monkeys

Rain Forest Monkeys
Rain Forest Monkeys
Here, and there.
When I'm in the Rain Forest,
I can see them everywhere!
They are so cute —
When you look at them,
I really think —
You should meet one!
Ooooh! Ooooh! Ahhhh! Ahhhh!

Davide Bazzani, Grade 1
Milton Terrace South Elementary School, NY

The Ocean

Strong and blue
Bold and beautiful

As the wind blows
Making loud sounds
I crash, tumble and flip

On sunny bright days
People get a beautiful view of me
As I tumble and dance

When there is a storm
I yell and scream

When summer comes
I feel warm and foamy

For I am
The ocean

Haley Mancill, Grade 3
Indian Lane Elementary School, PA

Puppy Days

When I had
a puppy it
was so fluffy
and soft like
a teddy bear, it
was so cute
like a baby,
he likes it
when I brush
his fur, he wags his tail
and he loves
when he sleeps
at the end
of my bed,
he loves it
when I kiss
him on the
head!

Mya Samuels, Grade 3
Public School 114 Ryder Elementary, NY

I Am the Ocean

I am the ocean
I bob up and down like a sea horse
I am the ocean
I am green, blue, and manatee gray
I am the ocean
I smell like salty fish
I am the ocean
I see the rest of me far away
I am the ocean
I am important because
I protect all underwater creatures
I am the Pacific Ocean.

Anna Grasso, Grade 3
Meeting House Hill School, CT

Toast — Hot

Toast,
Toast
Hot! HOT!
It
Burns
Like tea
A little
Butter
Mmmm
That,
Was good
Gulp!!

Emily Rosenburg, Grade 2
Tashua School, CT

Peeking Through a Hole

In my door
There's a little hole
About the size
Of a baby mole.
Peeking through it
Day and night,
Sunlight and moonlight
Pours through
And makes the house shine.

Liliko Uchida, Grade 3
Lincoln Street School, MA

Summer

Summer pops out with
The golden sun,
Children play,
Birds sing
When 12:00 hits, it's ice cream time.
Sitting in the park,
Looking out at nature
Flowers grow, people say,
"Wow! It's hot outside!"
Some people walking with ice cream

Zavier Peters, Grade 2
Public School 40 Samuel Huntington, NY

True Friend

We met on line had a good time chatting
We became good friends
Time went on and we're still here
I truly believe you are someone dear
Here is something I like to share
With you for all your love and kindness too
It's a symbol of friendship we share
Together a friendship I hope will last forever
And although we live so far apart
Always remember you hold a place in my heart

Brianna Rodriguez, Grade 3
Public School 115 Alexander Humboldt, NY

Summer

Lick, lick, lick —
ice cream on a hot day!
Buzz, buzz —
goes the bee flying by.
Splish, splash —
people jumping in the water.
Squirt, squirt —
time for sunscreen.
Ding, dong —
there goes the ice cream truck!

Cailin Mercier, Grade 1
Milton Terrace South Elementary School, NY

It's All About Me

My name is Kylie Wall
and I am 45 inches tall.
I have two fish named Lulu and Goldy,
and their tank is moldy.
When I grow up, I will be a vet
and take care of everyone's pets.
I'm six and a half, I'm almost seven,
I wish I had a dog because my old one is up in heaven.
My hair is blond, my eyes are blue
I still need to learn how to tie my shoe.
I go to St. Joan of Arc and I'm in 1B,
Do you like my poem? It's all about me.

Kylie Wall, Grade 1
St Joan of Arc School, PA

I Play too Much Video Games

I play too much video games
I am constantly moving around
It makes me hyper and jumpy
I don't know why I get jumpy
My mom says why are you so jumpy?
And I don't know why.

While I play, I forget where I am.
I get excited and keep playing.
I just play, play and play lots of video games.
I ignore whoever is around and keep playing my games.
I just love to play my video games.

Alexander Fragoso, Grade 3
Public School 131, NY

Books

Books are fun in your mind.
Books are here and there and everywhere.
Books are my favorite things in the whole world.
Every time you look at one you think you are in a magic world.
You could jump in a book and be in a jungle and start walking on a trail, and you
might see an elephant, a monkey, a panda, a lion or a tiger.
They could be in all different places, high places and low places.
When you use your imagination, books can bring you where nobody else is going
and wherever you want to be.

Isabella McGovern, Grade 3
Como Park Elementary School, NY

Green

Green is the color of the grass.
Green is like spring coming early.
Green is when I think sad!
Green is one of my favorite colors.
Green smells like snow coming soon.
Green tastes like beautiful grass in the summer!
Green sounds like joy to the world.
Green looks like a starting of a sunset.
Green feels like I'm going to BURST into tears!
Green makes me feel, just so sad!

Deanna Cusumano, Grade 3
Evergreen Elementary School, PA

Dogs

Dogs, dogs, dogs, dogs
They are your best friend because
They can play with you without complaining
They are good pets to have
Whenever you feel lonely
They keep you company
They are nice and kind
They are not hard to take care of
If you need a friend, just get a dog
Dogs, dogs, dogs, dogs

Melvin Ramirez, Grade 3
Public School 131, NY

Special Woman

Mommy, Mommy, Mommy
My mom is so much fun
Here comes the sun
Me and my mommy play every day
We love to dance and play
Me and my mommy do work
Mommy helps me with my homework
Mommy, Mommy, Mommy
I love you so much.
Mommy you're the special woman in my life!

Megan Kessler, Grade 3
Public School 232 The Walter Ward School, NY

Spring

Spring is here
Spring is here
Time for cheer.
Animals here and there
Everywhere!
The hot wind is blowing
And flowers blooming,
Spring rain showers
For the lovely flowers.
Spring rain showers,
Rainbow is like its powers!

Kenneth Phillips, Grade 2
Public School 235 Lenox, NY

Mountains

Mountains, mountains
so high, so high
climbing up
You made it to the top
you're falling down!
but you got your grip
you're climbing down
and you fall again
but you don't get your grip
Thank goodness...
you were only 5 feet up!

Sean Dickson, Grade 2
Primrose School, NY

Twilight

Night gets tired as day wakes up.
Two fishermen cast their lines.
The night is saying goodbye.
Robins shop for breakfast worms.
As they pour the special syrup.
Night and day whisper secrets.
Dusk deepens the color.
Dusk hisses on sprinklers.
Dawn is like the sea.
Great celebration to night.
Dusk sets tables.

Rain Lasch, Grade 3
Jeffrey Elementary School, CT

Elephants

E normous
L arge
E lephants have big ears
P rey and predator
H igh
A mammal
N ot small
T all
S mallest animals are not elephants

Jakob McCloskey, Grade 2
Central Elementary School, PA

Ice Wonder

I build an ice castle.
The blocks look like chunky dice,
An ice wonderland
like the North Pole in my lawn.

I pretend to be a silly snow girl
A cold snowball in my hand.
Pretty dress, pretty purse
I'm covered with coldness and loveliness.

Kaytlyn Renee Rasmussen, Grade 2
Carlyle C Ring Elementary School, NY

Hockey

Hockey
Wear lots of gear
Shooting on good goalies
Fun game and also tiring
Shoot! Score!

Kaitlyn Lisiecki, Grade 3
Clinton Street Elementary School, NY

Friendship

My friends and I are like dolphins
Swimming in the sea.
Diving and diving, having so much fun,
Making me feel like a rising sun.
Having fun splashing and splashing
In the sun.

Colette Maloney, Grade 3
Meadow Drive School, NY

Flakes

Flakes flakes into the lake.
Shake, shake they went into the lake.
Flakes, flakes take little shapes.
Lauren O'Hara, Grade 3
Meadow Drive School, NY

Bees

Bees fly and sting you,
Making and eating honey,
Yellow and black, too!
Sean Reynolds, Grade 2
Helen B Duffield Elementary School, NY

Green Balloon

Green balloon
Smooth and tough
Like a rubber duck
Helena Johnson, Grade 2
Fountaindale Elementary School, MD

Spring

No more big jackets,
Beautiful flowers blooming,
Playing a sports game.
Nicholas Miller, Grade 2
Helen B Duffield Elementary School, NY

Spring

Spring is hot and cool
It's a lively time of year
Flowers bloom brightly
Natalie Bourque, Grade 3
Lincoln Street School, MA

Snow

I have hot cocoa,
I have fun when it's winter,
Do not throw snowballs.
Frank Moceri, Grade 2
Helen B Duffield Elementary School, NY

Rain

Cold wet pouring down
It smells like morning at camp
It looks like wet ice
Nolan Weber, Grade 2
Klein Elementary School, PA

Clouds

Puffy in the sky,
Slowly the clouds are moving,
They look like cotton.
Ava Britt, Grade 2
Helen B Duffield Elementary School, NY

Rain

Rain is falling down
It falls from the dark black sky
It helps the plants grow
Shane Work, Grade 2
Klein Elementary School, PA

School

I play with my friends,
I buy ice cream at lunchtime,
I go on the slides!
Alyssa Brady, Grade 2
Helen B Duffield Elementary School, NY

Flowers

I see some flowers,
They are yellow and purple,
They grew and bloomed.
Isabella Robinson, Grade 2
Killingly Memorial School, CT

Nature

Nature gives us life
Golden flowers bloom in spring
Birds fly in peace.
Ace Crowell, Grade 1
Dartmouth Early Learning Center, MA

My Dad
You helped me ride my brand new bike
You calm me down when in a fight
You hug me tight when I am scared
And that showed me how much you cared.

You read to me every day
We go outside to run and play!
When I am hurt, you help me out
When you are mad, you do not shout.

When I am cold, you warm me up
When I am thirsty, you get a cup
When I am bored you play with me
When I am sick, you stay with me.

I wrote this poem because of love
I wrote this poem to tell a dove
I wrote this poem because I want to tell you
That I really, really love you!

Emma Kalajian, Grade 3
St Anna School, MA

Spring
I like spring it is fun,
you get ice cream every day,
you get to go to the beach,
spring is fun you get to play football and tennis like crazy,
I like to take a walk too,
squirrels and bears come out,
your garden grows,
baseball games start.

You get to ride a bike,
spring is so much fun,
you get to play golf and you see birds singing,
Easter is coming
the Easter bunny comes with eggs
we find eggs
we make eggs for church.

Nicholas Mochalski, Grade 2
Public School 232 The Walter Ward School, NY

Numbers

1, 2, three count with me,
4, 5, six it goes quick.
7, 8, nine you are doing fine.
10th, 11th, twelfth you can say it straight.
13, 14 and fifteen make room for sweet sixteen.
17, 18, and nineteen give us plenty to
make twenty.

Kalina Witkowska, Grade 3
St Maria Goretti School, PA

Fun in All Seasons

Summer
Hot, sunny
Swimming, playing, camping
Fall links summer and winter together
Drinking hot chocolate, ice skating, sledding
Cold, indoors
Winter

Emma Keating, Grade 2
St Madeleine Sophie School, NY

Water and Ground

Water
Blue, wet
Splashing, swimming, drinking
Animals need the water and ground to live
Playing, building, walking
Dry, dirty
Ground

Matthew Kordziel, Grade 3
St. Madeleine Sophie School, NY

Dogs

Dogs are funny, dogs are cute
they like to jump like a parachute.
They cuddle on your lap and sing "arf, arf."
They love and cherish you, lick your face and never
leave a single trace.
They know their place and they keep their space,
most have electric fences and great senses…

Angelina Balzano, Grade 3
Jeffrey Elementary School, CT

Football

Football
is
   fun
    to play
run
   whoosh
run run
touchdown
we won
yeah
we won

Max McGillicuddy, Grade 2
Tashua School, CT

A Quiet Bell

Do you know what's in a quiet bell?
What's in a quiet bell?
Inside a quiet bell,
There is Santa's sleigh
On Santa's sleigh,
There is a quiet bell
That rings
SO
So
so
soft.

Jenna Bradley, Grade 2
General Wayne Elementary School, PA

Spring

Once Spring comes around
Flowers start to bloom
The birds start to chirp
The sun comes out.

Now, everything is blooming
And when I awake
I smell the fresh air.

I see all of the bright colors around me
Now Summer is right around the corner.

Haylee Briggs, Grade 3
Central Elementary School, PA

Paperweight

Oh shimmering paperweight,
Your black dot is staring at me
Like an eye,
Two girls back to back,
Heads stuck together
Thinking about who's
On the other side,
Red, yellow, and blue background,
When I look inside you
A small town seen,
Where did you come from?

Molly Zito, Grade 2
John L Edwards School, NY

Flowers

Flowers, flowers, flowers,
you bloom in April showers.

You bloom on my apple tree,
oh, there will be sweet treats.

Flowers, flowers, flowers,
you heap like golden towers.

Mother's day is coming near,
roses for our mother dear.

Nanette Tran, Grade 2
Public School 69, NY

Road to Heaven

When I was a kid,
I thought the smoke from the planes
was the road to heaven.

The white cloud was the trail
for the spirits
to walk up to heaven.

And I thought the planes
were carrying the spirits
from their grave to heaven.

Seth Ziemke, Grade 2
Greenock Elementary School, PA

Aruba

Aruba
Really really hot like Italy
Go to the beach
Or the pool
Hot hot
Really hot
I need some shade
Lets get a drink
Like lemonade
mmmmm mmmmm
This tastes good
Sara Bartoli, Grade 2
Tashua School, CT

Summer!

The sun is high in the sky.
Below the kids play on the beach.
They fly kites,
Ride waves,
And have picnics with lemonade.
Butterflies fly,
Sports are played,
Camps start to open.
But rain clouds come.
We pack up our things
And start for home.
Lucy Verdone, Grade 3
John Ward Elementary School, MA

Rachel in Trouble

Hitting punching
turning off the lights
stop it
stop it
you're not being nice
you'll probably get in trouble
from doing all these things
go to your room
go to your room
"I'm not in trouble"
you say
Melanie Boschen, Grade 2
Fountaindale Elementary School, MD

My Sister

She jumps, she kicks
She smacks, she whips
She gives me the itch
She fights, she bites
At night she snores
On days she roars
It makes me mad
Not just a tad
But if you're bored
She'll make you glad
But I have to say
She's all right in her own way
For yes she is my baby sister
Damiana Crankshaw, Grade 2
Mayfield Elementary School, NY

Fridays

Morning
Tired
School
Friends
Pay attention
Lunch
Recess
Afternoon
Fun
Awake
Gym
Dinner
Stay up!
Sophia Boccadifuoco, Grade 2
Helen B Duffield Elementary School, NY

Luke

My brother
Funny dude
Loves basketball
Liked bowling
Likes raviolis
Turtle lover
My twin
Oliver Adey, Grade 1
Maureen M Welch Elementary School, PA

Midnight

The last light went out
Darkness crawls over me
And covers me like a blanket.
My eyes are open, yet there's nothing to see.

I drink it in
The wind teases me while
The trees laugh their crackling laughter.
The stars can't twinkle.
The moon is a thin sliver.
I drink it in.Yet I am not afraid. Why should I be?

Erica Daniels, Grade 3
Colebrook Primary School, NY

My Injury

Well in the winter we went to the park. We went to sled in the park that had high
hills.
I went down there was a vent. Guess what? I hit it. My little sister was fine.
My aupére picked me up blood gushed out of my head.
Richard called to the people walking, "Call 911." Then an ambulance came.
When I got to the hospital I went to the Emergency Room. I forgot what happened
after that.
I went in the car and said, "My foot hurts." I couldn't walk.
A doctor said to give me crutches.
I went to the doctor. They said, "We don't have crutches."
There was not one six year old crutch in the whole state of Pennsylvania!
So I got carried everywhere. Then I was fine.

Luke Racicky, Grade 1
Wyoming Valley Montessori School, PA

Ice Cream Flavors

Strawberry, vanilla, chocolate, mint
Maybe I need a hint
Of the kind of ice cream I should pick.
I need ice cream really quick!

Strawberry, vanilla, chocolate, cookie dough,
Maybe I need to go
To the ice cream store
To get the ice cream I adore.

Madelaine Becker, Grade 2
Carlyle C Ring Elementary School, NY

Spring
Telltale V-shape in the sky,
Canadian Geese have arrived.
Red Winged Blackbird perched on a reed.
Robin nesting in the tree.
Sure signs spring is here.
Ethan Roseberry, Grade 3
Brewster Pierce Memorial School, VT

Diamond
Diamond
Beautiful, shiny
Glowing, sparkling, shining
Diamonds are so beautiful
Jewel
Shelby Taylor, Grade 1
Buckley Country Day School, NY

Izzy
Izzy
Cute, cuddly
Running, crawling, eating
Everyone loves her!
Baby
Olivia Alvira, Grade 3
Brant Elementary School, NY

My Dad
Daddy
Tall, Hilarious
Joking, Playing, Shopping
Loves taking long rides into the country
Arthur
Artezia Montour, Grade 3
Brant Elementary School, NY

Easter
Do you like Easter?
Well, I really like Easter.
Eggs and jelly beans.
Everything is colorful.
Easter, Easter it is fun.
Joseph Powierski, Grade 3
Penn-Kidder Campus, PA

Cotton Candy
Blue,
Pink,
Purple,
Juicy,
Sweet like sugar,
Scrumptious,
Soft,
Waiting for me!
Christopher Coburn, Grade 2
Helen B Duffield Elementary School, NY

Playing Outside
I am making a snowman and hear clear
pointy icicles falling down. I see flying
snowballs and smoke coming out of
chimneys. There are big yellow snow
plows on the streets. The wind is
blowing me over. Now I hear people
laughing. There are sleds skimming and
the wind is howling.
Jaeden Lampro, Grade 3
Craneville School, MA

A Magical Winter
I see ice cracking while the ice
skaters glide. I go inside and feel the
warm wood fire on my red cheeks.
I like to sip hot cocoa when it's cold out.
I like to go sledding when the snow is
just right for sledding (which is powder).
I also like packing which is right for
building snowmen.
Tanner Hill, Grade 3
Craneville School, MA

Winter
Winter comes as fast as the wind
And stays it seems for years and years,
While the soft snow falls all sparkly white
Like a soft blanket falling from the sky
And covering the ground.
Halina Rhodes, Grade 3
Cottage Street School, MA

Snow Is Like...

Snow is bright like the sun.
Snow is also white just like a polar bear.
Snow covers the sidewalk!
Winter is before the spring.
I like snow because it is fun.
Edward Wu, Grade 1
The Delphi Academy, MA

Dogs

Dogs in the park.
Dogs in the house.
Dogs in the yard.
Dogs on the street.
Dogs in the store eating treats.
Lucy Nevin, Grade 1
St Rose School, CT

Fairy Friends

Fairy
little friend
up at night
you're loving and kind
Dreamy
Abigayle Watson, Grade 1
St Rose School, CT

Rain

Rain is beautiful
Rain is slippery
Rain is wet and cold
What do you wear?
You wear a coat!
Alex Topper, Grade 1
The Tobin School, MA

Rocking and Rolling

One day there was a guy with a clover,
That was run over by a boulder,
He had a sister named Pat,
That had a friend bat,
And the boulder had a cup holder.
Connor Dunn, Grade 3
Saint Rose School, CT

Wishing on a Star

I like stars because they glow in the dark
Stars shoot through the night sky
If you wish upon a star it will come true
Or it won't come true
If you are sleeping it may come true
Mackenzie McSpirit, Grade 2
Mayfield Elementary School, NY

Easter

I like jelly beans
Tutti-frutti jelly beans
Jelly beans are cool
Lots of colorful flavors
I think Easter is the best.
Mason Farnell, Grade 3
Penn-Kidder Campus, PA

Leprechauns

There was a leprechaun named Matt,
Who had a friend whose name was Pat,
Pat and Matt had a friend,
They were friends until the end,
And Matt never, ever sat.
Kristen Cirone, Grade 3
St Rose School, CT

My Friends

My friend and I are like birds
in the sky.
Soaring and dipping into the water.
Having fun and playing.
We are never mean to each other.
Anthony Scibelli, Grade 3
Meadow Drive School, NY

Leprechaun World

Come to Leprechaun World on Tuesday,
We have a good TV that's blue ray,
You have to cross the rainbow,
Don't be too slow though,
Remember you always have to go-go.
Savannah LaFerriere, Grade 3
St Rose School, CT

Incomplete

A city without people, a church without a steeple.
A fish without a swish, good without a dish.
A school without kids, jars without lids.
Pools without water, a boy without a father.
A volcano without lava, fruit salad without guava.
A baby without a pacifier, a necklace without a sapphire.
Wings without a plane, a bowling alley without a lane.
A game without rules, a toddler without drools.
A book without pages, people without ages.
Bees without stings, fingers without rings.
Shoes without feet, a bird without a tweet.
Stamps without ink, an eye without a blink.
A guy without a suit, a word without a root.
A mouth without taste, a toothbrush without toothpaste.

Eric Weisz, Grade 3
West Branch School, PA

What a Friend Is Like

A best friend, like mine, is someone who...
Stops by to see if you're all right,
Cares about you,
Who shares moments of
happiness and sadness with you,
and
Is always there to help you.
And now I met one,
the only one,
Shania.
And now she lives on at 10 years old,
and still...
my
BFF!

Anna Donovan, Grade 3
Sarah Dyer Barnes School, RI

Peace

Peace is like a no sign or no people calling you names
Peace looks like people being free
It sounds like birds and
It can be great but,
Peace is always around.

Jacob Goldman, Grade 3
Coram Elementary School, NY

Autumn Nature
Plumpy, orangish pumpkins
Leaves on the ground
Flying from the ground to the ground
Yellow dandelions falling from the ground
Crunchy, crackling, fluttering, twittering
Falling from the ground.

Matthew Rubino, Grade 3
Jeffrey Elementary School, CT

Giggling
Friendship is like a pretty violet
Friendship tastes like hot chocolate on a cold day
It smells like the first day of summer
It reminds me of my heart pounding
It sounds like best friends playing together
Friendship makes me feel like giggling

Abby Williamson, Grade 2
Klein Elementary School, PA

Christmas
I saw my sister throwing a snow ball
It went on my face and hit my eye
I see lots of girls under a tree
Somebody brings gifts in the night
We eat candy canes and decorate
We stay in our pj's every Christmas

Ivanese Perez, Grade 3
Public School 115 Alexander Humboldt, NY

Christmas
Presents everywhere
Opening presents
Giving cookies to Santa
Hot chocolate, marshmallows
Yummy
I love Christmas!

Kayla Noboa, Grade 3
Public School 115 Alexander Humboldt, NY

My Baby Brother
I love my baby brother
Like no other.
I could play
With him all day.
Marcos Cabrera, Grade 2
Public School 1 The Bergen School, NY

Spring
Jumping, Playing
Walking, running, skipping
Having fun in the park
Trees bloom
Gianna LaMonica, Grade 3
Our Lady of Hope School, NY

Pearls
Pearls are shiny,
Pearls are bright,
Pearls are sparkly
just right!
Celena Pawling, Grade 3
St Maria Goretti School, PA

Baseball
Fun, Long
Batting, pitching, fielding
I like to play baseball
Fun
Anthony Cipri, Grade 3
Our Lady of Hope School, NY

Spring
Oh spring
Can you sing
Can you fly a kite
In the night
Michele Evangelista, Grade 3
Our Lady of Hope School, NY

Spring's Song
The butterflies will flap their wings
The flowers ring
The birds will sing
To the Spring!
Lauren Guarneri, Grade 3
Our Lady of Hope School, NY

My Baby Sister
My baby sister is tiny.
My baby sister can't talk.
My baby sister has no teeth.
My baby sister can roll.
Jeffrey Johnson, Grade 2
Tashua School, CT

Spring Is Here
Winter is gone, Spring is here
The sun is out, the flowers are near
I see the bright sun
Let's have some fun!
James Loeffel, Grade 3
Our Lady of Hope School, NY

Spring Is Fun
Here comes the sun
Let's go to the park and run
We will play with my cat Bun
Everyone will have fun
Sara Gomez, Grade 3
Our Lady of Hope School, NY

Cotton Candy
Pink
Cotton candy
Sticking to my mouth
A carnival is yummy!
Stella Sabo, Grade 1
St Rose School, CT

Easter

E gg coloring
A pril showers
S pring
T reats in baskets
E aster bunnies
R abbits everywhere hopping
Christopher Powell, Grade 3
St Agatha School, NY

Hockey

Have fun. Just do not get hurt!
Old sport, started in 1875.
Center man can go anywhere.
Keep your self in shape!
Exercising helps you skate.
You should never give up!
Brady Fitzpatrick, Grade 3
Colebrook Primary School, NY

Balloon

Colorful balloon,
Up in the sky,
Through the mountains and houses;
Decorative balloon,
Sailing in the air,
Up so high.
Najia Choudhary, Grade 2
Helen B Duffield Elementary School, NY

Family

F un
A wesome
M emory making
I mportant
L oving
Y our favorite
Alexander Beechey, Grade 3
Colebrook Primary School, NY

Spring

S ky is blue
P retty flowers
R ain
I have a birthday
N ice outside
G reen grass
Amaya Garcia, Grade 1
St Agatha School, NY

Dance

I like to dance,
I dance and prance.
I take jazz and ballet,
I dance all the way.
I'm not saying don't run,
Dancing is just really fun!
Victoria Garland, Grade 2
St Stephen's School, NY

Swimming

dive, fun
floating, sliding, racing
paddle with your arms
pool fun
Sierra Shrauger, Grade 2
Caryl E Adams Primary School, NY

Cubby

A cubby is where you keep your things
Like backpacks, books, and shoes
A cubby is like a friend to you
It keeps your things safe too
Riya Subbaiah, Grade 1
Buckley Country Day School, NY

Roses Poses

I smell the roses
They have a wonderful smell
The roses bloom fast
Jonathan Ngaruiya, Grade 1
St Louis Elementary School, MA

Flower Colors

Flowers are pretty
Purple is my favorite
I like the trees too
Sydney Langlois, Grade 1
St Louis Elementary School, MA

A Shamrock

A shamrock is as green as
green apples,
leaves,
green peppers,
and nail polish.
A shamrock is green like
crickets,
grass hoppers,
dollars,
and limes.
A shamrock is GREEN!
Madison Taylor, Grade 3
Mary J Tanner School, NY

Autumn

High, high, high
are the leaves in the tree.
Red, orange, brown, yellow.
These are the colors in autumn.

Down, down, down they fall.
This is what happens in autumn.

Finally they blow away,
to somewhere far away.
This is what happens in autumn.
Laura Kelly, Grade 2
St. Teresa of Avila School, PA

Money

Money is like
That little green stuff
That we spend
When we
Buy something.

The gold coins
That are worth
One dollar
Are golder
Than gold.
Colten Cicarelli, Grade 1
St Rose School, CT

Blue

Blue is the color of the sky.
Blue is the color of the ocean.
Blue is the color of Neptune.
Blue is the color of blue birds.
Blue smells like blue bells.
Blue tastes like blueberries.
Blue sounds like the crashing waves.
Blue feels like I'm swimming.
Blue makes me feel happy.
Blue looks like Jamaican waters.
Blue is my favorite color.
Nicholas DiLeonardo, Grade 3
Evergreen Elementary School, PA

Sea Shell

I am bored
I want to move
I'm stuck here
just sitting
in the sand
a star fish stuck to me
I want to move from
this spot
hear a wave
I have moved
My day is no longer boring
Caroline Thomson, Grade 3
Buckley Country Day School, NY

Quarters

Quarters jingle
in my pocket
waiting to
be spent
It is
silver
It is
round
with
George Washington's
head
Hunter Niebuhr, Grade 2
Tashua School, CT

Elizabeth Wallace Is My Name

Elizabeth Wallace is my name.
I have two cats and they are tame.
In China I was born.
My favorite vegetable is corn.
I like to swim at the beach.
My favorite fruit is the peach.
Disney World is my favorite place.
You can tell by the smile on my face.

Elizabeth Wallace, Grade 1
St Joan of Arc School, PA

Michelle

M ay is my favorite time
I love cats
C aring
H elpful
E njoys playing
L ikes ice cream
L oving person
E nergetic

Michelle Raytsis, Grade 3
Penn-Kidder Campus, PA

Snowflake

Snowflake, Snowflake
with that soft fur
and golden eyes
that stare at me
all the time
who snuggles with me
and that tail wagging
when she sees me!

Madison Kasch, Grade 2
Pine Tree Elementary School, NY

Winter

I want to build a snowman
But I don't know if I can.

I made a big snowball
I thought it might just fall.

Got a carrot for his nose
But my toes almost froze.

Danielle Shapiro, Grade 3
Penn Kidder Campus, PA

Polar Bears

fast
running in the snow
fierce
showing his claws
hunting seals
to eat
standing up tall
on his hind feet

Timmy McCrae Jr., Grade 2
Tashua School, CT

Baseball

B at
A ctive
S hort stop
E ighth inning
B all
A fast ball
L eft field
L ast inning in the game!

Matthew Morris, Grade 3
The Edgartown School, MA

Monkey

Monkey
hairy, funny
eat bananas all day
eating and swinging all day long
primate

Bethsaida Anderson, Grade 3
Clinton Street Elementary School, NY

Flowers

Flowers
pretty colors
in the garden it grows
warms my heart when I see flowers
bouquet

Claire Guindon, Grade 3
Clinton Street Elementary School, NY

China
It will never sink.
Land is as great as can be.
Don't use the wrong tone.
Simon Maslak, Grade 3
Como Park Elementary School, NY

Dad
Dad, you are
So fun! I love you,
Today and forever.
Ben Rinehart, Grade 3
John T Waugh Elementary School, NY

Spring
Bees are buzzing here,
Flowers blooming everywhere,
Going to the park.
Christian Rivera, Grade 2
Helen B Duffield Elementary School, NY

Hawaii
The palm trees blowing in Hawaii
It's so glorious
The water is shining blue
N'dia Neal, Grade 3
Colebrook Primary School, NY

Pine Cones
They make cool noises,
when you step on them, they crack.
They are very small.
Samuel Bedrosian, Grade 2
Cornerstone Academy, MA

Marigolds
Watching in the shade.
Goldest in early spring-time.
Annual flower.
Lydia Partenio, Grade 2
Long Meadow Elementary School, CT

Black-eyed Chickadee
Eyes as black as night
Black-eyed chickadees fly high,
Jumping into flight.
Nishka Pant, Grade 2
Cornerstone Academy, MA

Magical Garden
A soft place to be
Waving at me in the sun
A magical place
Julia Lenahan, Grade 3
Colebrook Primary School, NY

Birds
They flutter around,
gliding in the humid air,
looking for their food.
Davin Evans, Grade 3
Cornerstone Academy, MA

A Tunnel
A tunnel of trees
Green grass glowing in tunnel
I follow a path
Chase Herrgesell, Grade 3
Colebrook Primary School, NY

Birds
Birds are very cute.
They make beautiful noises.
They love to lay eggs.
Riley Fields, Grade 2
Cornerstone Academy, MA

Emma
Cute, tiny
Loving, caring, talking
A little running machine.
Rain Galanti, Grade 3
Colebrook Primary School, NY

Spring Is Here

Spring is here
Time to Cheer
Flowers are blooming
The grass is greener
Birds are chirping all around
So that we smile and take away our frown.
Spring is here
Spring is here
So let's all cheer!

Maia George, Grade 2
Public School 235 Lenox, NY

Ice Cream

In the winter you don't eat ice
Cream.
Eat a lot of ice cream and you'll get a stomach ache.

Carrying it everywhere.
Racing to Brighams.
Excellent with whipped cream.
And a cherry on top.
Marching through the world with ice cream.

Chloe Ho, Grade 3
Sacred Heart School, MA

The Moon Is a Silver Balloon

The moon is a tiny silver balloon
When it's cloudy the balloon hides because he's shy
When it's day the balloon pops
And the next night there's a new balloon inflated
But this time he's smaller and he gets even smaller
And then there's a new one inflated and it's full again

Georgia Pennington, Grade 2
North Street School, CT

Hurt

Hurt is when one's heart has a hole pierced through.
With a stinging that swells up their insides,
and kills the happiness on the outside leaving an empty soul.
And let's the burn of the rage and the fury in to steal the peace
that was once in their heart, not anymore.

Logan Burdette, Grade 3
Runnymede Elementary School, MD

Winter

I push my sister on her sleigh
When she went down she said, "Hurray."

She went on a bigger slide; she had a fright
When she was done she had frost bite.

When we got home late at night
I went to bed and said, "Don't let the frost bite."

Austin Williams, Grade 3
Penn-Kidder Campus, PA

Earth Day!

Please, oh please don't litter on me,
For I am Earth and I hate your yucky trash.
Please recycle — it will only be best.
Don't you love me and my trees?
It's a great sunny day,
Pick up the trash.
Come on it's Earth day,
It's a blast!!

Jenny Landells, Grade 3
Shady Grove Elementary School, PA

Rhinos

Rhinos can weigh up to 10,000 pounds,
And that would be scary if they were chargin' at you.
When they walk around,
They shake the ground,
their feet pick up bugs, which crawl into their mouths.
Some people believe,
That their horn is magical,
so they kill the Rhino, and take the horn.

Kaitlin Morehouse, Grade 3
Shady Grove Elementary School, PA

Cotton Candy

Cotton candy is yummy and sweet to eat,
It is like a cotton ball as you can see;
You probably wouldn't know which color you like,
When the man said, "Do you like green, blue, or white?"
I chose the blue because it looks cool.

Kayla Singh, Grade 2
Helen B Duffield Elementary School, NY

Friends

Friends are people who care for you.
They cheer you up when you are blue.
Friends enjoy the same things when it comes to having fun.
When friends have sleepovers they're always on the run.
Everyone should have a best friend
To share your life to the end.
Friends are people who care for you.
They cheer you up when you are blue.

Abbey Mae Gardiner, Grade 2
Carlyle C Ring Elementary School, NY

Winter Is...

Winter is sleigh riding on a big hill.
Winter is building snow forts in my backyard.
Winter is playing and making snow angels.
Winter is coming inside and drinking hot cocoa.
Winter is watching the fires in our fireplace.
Winter is getting presents for Christmas.
Winter is Jesus' birthday.
Winter is fun!

William Gannon, Grade 1
All Saints Catholic Academy, NY

Killer Earthquakes

I am terrible.
I knock down buildings —
They fall on people.
I am scary.
I shake the ground —
Then, there are cracks all around!
I am a killer Earthquake,
Watch Out!

Garrett Moore, Grade 1
Milton Terrace South Elementary School, NY

I Love You

I love you the bluest...
I love you more than the shiny seas.
I love you more than the bright blue sky.
The touch of a comfortable blue couch reminds me of you.
The taste of a blueberry reminds me of you.

Eric Connolly, Grade 3
Southold Elementary School, NY

What Is Pink?

Pink is the color of a clean sweet cat nose.
Pink is the sister of Purple.
Pink is the child of red.
Pink is the glorious sun setting on the horizon.
Redish Orange is the father of Pink.
Pink is the inside of a dog's ear.
Pink is the color of apple blossoms.
Pink is the color of sweet smelling flowers.

Annalise Irwin, Grade 3
Colebrook Primary School, NY

Better Me!

I like to
Play basketball.
I love the games.
When we go to
An away game
We are going to win!
I feel strong
Inside when I play.

Almasi Johnson, Grade 2
New York Institute for Special Education, NY

Florida in Summer

Wipeout is the best place
In the whole, wide world.

There were a lot of rides
In the park.

My favorite ride was
The Wave Pool.

Jalen Cordero, Grade 3
New York Institute for Special Education, NY

At the Beach

Splish! Splash! goes the waves on the beach
The peaceful sun and palm trees lay in back
Blue skies and waters
Crabs and star fish crawl under my feet
It feels so great to go to the beach!

AnnaBella Ball, Grade 2
Mayfield Elementary School, NY

Spring Is Here
The leaves are falling
kids are screaming in the park
having so much fun playing
The leaves are beautiful
they make a pile so
we can jump in
the leaves go flying everywhere
but when they are finished
they sweep them up so
they don't make a mess.

Nicole Ciscart, Grade 2
Public School 232 The Walter Ward School, NY

Nightmare
A nightmare is like a by accident dream.
A nightmare only comes
when you were mean or sad or mad, maybe bad.
The only way to get rid of the nightmare
is to count to ten and breathe.
A nightmare is not on purpose.
It's all yours.
A nightmare is a very scary dream
that you will never forget.

Kierlyn Seeley, Grade 2
Pine Tree Elementary School, NY

Ocean
The waves move
In and out
Crashing as they
Wash the
Sandcastles of the day
Away.

Nelyanna Kercado, Grade 3
Public School 40 Samuel Huntington, NY

Mr. Beck
I have a gym teacher named Mr. Beck
When he was playin' basketball, he broke his neck
And now he has a cast
Now he doesn't run very fast

Daniel Claypool, Grade 2
Klein Elementary School, PA

Baseball

B ubble gum.
A t the field.
S unny sun shine.
E ating seeds.
B atting balls.
A t the mound.
L eft and right.
L imping around the bases.
Summer Cardoza, Grade 3
The Edgartown School, MA

Planting

P retty flower
L ove
A nimals
N esting
T ennis
I ncredible
N ice weather
G ardening
Meghan Delphous, Grade 3
The Edgartown School, MA

Colors

As I was walking by, hesitating,
What colors should I make?
A deep feeling of red,
A puddle deep and pink
Like a wonderful pink waterfall,
or
Tear drops of blue tears?
Maybe just colors
Sydney Hernandez, Grade 3
The Brooklyn Charter School, NY

Teacher

Teacher, Teacher
You are so, so nice.
When I am hurt
you are there for me.
Your hugs make me so happy.
You are smart, kind and friendly.
You are a nice teacher and the
BEST too!
Yanet Garcia, Grade 2
Pine Tree Elementary School, NY

Spring Is Fun

Spring is fun
Spring is fun
My sneakers are on.
My slippers are off.
My scarf is lost.
Spring is here!
Spring is here!
Have fun!
Reanna Hawker, Grade 2
Public School 235 Lenox, NY

Riley

Riley likes to play in the sun,
He thinks it is fun.
He likes to eat,
Riley likes to eat meat.
Riley likes to play ball,
Riley just stares at them all.
Riley is my dog,
He has a chew toy log.
Katie Sullivan, Grade 2
St Stephen's School, NY

Rabbits

Rabbits
cute and fluffy
they're are so bouncy too
they're sweet, nice, have sharp teeth
awesome
Rebekah Rennard, Grade 3
Clinton Street Elementary School, NY

Turtles

Turtles
scaly hard shell
very slowing moving
cute slow moving amphibians
creatures
Lucrezia Fruci, Grade 3
Clinton Street Elementary School, NY

Snow

Snow, Snow
watch it as it grows
Snowflakes tumble down.
I always watch it
as it goes.
When snow melts
it looks so low.
But when it comes
"Watch out for snow!"
Emily Helen Fradellos, Grade 3
The Delphi Academy, MA

Ice Cream

I ce cream with
C aramel dip
E xtremely tasty

C rispy cones
R ed cherry dip
E xtraordinary fudge melting
A mazing chocolate
M y ice cream is tasting yummy!
Alexis Condon, Grade 3
The Edgartown School, MA

Rain

Shiny diamonds fill my
heart with happiness.

The humidity fills the air.

I can't wait to see what
flowers bloom.

Fills the bird baths.
Lilly Quilty, Grade 2
The Tobin School, MA

I'm Hungry!

My tummy is starting to growl.
I'm hungry! I'm hungry! I'm hungry!

I wonder what's for lunch!
I'm hungry! I'm hungry! I'm hungry!

Will it be pasta or pizza or fish???
Why can't I just make a wish?
I'm hungry! I'm hungry! I'm hungry!!!
Samantha Berra, Grade 2
Pine Tree Elementary School, NY

Surfing

Surfing
Sunny, bumpy
Surf, flip, turn
My surf board is nice.
Me
Julia Myers, Grade 2
The Fourth Presbyterian School, MD

Easter

Easter is so fun,
There are bright, colorful eggs,
Blue, pink, green eggs too,
The birds sing a little tune.
The butterflies will fly high.
Branden Garner, Grade 3
Penn-Kidder Campus, PA

Rainbow

Apple
Orange cat
Gold
Leprechaun
Blue fish
Purple marker
Sheylanie Cedeño, Kindergarten
Robert M Hughes School, MA

I Like Lots of Things

I like ribs and candy
I like Chinese food and ice cream.
But I do not like salmon!
I like moose and spiders.
I like lions and penguins.
But I love cats!
Steven Brown, Grade 1
Maureen M Welch Elementary School, PA

You

You
You can.
You do.
You fly.
You run.
You walk.
And I…
Love.

Marissa DiCondina, Grade 3
Salford Hills Elementary School, PA

Rain

I love rain because
without rain plants can't grow

I love rain because
without rain we can't live

I love rain because
it fills my heart with love

Darren Quilty, Grade 1
The Tobin School, MA

Love Is Warm

Love is great
Love is peaceful.
It's so warm,
It starts a fire in your heart.
Love makes you happy,
When you're sad.
When you're sad,
Love always brings you warmth!

Andrew Newman, Grade 3
Willits Elementary School, NY

Spring!

S uper smelling,
P retty flowers,
R unning and playing,
I n the sunshine,
N ever ending,
G reat days,

in spring!

Addy Hayman, Grade 3
The Edgartown School, MA

My Grandma

My Grandma
Loves to Paint
Every day
She makes
Things as beautiful
As the sun
My Grandma
Has a talent!!!

Lucas Gelmetti, Grade 2
Tashua School, CT

Baseball

B ase
A t base
S o fun
E xciting
B all
A home run
L eft field
L efty

Lukah Vieira, Grade 3
The Edgartown School, MA

Peace

Peace is like a sign of love
Peace looks like wonderland
It looks like a hundred birds and
It can be heaven
Peace is always a good thing.

Kerri Cox, Grade 3
Coram Elementary School, NY

Peace

Peace is like a flowing river
Peace looks like beautiful gold
It sounds like music and
It can be graceful but,
Peace is always nice to have.

Peter Furgal, Grade 3
Coram Elementary School, NY

Fire

Red and hot
Big and horrifying

I destroy buildings
While humans flee from my arms

I can hear sirens blazing
Soon I will die

My body is shrinking
Water is killing me

There is a crowd watching me
I am sad

It takes hours
Until I die

But until then…
I am fire

Tom Kuntz, Grade 3
Indian Lane Elementary School, PA

Super Hero

Dad says: "Go to Sleep," but instead
I lie in bed,
pretending…

I am a super hero
saving the world
from danger
from a bad guy.

My cape is blue and green
with red stripes
like fire.
It makes me feel
proud.

I am saving a little boy
from a bully.
He is a nice little boy.
The bully is mean.
I am a hero.

Gerardo Claure, Grade 3
Number 2 School, NY

Grandparents

I wait at the window
I wait for them
I wait
I wait
I wait
Where are you?
Where are you?
I yell to myself.
Then I turn my
back
for
a
sec
Wait it is true
THEY'RE HERE!
MY GRANDPARENTS ARE HERE!
NO MORE WAITING!!!!!!!!!!!!

Johnny Fleming, Grade 2
Pine Tree Elementary School, NY

The Silver Star

The silver star
is a soft baby star
that needs a lullaby.
It sparkles and shines
and lives way up in the sky.
Her name is Stella
she has a sister named Bella,
they learn how to fly.
Stella learns to dance in the sky.
She will sparkle and dance
when she hears the song
Twinkle Lullaby.
Then she sleeps in her star room
talking to herself
Is there a reason why?
Oh I love you Stella
I'll croon you a sweet lullaby.

Erin Palmer, Grade 3
The Tobin School, MA

Green
Green feels like smooth pears,
Green looks like broccoli,
Peppers, snakes and frogs.
Green is the color the priest wears
In ordinary time.
Vincent Coolberth, Grade 1
St Anna School, MA

Turtle
Turtle
inside, outside
walks and walks
sleeping after the race
Turtle
Ryan Wagnblas, Grade 1
St Rose School, CT

Spring
Hello to planting in my garden,
Hello to violets and roses,
Hello to soccer fields and riding my bike,
Hello to insects and warm weather,
Good-bye to dark, gray clouds!
Andrew Gardiner, Grade 1
St Anna School, MA

Lime Green
Lime green is like a lime
Sour and good
Slimmer from Ghostbusters
A popsicle —
refreshing in the summer
Michael Procopis, Grade 2
Primrose School, NY

Monique
There once was a girl named Monique.
She looked like a very old antique.
She had a lot of wrinkles,
And she loved her sprinkles,
That's why Monique was so unique.
Monique Cormier, Grade 3
St Anna School, MA

Cute Butterflies
Butterflies
Cute, Wonderful
Changing, Flying, Colorful
Butterflies have pretty patterns.
Fast flying butterflies.
Hayley Lambert, Grade 3
Our Lady of Hope School, NY

Flowers
Flowers
Pretty colors
Planting, growing, blooming
Bees get their nectar from flowers
Lovely
Nicholas Borlie, Grade 3
St Clement Mary Hofbauer School, MD

Animals Always in Action
Camels carrying cargo.
Snakes slithering in the swamp.
Raccoons running rapidly.
Leopards leaping lightly.
And piranhas pursuing their prey.
Aaron Maier, Grade 2
Home School, PA

Football
Football is a game of excitement
"Hut! Hut! Hike!" yells the quarterback
As he throws it through the park…
CAUGHT!
TOUCHDOWN!
Jack Sibilia, Grade 2
Primrose School, NY

Balloon
The thick, colorful balloon,
Filled with helium,
Glided through the cold, breezy day;
It sailed for days and nights,
Until it got stuck in a tree.
Alexander Ungar, Grade 2
Helen B Duffield Elementary School, NY

Biography

I am a good video game player and gymnast
who's good at climbing — like rock climbing —
and I like cars.

Here's something I care about deeply: training my dog.
Here's something I need deeply— more video games and toys!

I'd like to give toys to the needy and give presents.
I'd like to be helpful to everyone
I'd like people to stop throwing trash, stop killing animals and
stop cutting down trees where birds make their homes.

I live in Queens, New York

Joshua Elgandy, Grade 3
New York Institute for Special Education, NY

War

I once was flying high,
up in the baby blue sky
in my big booming bomber!
I fired my bombs!
One! Two! Three! Four!
I hate this war!
Boom! Bang! Crash! Smash!
The enemy began to scream,
"I'm not on your team!"
We were winning
in this inning.
I wish this war was over!
Boom! Bang! Crash! Smash!

Alex Seip, Grade 3
Emmanuel Baptist Christian Academy, PA

Halloween

Halloween. What a fun holiday!
Getting scared, having fun, getting candy
Walking around with a costume
Seeing different things
Witches, fairies, goblins, princesses
And eating candy
Halloween. What a fun holiday!

Mayreny Rodriguez, Grade 3
Public School 115 Alexander Humboldt, NY

Books

Every book
is a
magical book.
When you
read the
words on the paper
it takes you
places you have
never gone
before.

William Lennon, Grade 2
Pine Tree Elementary School, NY

Winter

Snow, oh snow,
So shiny and white,
Hard to plow,
What a beautiful sight!
It is so bright outside the window!
Up and down the hills we go,
Sledding all day!
It was fun to play!
The sun goes away.
Oh, how it was a wonderful day!

Kloei Logan, Grade 3
John T Waugh Elementary School, NY

Bacon

Bacon, Bacon, Bacon
You're so good
and juicy!
Why do you have
to be so good?
Bacon, Bacon, Bacon
Even though I'm full
I always have room
for you!
Bacon, Bacon, Bacon!

Neiko Welch, Grade 2
Pine Tree Elementary School, NY

All About Me

Nicholas is my first name
Baseball is my favorite game
My eyes are blue
I love school too
This year I will be eight
And it will be great
For a pet I'd like a snake
Maybe I could have it on my cake
My poem is done
And I have had a lot of fun

Nicholas Hamilton, Grade 1
St Joan of Arc School, PA

The Apple Party

Apples
Brown
Colorful
Dancing
Eating
Flying
Getting
Hats
In
July.

Nicholas Kindya, Grade 3
Our Lady of Hope School, NY

The Owl

Hoo, Hoo
He comes
out at
night to
see all
his friends.
Hurry up!
The sun is up.
He's going
to bed.

Rebecca Murphy, Grade 2
Pine Tree Elementary School, NY

St. Patrick's Day

On St. Patrick's Day there is green.
More than you have ever seen.

The leprechaun leaves lots of tricks,
and that's how he gets his kicks.

Sometimes the leprechaun leaves some presents,
and you might just find them in your residence.

There are lots of leprechauns in the world,
to play tricks on the boys and girls.

In the morning there is lots of tricks and sometimes you might find a treat.
It could be a treat or something to eat.

Tanner Till, Grade 3
Ellicott Road Elementary School, NY

Piano Practice

I love piano, it's lots of fun.
I like the way my fingers run.
Across the keys they swirl and prance,
They are doing a little dance.

But the black and white keys are so dull.
Don't worry their music is colorful.
It sounds so pretty, the notes low and high,
So pretty it sounds like the beautiful sky.

The song I am playing is called "Monkey,"
Ugh, it was supposed to be F, not E.
Piano is joy and music made to blend,
I wish piano practice would never end.

Sophia Harne, Grade 3
Home School, NH

Snow

I fall down on you.
How cold I am.
Here comes more of me.
Like a blanket oh how you jump in me.
Oh how I love kids and how you play in my coldness.

Jacob LaPietra, Grade 3
Colebrook Primary School, NY

Spring

Rain is falling
birds are chirping.
I can feel the fresh air coming at me.
The sun is shining down on me.
Everybody comes out to play with me.

Christian Pichardo, Grade 2
Public School 232 The Walter Ward School, NY

Peace

Peace is laying on my trampoline on a dark summer night,
watching stars glowing at night by the fire,
settling a fight with words, not fists,
laying on a hammock blowing bubbles,
and laying on my bed watching TV alone.

Maygan Robinson, Grade 2
Wells Central School, NY

Peace

Peace is playing with my Legos on a rainy day,
playing fetch with my dog outside,
Ken and Joanne pushing me on the swing,
riding my bike in a circle around our park,
and reading a book by myself.

Dylan Heaney, Grade 2
Wells Central School, NY

Summer

I see the beautiful bright sun and pretty people tanning,
I hear people jumping in the pool and birds' beautiful chirping,
I taste cool lemonade and yummy strawberries,
I smell fresh air and nice flowers,
I feel soft sand and hard sea shells.

Alyssa Loveland, Grade 3
Mary J Tanner School, NY

Stuffed Animals

Stuffed animals, stuffed animals are the best.
I love them so much they help me rest.
I like big, little, tall, and small.
They are fluffy, puffy, cuddly, and snuggly.
I love to collect them all.

Molly Brett, Grade 3
St Barnabas Elementary School, NY

The Good Tree
Trees are good
Trees are great
They make us feel good
All night and all day.
Lucas Weller, Grade 3
Ridgeway Elementary School, MD

Spinach
Spinach
Green
My dad eats
it all.
Nicole Sountis, Grade 2
Pine Tree Elementary School, NY

Spring
Buds growing on trees
Flowers finally blooming
Spring is here at last
Patrick Connolly, Grade 3
Southold Elementary School, NY

Sweet
The flower was pink
and smelled like candy ice cream.
Sweet and sugary.
Eliza Odum, Grade 2
Simpson-Waverly School, CT

Worms
Worms crawling around
squirming, crawling in the dirt.
Worms are weird.
Thomas Harlee, Grade 2
Simpson-Waverly School, CT

Escape
The furry, brown mouse
scurries past the hungry snake
hiding in the grass.
Rennarda Washington, Grade 2
Simpson-Waverly School, CT

Magic Island
Go to Magic Island
and escape from the chilly fall.
Go to Magic Island
and have a big ball!
Go to Magic Island
and when you go away,
remember to come back the next day!
Samantha Beaulieu, Grade 3
Odyssey Day School, MA

Games
Games are fun.
Games have names.
In games you can run.
Games, games and games.
There are tons and tons.
Sometimes you can wish.
Wow you won.
Maggie Kell, Grade 3
St Maria Goretti School, PA

Jump Rope
Jump rope
Jump rope
Back and forth
When I jump rope
I even do tricks
Jump rope
Jump rope
Daniel Lippman, Grade 2
Tashua School, CT

The Sweet Air
The sun is shining on the sprouts
Spring is here!
Air, air, air is sweet
Sun shining on my back
Spring is hot
Butterflies are floating in the air
Bees are singing
Gianna Messina, Grade 2
Helen B Duffield Elementary School, NY

Seasons

The snow is falling softly down,
The wind is blowing round and round.
The ground is turning snowy white,
Snowing through the day and night.

In Spring the days grow longer,
In Spring the weather grows warmer.
There is only a soft breeze,
Sprout a flower please.

Swimming swimming in the summer,
Happy happy days grow longer.
Warmer warmer every day,
Come on let's go play.

Leaves are falling every day,
Animals flying south away.
School is starting in the fall,
Fall is a wonderful season after all.

Jessica Wang, Grade 2
Maureen M Welch Elementary School, PA

Titanic

The titanic is sinking,
It's going down,
Water is all around.

The bulkheads aren't working
We're scared
And we're sad.

The lifeboats are leaving
Third class is trapped
By the gates of the ship.

The Carpathia is coming
That's not bad
I'm not so sure about that

Rockets are firing
The bottom is breached
We are praying to God that we will live.

Joshua Corey, Grade 2
Greenock Elementary School, PA

Ice Cream

Ice cream,
Ice cream,
with Reese's chunks.
Ice cream,
Ice cream
vanilla in a cup.
Ice cream,
Ice cream
Munchity
Munchity
CRUNCH!!!!!
MUNCH!!!!!
Mmmmmm!!!
Yummy!!!!!
Ice cream,
Ice cream,
I need more
Ice cream!!!

Nicholas Culhane, Grade 2
Pine Tree Elementary School, NY

Operation Dinosaurs

See them fight.
Hear them roar.
Prehistoric
dinosaur.
Watch
out
cause
they're
right
next
door.
Boom,
smash,
bite
or
roar.
Prehistoric
dinosaur.

Michael Robinson, Grade 2
Public School 235 Lenox, NY

Snowy Day

Fluffy
Puffy
I jump into a cloud of snow
I'm loving it
I'm fluffing it
Till the day grows dark
I quietly fall asleep Zzzz…

Sofia O'Bryant, Grade 2
Public School 69, NY

Spring

Spring
Birds
Chirp
Chirp
Chirp
Cherry blossoms bloom
I love spring

Lauren Kashinsky, Grade 1
Buckley Country Day School, NY

Inch Worms

Inching, inching
Inching up a tree.
Hanging, hanging
Hanging down from
Thread just for me
To look at and
Watch nature grow.

Isabella Marrale, Grade 1
Buckley Country Day School, NY

Ocean and Desert

Ocean
Beautiful, blue
Swimming, surfing, scuba diving
Fish, seaweed, cactus, snakes
Slithering, sweating, sculpting
Dry, hot
Desert

Kaylee Peacock, Grade 3
Brant Elementary School, NY

Carnivores and Herbivores

Carnivores
Meat, fangs
Eating, running, chewing
Bears, wolves, deer, chipmunks
Feeding, dashing, licking
Plants, teeth
Herbivores

Doralea Kettle, Grade 3
Brant Elementary School, NY

Peace and War

Peace
Calm, quiet
Helping, loving, caring
Friends, family, enemy, foe
Hating, fighting, feuding
Chaos, loud
War

Kamree Bomberry, Grade 3
Brant Elementary School, NY

Small Creatures Below

Arachnids
Peaceful, hairy
Frightening, catching, spinning
Eight legs, fangs, six legs, stingers
Annoying, bothering, pollinating
Mean, pests
Bees

Cyrus Farner, Grade 3
Brant Elementary School, NY

Love and Hate

Love
Hearts, smiles
Caring, hugging, kissing
Roses, happy, mean, angry
Kicking, fighting, punching
Darkness, frowns
Hate

Caitlin Burbige, Grade 3
Brant Elementary School, NY

Outside by Nature

Flowers shivering
Trees waving
Sun hot
Nasty wind
Beautiful flowers
Bunnies hopping
Moon shining
Flowers blooming
Ants moving
Mr. Tree flowering
Flowers exciting
Trees fun
Leaves floating

Brianna Murante, Grade 2
Helen B Duffield Elementary School, NY

In Nature

I once went into the grass and woods
I found a soundless acorn
On the ground
With black, red leaves
With ferns, flower petals
With light pink
A little white
With berries, stems
Red, black, green, yellow, pink, white
Brown leaves
That are small
Big huge seeds like little seeds
Small seeds, big seeds.

Gideon Charles, Grade 3
Jeffrey Elementary School, CT

Sunny Day

Leaves blowing all around
Trees dancing all around
No one on the playground
The sky is blue
Hearing airplanes
Bugs flying everywhere
Fighting bees, "Get off bee!"
At the park kids run and laugh
Everywhere trucks cling and clang
The sweet air is very sweet
Flowers born
The happy sun
Then very quiet

Isabella Rivera, Grade 2
Helen B Duffield Elementary School, NY

A Circle of Fun

Fall, I love fall.
Make a pile of leaves
Then jump in.
Winter comes
Long white snow
Snowballs fly
Then comes spring
Flowers grow
Bees come too.
Summer's next
Jump in the pool and get cool.
Fall, winter, spring, summer
A circle of fun.

Elijah Swift, Grade 1
Dartmouth Early Learning Center, MA

Sun

Sun
Yellow, hot
Burning, warming, life giving
Light by day, light by night
Reflecting, shining, changing
Silver, cold
Moon

Kendall Fleming, Grade 2
St. Madeleine Sophie School, NY

My Dog Lucky

Fluffy tail
Golden like the sun
Black and rounded eyes
Small paws but a fast runner
Loves to bark
Friendly and a good friend
My dog Lucky

Devin Trigueros, Grade 3
Public School 131, NY

Undertaker WWE

Nearly seven feet tall
300 pounds
long black hair
green eyes
wears gloves
on his fist
dressed in black
super star of WWE
3 title belts
choke slam
tombstone pike driver
old school
side walk slam
my favorite wrestler
Undertaker
  Ricky Mariani, Grade 2
   Tashua School, CT

The Ocean

Blue and clear
Big and bold

I stomp down on the ground
As I crush little bits of sand

I sneak up on the people
As they play and relax in me

I get angry during a storm
Crashing my body
Until the storm is over

For I am
The ocean
  Connor Elliott, Grade 3
Indian Lane Elementary School, PA

Horses

Horses run so fast
They are as fast as the wind
Horses make me smile
  Fabia Mahmud, Grade 2
   Public School 69, NY

Hamsters at Night

waking up
running
in the wheel
climbing up
to their food.

storing food
in their cheeks
getting ready
for day.

getting cozy
in a place
where they
won't be
found.
  Hunter Maddock, Grade 2
Fountaindale Elementary School, MD

Easter

E gg coloring
A pril
S pring
T reats
E aster hunt
R ainbow
  Vanessa Taveras, Grade 1
   St Agatha School, NY

Rain Falling

Shiny crystals fill the air.
It fills my heart with warmth.

Flowers blooming all around me.
Dew drops on leaves and grass.

Black clouds fill the air.
I love the way it soaks me.

It's wet and slippery.
That's the way I love rain.
  Sadie Vaughn, Grade 2
   The Tobin School, MA

My Friend Sophia!

The friend I am talking about
Knows she can trust me,
The friend I am talking about
Cares a lot about me,
The friend I am talking about
Helps me when I need help,
The friend I am talking about
Supports me,
The friend I am talking about
Sticks up for me,
The friend I am talking about
Doesn't interrupt me,
The friend I am talking about
Never tries to change me for who I am,
The friend I am talking about
Does those things to make me feel like I am
A true friend to her,
I will remember
My best friend Sophia.

Kyra Mattera, Grade 3
Sarah Dyer Barnes School, RI

Aqua

Aqua is for aqua eyes
that seek adventure.
Aqua is for the turquoise gem.
Aqua is for the northern lights
that dance across the winter nights.
Aqua is for the robin's eggs
that rest in a cozy nest.
Aqua's for the aqua night
that during the day is hid from sight.
Aqua is for silky roses
in a wedding bride's bouquet.
Aqua is for an aqua sky
that rests out in our atmosphere.
Aqua's for an aqua wish
that lies upon a wishing star.
Aqua's for the world's great oceans
Aqua is for aqua objects shining in the sun.

Katie Shull, Grade 3
West Branch School, PA

Snow Day

Today is a snow day.
Snow is the hero of today.
Make way snow!
I'm playing in you
Until my mother shouts
"Karie Mashoo!"
I sit next to the fireplace with my shih tzu
With the snow still
Falling, falling.
My nose is as red as fireworks.
That doesn't stop me
From drinking hot chocolate.

Emily Evangelakos, Grade 3
John Ward Elementary School, MA

The Caterpillar

Nibble, Nibble! from a caterpillar's teeth
Slurping, slurping from a peaceful
flower's leaf
Flitter flatter I'm free I'm free
Shutter shutter finally I can forget
living in a tree
Flap flap I can fly
And see the little cars zooming and
passing by
After a cloudy day the sky is filled with
the glorious sun
A new day has begun

Mia Crankshaw, Grade 2
Mayfield Elementary School, NY

Seasons

Seasons are great!
I love the seasons,
I bet you do too!

I watch the sun go down
Through all the seasons

I love winter the best
Snow glittering in the sun

Genevieve Rioux, Grade 1
Dartmouth Early Learning Center, MA

Nice

Nice is brown.
It tastes like Mom's chocolate cake.
It smells like a rose.
It's fluffy like my feather pillow.
It sounds like a music box.
Nice is a purple sunset sky.

Hunter Lee, Grade 3
Asa C Adams School, ME

Anger

Anger is black.
It tastes like a sour drink.
It smells like rotting food.
It feels all bumpy and gross.
It sounds like a horrible song.
Anger is raggedy clothes.

Braeden Selby, Grade 3
Asa C Adams School, ME

Peaceful

Peaceful is light pink.
It tastes like pink lemonade.
It smells like a rose.
It feels like a baby's soft skin.
It sounds like the humming of the wind.
Peaceful is a soft cloud.

Caitlin Tyrrell, Grade 3
Asa C Adams School, ME

Cookie

Sweet,
Crunchy,
Tasty,
Cookie.

Sean McCormick, Grade 2
Helen B Duffield Elementary School, NY

Fall

Fall is very cool.
Apple trees bloom in autumn.
I like fall a lot.

Michael Gilbert, Grade 2
The Fourth Presbyterian School, MD

Snowflakes

Snowflake, snowflake
Where are you now?
Maybe you are on a boat bow?
Snowflake, snowflake
Follow me please.
Some of the snowflakes are coming to tease.
Snowflake, snowflake
I really like you.
Snowflake, snowflake
Snowballs are coming, too.
Snowflake, snowflake
Let's go hide.
Follow me now,
Come on inside!

Katerina Poulopoulos, Grade 3
Delphi Academy, MA

The Great Big School

Once there was a great big school with a great big teacher and a great big class.
The great big class had their great big notebooks that are based on science and
    based on math.
The great big teacher's name was Mrs. Smith and the great big class had sixteen kids.
Oh, I forgot, the great big white board and the great big desk with the popsicle sticks.
Next there was a great big sink with the water fountain and the soap that was pink.
Next there was the great big posters on the great big desk with the lava lamp!
I'm at the great big trash can next to the recycling bin and the water fountain.
Next there was the weather chart with the big sharp teeth and the fish beneath.
Next there is the great big lights with the ABCs and the banner rights.
And that is all we have today see you again another day.
See you again, it's time to go. Let's go and run out into the snow.

Alina Chmura and Camille Sweet, Grade 2
Thatcher Brook Primary School, VT

Shorkie

Shorkie
yorkie, shih tzu
playing, sleeping, eating
a little dog that is funny
small dog

Erika Switzer, Grade 3
Clinton Street Elementary School, NY

My Friend

My friend is nice
Very nice
She helps me up
When I fall down
I help her up when she
Falls down
When I have no one
To play with
She plays with me
When she has no one to play with
I play with her
We are best friends.

Melissa Fernandes, Grade 2
Tashua School, CT

My Cousin's Birthday

It's my cousin's birthday
The building he's in is a large mountain
The car stops
In the building we go
1 by 1 the guests came
And played a fun game
We danced to a song
Noises everywhere ahh!
The cake was as big as a mini fan
2 cakes not 1
He finally turned 5
It's my cousin's birthday

Mantjita Camara, Grade 3
Public School 114 Ryder Elementary, NY

I Am a River

I am a river
I go through miles
Through canyons,
Mountains and grassy fields
The sun reflects off of me
People swim in me
People drink from me
I am a river and
That's what I'll always be.

Ryan Nason, Grade 3
Meeting House Hill School, CT

Colored Eggs

C andy baskets
O utside having fun
L aughter
O utside in the sun
R abbits, rabbits everywhere
E aster is fun
D igging in the garden

E veryone eating candy
G reen grass
G reetings
S unny days

Haley DellaTorre, Grade 3
St Agatha School, NY

Crystal Rock

Oh glittery rock,
You look like painted mountains,
Purple
Above the sparkly, frozen pond,
Icicles
Grow,
Grow,
Growing,
Gleaming shades of purple,
Your spikes
Brighten the dark sky,
Where did you come from?

Katie Jepsen, Grade 2
John L Edwards School, NY

Seasons

Summer, spring, fall, winter!
I love all the seasons,
As they go by, one by one.
Summer is when we go swimming.
Spring is when the flowers bloom.
Fall is when we go camping.
Winter we get to play in the snow.
I love all the seasons,
As they go by — one by one.

Alaina Tautkus, Grade 1
Crystal Lake Elementary School, CT

The Funny Bunny

Oh, I had a little bunny.
I got it from the pet store.
It looked a little funny.
My mom said "Let's call him, Roar."

Olivia L. Chen, Grade 2
Public School 205 Alexander Graham Bell, NY

Summer Is Fun at the Beach

Summer slides in with June
People go to the beach
go play at the beach
to make sand castles.

Abraham Phillips, Grade 2
Public School 40 Samuel Huntington, NY

Homework

We have homework every night
My teacher says it will make us very bright.
I'm sure my teacher is right,
But all this homework is a fright!

Zaeem Chaudhry, Grade 2
Public School 1 The Bergen School, NY

Rain Sparkles

Each raindrop is special to me.
I dream of crystals falling down on the grass like dew drops.
I love rain because it saves lots and lots of nature and animals.
Rain is made from lakes, oceans and seas.

Amy Palmer, Grade 2
The Tobin School, MA

Summer

Summer drops in with
Pools, towels, and the hot sun
It is summer,
Before summer is spring

Kevin Nelson, Grade 2
Public School 40 Samuel Huntington, NY

I See

I see a car
I see a train
I see some clouds
I see the rain
I see the bus
I see the stores
I see the roof
I see the floors
    Samuel Flores, Grade 2
Public School 1 The Bergen School, NY

It's Getting Cold

Summer is over
It's getting cold
It's only fall,
But behold!
The winter will be
Here with falling snow
The winds will blow
And lots of snowmen will glow.
   Christian Gutierrez, Grade 2
Public School 1 The Bergen School, NY

Legos and Chocolate

My name is Robbie.
Playing with Legos is my hobby.
I like to draw and read.
Oh, I wish I had a hamster to feed.
Brown is the color of my hair and eyes,
but the color blue wins the prize.
Mac and cheese is good to eat,
but chocolate is my favorite treat.
    Robert Owens, Grade 1
    St Joan of Arc School, PA

Geckos

Geckos
small animals
running all over trees
I love seeing awesome geckos
Lizards
    Matthew Pitiss, Grade 3
Clinton Street Elementary School, NY

Egg Hunt

E aster is a wonderful time
G reen colored eggs
G rass grows into bushes

H appiness comes to the world
U celebrate Easter with family
N ew life comes to plants
T reats in baskets filled to the top
    Karina Guerrero, Grade 2
    St Agatha School, NY

What I Like

My eyes are blue and I am tall.
My favorite sports are soccer and baseball.
My dog and I like to run.
We think it is very fun.
My favorite snack is salsa and chips.
It tastes so good and fun to dip.
After my snack it is Legos!
I build and build until my shelf is filled.
    John Hanosek, Grade 1
    St Joan of Arc School, PA

Mom

mom cleans
mom works
we are
best
friends
she is like a flower blooming
she is like the sun shining
my mom
    Emma Lilley, Grade 2
    Tashua School, CT

Puppy

puppy
cute and fluffy
running out of control
getting scared when sees a kitty
morkie
    Hope Wojtkowiak, Grade 3
Clinton Street Elementary School, NY

Outside in the Snow

The pine trees are cracking because the
wind is blowing them back and forth.
You can smell the gas of the
snowmobiles as they drive by. The sun
isn't so bright because it is blocked by
the needles on the tree. Kids are sledding
down the mountain fighting the crisp air.
Everyone is bundled up to keep warm.

Alex Martin, Grade 3
Craneville School, MA

Winter Time

Chestnuts roasting by the fire,
and churches singing choir.
It is very cold,
and the age old stories being told.
The tinsel on the tree,
that was hung by me.
It is that special season,
and that is the reason to be good.

Gilen Prett, Grade 3
Craneville School, MA

The Wild Horse

Shiny colors in the sky,
Marvelous flowers on the ground,
Three beautiful butterflies
Floating near
A glowing, pony with his sparkly tail
Touching dazzling rocks,
The beautiful voice of a bird
Is heard in the distance

Amber Smith, Grade 2
John L Edwards School, NY

My Daddy

My daddy's gone
he won't come home

the bad weather
is making him stay

he might come home on Sunday
but I don't think he's coming

Logan Nunes, Grade 2
Fountaindale Elementary School, MD

Crazy Cat

The cat is crazy
Just a bit,
Black as the night,
Playing with a squiggly toy
Knocking things over,
Yelling,
Mom says
Stop!

Jazminia Cintron, Grade 2
John L Edwards School, NY

Fun with Friends

Oh, friends are fun
To play with in the sun.
I like to play with Christina;
We go to the hockey arena.
I live in her neighborhood.
We want to go to Hollywood.
I am a rocker!
She likes to play soccer.

Rebecca Perry, Grade 3
John T Waugh Elementary School, NY

The Nightmare

There was a tall man named Ned
That rode down a hill in his bed
He screamed with his might
With a terrible fright
But he was really just dreaming in bed

Joseph Willson, Grade 3
Craneville School, MA

Puppy

Brownie
Chewy and moist
Tastes like Heaven
So good, delicious and sweet
Amazing

Samantha Kiszewski, Grade 3
Clinton Street Elementary School, NY

Penguin

Penguin, I love how you waddle around.
When you walk on the ice,
Don't slip and drown!
Please, make sure the ice
Is thick and strong,
So you can walk on it
All day long.
Hold your egg to keep it warm
Before the terrible winter storm!
Branden Hutchinson, Grade 3
John T Waugh Elementary School, NY

Coconut

Oh coconut,
You look like tree bark
Glistening in the moonlight,
Shaped like a football
Fallen from a palm tree,
Written messages
From daughter to mother,
Colorful, painted pictures,
Who drew on you?
Taylor Wallace, Grade 2
John L Edwards School, NY

Art

Splitter splatter
Paint is the batter
Make a creation in a freeing situation

Orange, red, yellow, and blue
You can choose any hue
Mix and match
Make a new batch
Artistry is a happy catch
Gracie McBride, Grade 2
Memorial School, NH

Emmie

So fluffy and warm
So soft and cute
So cozy

She has the world's
Wettest nose my dog
Emmie.

I can't stop hugging her.
Lucille Covington, Grade 2
Fountaindale Elementary School, MD

Pit Bull

Pit Bull
Playful, trouble
Nasty, strongest jaw, good
Full of energy, happy now
Riley
Paige Szekely, Grade 3
Clinton Street Elementary School, NY

Ashly

Ashly
My greatest friend.
Helps me read, write and draw.
She called me over the summer
Awesome.
Paige Brzezinski, Grade 3
Clinton Street Elementary School, NY

Poor Children

I feel so bad for the children who are poor
They don't have toys for sure.
I would give them all they need
Clothes and toys and puppies to feed.
I would give them lots of food
And an apartment to live in for good.
Ivan Santos, Grade 3
Public School 1 The Bergen School, NY

My Imaginary Tree

I love my imaginary apple tree.
It is awesome.
I like to sit under the tree
Eating apples in the shade
I wish this tree was real.
I just love apples!
Tyler Chilton, Grade 3
Ridgeway Elementary School, MD

Crystal Ball

sitting bored
a little boy
not knowing what to write
finally he picks up his magic pen
ready to look in the shiny crystal ball
for shiny future poems

Yuuki Endo, Grade 3
Thoreau Elementary School, MA

Spring

S pring
P laying on swings
R unning till you can't stop
I t's the beautiful flowers
N o more snow
G et exercise by swimming!

Kate La Plume, Grade 3
The Edgartown School, MA

Spring Is Here

S tart of lacrosse
P lay outside late
R ide my bike
I ce cream at the Dairy Queen
N ights grow later
G reen grass

Brendan Morris, Grade 3
The Edgartown School, MA

I Am a Wolf

I am a wolf.
I howl at night.
I live on the mountain,
And give people a fright.

Emily Barata, Grade 3
Meeting House Hill School, CT

Waiting

Wind waited until the coast was clear
so it could rush
to the sea

Logan Schulman, Grade 3
Thoreau Elementary School, MA

When I Read a Book

When I read a book
The things that make me happy
Are that I learn new words
The words are very interesting
And it's fun

It's very exciting to know what happens
And sometimes scary

There are some books I really like
And sometimes I don't like some books
But they're still fun and interesting

Lilliana Tarillo, Grade 1
La Scuola D'Italia G. Marconi, NY

Colored Eggs

C hocolate is nice
O utdoors can be breezy
L iving in peace
O utside is a good place to be
R abbits hop around
E aster is a happy time
D ressing up for Easter

E ggs are painted
G reen is a good color
G rass is the color green
S pring is a time of new life

Isabella Balgobin, Grade 2
St Agatha School, NY

Watermelon

Water,
Flavored ice,
Sour,
Sweet,
Red,
Green,
Drippy,
Crunchy,
Watermelon.

Kaitlyn Fazio, Grade 2
Helen B Duffield Elementary School, NY

The Promenade
The wind is blowing against the ground
Peace fills the air like it
My sun blends in with clouds
Smells of food come from all around
As I cross the Queensboro Bridge
The dogs running free as they please
Brearley stands tall and watches them play
The dog park that stands near
A helicopter flying in the sky stops to say hi
Then flies away into the sky
I hear the workers doing their job
Having fun that's all that matters
The sun shines bright and the cold sacred night
Night and day I stand in the air
as a single feather simply passes by
I hear the cars on the FDR
The wind is still blowing
We're still sharing peace
That's all that matters

Ella Cohen, Grade 2
Brearley School, NY

Springtime
The wind blows gently in my face and makes a smile appear;
I see the water run down the stream gently inviting me to come in.
When the flowers bloom they ring my heart with joy.
And when I see the new bulbs grow I jump with happiness.
I love spring time.

I sleep in grass and when I look up in the sky the moon and sun seem to smile
down on my face. Soon I can see rays of light through my hands when I put them
    up in the air.
The butterflies swarm around me as I play.
When I laugh the world turns brighter and shines in my face.
I see the world turn green and bright and know right away the winter is over.
I love spring time.

As we dance in the sun light we bathe in it too.
The world is growing and recovering again from the winter.
I climb the trees and pick the fruits that hang outside my window.
I love spring time.

Lauren Kaveri May, Grade 3
Chestnutwold Elementary School, PA

My Dad

He sings me
that song and
it makes me
so
so
peaceful.

He reads me that story
and I
dream
about it.

He gives me
that good night kiss
and I dream about him
singing that song
reading that book
and giving me
that good
night
kiss

Alexandra C. Gregory, Grade 2
Fountaindale Elementary School, MD

Hours at Church

Bored, I'm bored
nothing to do
bored, I'm bored
nothing to say
you can only say
I have to go to
the bathroom
to get out of it
so bored
I'd rather be at home
Noise, the preacher talking
on and on

I'd rather
be at home
It's quiet,
quiet at home
it feels like 5000 hours
It's church, it's church
Say your prayer to God
God get me out of here!

Kortny Coleman, Grade 2
Tashua School, CT

Friends Forever

They like to joke with me.
I laugh at their humor.

They like to live in the moment.
I do, too.

They get confused over little things.
I laugh at their expression.

They're there when it counts.
I applaud them for their support.

But who are they?
My best friends.

Friends forever.

Kaiyes Bhuiyan, Grade 3
Public School 3 Bedford Village, NY

Kira Moved Away

Kira moved
away.
I miss her!

Kira was very, very
nice.
I miss her!

Kira was my best friend
In the whole
world.
I miss her!

I love Kira so, so much!
I miss her
a lot!!!

Julia Wilkinson, Grade 2
Pine Tree Elementary School, NY

Darkness

I've seen something so horrible.
I've seen something so terrible.
Like your bad thoughts and nightmares
Are gazing at you.
Those horrible thoughts just
Gazing at you.

I've seen something so sinister.
I've seen something so evil.
Like a snake's about to bite you.
You feel very sad.
The sinister snake is about
To bite you.

The Darkness has reached us!
There's nothing to do, but sit and
Let the evil go by us.
The crows flap around staying
Camouflaged in the Darkness.
The Darknesssssssss.

Janey Moody, Grade 3
African Road Elementary School, NY

Lightning

Fierce and powerful
Gigantic and destructive

On cloudy days
I come down to grab the ground
With my large hands

I dance when I hear
The raindrops
Falling to the ground

I jump to the surface of the Earth
Startling people
Destroying anything in my path

For I am
Lightning

Lindsay Cave, Grade 3
Indian Lane Elementary School, PA

Mommy

Mommy,
As kind as a
Flower that bloomed
Always cooks
Delicious food.

Wakes me
At 7:00 am
For school.
Let's me
Go outside
When I'm done
With my homework.

She loves me
Like I'm her
Little doll.

She will always
Love me.

Despina Tsiamtsiouris, Grade 2
Buckley Country Day School, NY

Going on a Trip

Mom is packing.
Pack, pack, pack.
Dad is showering.
Shhh, shhh, shhh.
Before we go on our trip.

Johnny and me
are sleeping.
Hmmmmmm.
Johnny wakes up before me.
Before we go on our trip.

We get in the car
And buckle up.
Click!
We also take a nap.
Before we go on our trip.

Isabella Otero, Grade 2
Pine Tree Elementary School, NY

My Sneakers
Purple and white
big as a delight
black cool laces
that sparkle
like a star
and designs
on it, it has
flowers on it
like a rainbow
Sasha Datilus, Grade 3
Public School 114 Ryder Elementary, NY

Penguins
Penguins are cute it looks
like they are wearing a
black and white suit,
and they have black and white
hair upon their head that is so cute.
44 penguins in a line,
They can be so fine.
In their tuxedo suits
they are so darn cute
Victoria Forbes, Grade 3
St Maria Goretti School, PA

June
June
Humid, shady
Playing, celebrating, blooming
Go to the beach.
Sun
Anna Looney, Grade 2
The Fourth Presbyterian School, MD

My Friends
My friends and I are like
fireflies,
Lighting up the night sky.
Having fun, and exploring the night.
Having a blast and checking out
everything in sight.
Gabriella Caicedo, Grade 3
Meadow Drive School, NY

Skiing
Getting up
getting up
and
down
we go
racing
down
and
away we go!
Jaime Tolk, Grade 2
Tashua School, CT

Leopard
leopard
tiger
fight
leopard win
leopard eat
eat
eat
eat
leopard has a cub
Alexander Torricos, Grade 2
Tashua School, CT

My Mom
The nicest
Helps me
Snuggles me
Caring, sweet and kind
My mom.
Hannah Chaney, Grade 2
Fountaindale Elementary School, MD

Sad
Sad is dark gray.
It tastes like hot Dr. Pepper.
It smells like fish.
It feels like swimming in a cold sea.
It sounds like thunder.
Sad is a dark and dreary sky.
Nicholas Fox, Grade 3
Asa C Adams School, ME

Flowers

Flowers are pretty —
and, oh so nice.
They are amazing —
and, oh so colorful.
They are red, white, and blue —
and, ohhh sooo cool!

Makena Evans, Grade 1
Milton Terrace South Elementary School, NY

Peaceful

Peaceful is the color of the deep blue sea.
It tastes like salty ocean water.
It smells like ocean air.
It feels like the soft touch of a dolphin.
It's quiet like a beach in the early morning.
Peaceful is the beautiful, beautiful blue sea.

Brooklyne White, Grade 3
Asa C Adams School, ME

A Real Friend

A real friend helps you when you're stuck
A real friend cheers you up when you're down
A real friend doesn't tell other people your secrets!
A real friend never lies to you
Last but not least, a real friend plays with you.
A real friend

Kenny Hawkins, Grade 3
Sarah Dyer Barnes School, RI

Downy the Cat

Downy the cat is getting fat
He loves to play all day
He has short claws he also does
not break any laws.

Alexis Melendez, Grade 2
Public School 205 Alexander Graham Bell, NY

Stars

Stars are really bright.
Stars are located in space.
I like stars a lot.

Adrian Claburn, Grade 2
Fonda-Fultonville Elementary School, NY

Spring

Spring
Flowers, Trees
Playing, Giggling, Laughing
Flowers are Blooming
Springtime
Jennifer Capria, Grade 3
Our Lady of Hope School, NY

Flower Petals

Flower petals are in my pool
That shows me it's springtime
It makes me want to burst in happiness
Spring break is here
That means no school
Daniel Lake, Grade 3
Our Lady of Hope School, NY

Springtime

Springtime
Pretty, green leaves
Blooming, planting, smelling
We will garden in our backyard.
Flowers
Chidi Iwudyke, Grade 3
St Clement Mary Hofbauer School, MD

Easter

Bunnies
Furry, fluffy
Hopping, hiding, finding
All are jolly on Easter day
Candy
Abigail Heagy, Grade 3
St Clement Mary Hofbauer School, MD

Swimming

Swimming
Wet water fun
Diving, kicking, jumping
Fun in gallons of blue water
Big pools
Jillian Toomey, Grade 3
St Clement Mary Hofbauer School, MD

Ice Skating

Gliding across the ice
Is really, really nice.
Spin, glide, jump, slip, and fall.
Those are most of the skating moves,
Or maybe all.
Cassandra Kouletsis, Grade 3
Heron Pond Elementary School, NH

Earth

Earth moving around
A bird sitting in a tree
Running around
Taking care of Earth
Having a clean Earth
John Johnson, Grade 3
Shady Grove Elementary School, PA

Save the Earth

E arth is cool, save it!
A nyone, everyone, save the earth!
R ight away, save the earth!
T he earth goddess is Gaea.
H elp save the earth!
Jagger Doll, Grade 3
Shady Grove Elementary School, PA

Dog and Cat

There once was a dog and a cat,
Who got upset because of a hat.
Then one day,
The dog did say,
"Let us share!" and that was that.
Hannah Cawley, Grade 1
Mater Christi School, VT

Myself

I like to snowmobile
And to cross-country ski
And to swim
And to go to school
And to bike
Liam Guyette, Grade 1
Thatcher Brook Primary School, VT

If I Could Go into the Future

If I could go into the future,
I would see myself as a hockey player for the Pittsburgh Penguins.
I would be the captain.
We would have just won our 29th Stanley Cup.
We would beat the Detroit Red Wings.
The year after, we would win again.
We would go into the 2037 season World Record Book.
I would be the oldest man to win 30 Stanley Cups.

Brendan Erka, Grade 2
Wyland Elementary School, PA

Spring

Spring warm and bright
playing tag is fun in spring
Riding our bikes
you feel the beautiful wind
on your face
It's fun playing
with water in spring
Never cold in spring.

Brandon Atehortua, Grade 2
Public School 232 The Walter Ward School, NY

Christmas

Hot chocolate, marshmallows
Candy canes, chocolate cookies
Yum, I love this thing
I love my Christmas
I love to see Santa
I love this day off
I am going to cry
Cheer me up — Merry Christmas!

Arlene Capellan, Grade 3
Public School 115 Alexander Humboldt, NY

Buddy

Big black and brown
gets into stuff
lots of energy
likes to lick
I love Buddy!

Victoria St. John, Kindergarten
Mary Burgess Neal Elementary School, MD

Flowers
Flowers
Little, colorful
Seeing, touching, opening
Blooming of beautiful daisies.
Daffodils
Halle Saf, Grade 3
Chestnut Street Elementary School, PA

Lion
Lion
Fierce and scary
Very fast runner, jumper
I hope someday I will see one
So cool
Baylee DiCioccio, Grade 3
Clinton Street Elementary School, NY

Root Beer
Root beer
Fizzy, sweet
It tastes good.
It is very yummy.
Birch beer
Cleo Tuckey, Grade 3
Evergreen Elementary School, PA

Snow
I gently settle down on
the branches like a falling leaf.
I gently get covered
by more and more of me.
I gently settle down.
Jack Sullivan, Grade 3
Colebrook Primary School, NY

Spring
Spring
Warm, short
Swinging, sliding, fishing
In spring I swing.
Season
Isaac Gullifer, Grade 3
Chestnut Street Elementary School, PA

Cupcakes
Cupcake
sweet and tasty
delicious and tasty
pink and sweet and awesome
dessert
Mercedes Smith, Grade 3
Clinton Street Elementary School, NY

Spring
Spring
Warm, grassy
Running, jumping, playing
Buds sprout on trees.
Season.
Nikolas Bernhard, Grade 3
Chestnut Street Elementary School, PA

Snowflakes
The little boy across the street
Caught snowflakes on his tongue
On a cold winter day
On his driveway.
He wanted to catch snow.
Emma Groomes, Grade 3
Evergreen Elementary School, PA

What Is Orange?
Orange is the sun.
Orange is an orange too.
Orange is the meaning for happy.
Orange is the mother of yellow.
Orange is the smell of orange juice.
Amanda Northup, Grade 3
Colebrook Primary School, NY

Winter
Winter
Freezing outside
Snowmen, snowball fights
Fun sledding down hills
Frosty
Ciara Farley, Grade 1
All Saints Catholic Academy, NY

Death

Rain is coming soon,
Love is unwanted by now,
Mercy to the unloved,
Rain falls on them unpitiful.
Breaks of silence,
Nothing can tie up what has been done, and it is done.
Hatred opens it's mouth and swallows the Earth, the Universe, the Hope.
Love...
Is dead.

Clio Callimanopulos, Grade 3
Public School 6 Lillie Deveraux Blake, NY

Summer

Ice cream trucks are out
the park kids are riding bikes
kids are running around
the warm air surrounds them.
The leaves are growing on trees
the warm and hot air feels great
the schools are closing
the children are happy
the schools are closed until September!

Elijah Kabba, Grade 2
Public School 232 The Walter Ward School, NY

Branches

Branches swoosh, swoosh,
The branches reach for the sky
Like hands reaching for the ceiling
Bare from mean old Mr. Winter.
The wind sings a jazzy tune to the branches
That makes them dance.

Joshua Loomis, Grade 2
Carlyle C Ring Elementary School, NY

Fall

Crickle, Crackle
Drip, Drop, BOO!
Crunch, Crunch —
Whoooooooosh goes the wind...
I love Fall!

Ali Tetreault, Grade 1
Milton Terrace South Elementary School, NY

Soccer

S coring a goal
O utstanding saves
C ool goal
C ounting the goals
E ither you pass it or shoot
R unning around
John Habekost, Grade 3
The Edgartown School, MA

Spring Is Here!

Spring is here!
Yes it's here.
I love spring
Yes I do.
Do you love spring
I bet you do!
Kazara Aldeborgh, Grade 3
The Edgartown School, MA

Spring

Spring is almost here,
I can't wait to cheer!
Now we can play outside every day,
Even play outside with clay.
Slide on a slide, swing on a swing…
Oh how I love spring!
Taylor Magee, Grade 2
Carlyle C Ring Elementary School, NY

Spring

I love to dance in spring
With a pretty velvet string.
Look at that pretty sunshine
Springtime is always so fine.
Julia Guarniere, Grade 3
Heron Pond Elementary School, NH

Spring

Birds fly north for warmth;
singing to wake us all up.
Sun melting the snow.
Sabastian Beach, Grade 2
Wells Central School, NY

Peanut Butter

When you open a jar of peanut butter
the smell hits you like a flutter or like
a bunch of butterflies tickling your face.
And when you take your first bite it's like
swimming in an ocean of yumminess.
That is the magic of peanut butter.
Owen Hodkinson, Grade 2
Caryl E Adams Primary School, NY

Chinese Lantern

A little Chinese lantern
So sweet
As light as a leaf
As fragile as a baby
As small as a mouse
So beautiful and little.
Joyce Li, Grade 1
The Delphi Academy, MA

Friendship

Friendship is a light pink
Friendship tastes like salmon
Friendship smells like tulips
Friendship looks like dancing
Friendship sounds like laughter
Friendship feels like a hug
Tyna Wasserman, Grade 2
Klein Elementary School, PA

Ice Cream

It melts in your mouth
It is cold
You can choose any flavor
I like chocolate best
Tyler East, Grade 2
Klein Elementary School, PA

Seven

I will be seven. I will
have fun and the party
will be like heaven!
Adela Gutierrez, Grade 1
Park Avenue School, NY

Horses

H orses are pets
O utstanding horses!
R unning in a field
S uper horses!
E at hay and grass
S tupendous horses!

Ashlee Toth, Grade 2
Central Elementary School, PA

Spring

S unny
P retty plants
R ainbows
I ndigo flowers
N ice weather
G rowing gardens

Krisalyn Rhodes, Grade 3
Chestnut Street Elementary School, PA

Hockey

Hockey is puzzling
It tastes like snacks
It sounds like everybody charging
It smells like winning
It looks like scoring
It makes me feel good.

Argen Gian I. Detoito, Grade 3
Evergreen Elementary School, PA

Water slides

Water slides
Yippee!
Yippee!
Yippidy slippidy watery
Whoosh! Shark chomp!
Chomp!

Ryan Lamy, Grade 2
Tashua School, CT

Spring

S unny
P lants
R aining
I nsects coming out
N ew grass
G ardening starts

Zachary Zilkofski, Grade 3
Chestnut Street Elementary School, PA

Spring

S ometimes sunny
P erfect weather
R ainy
I see flowers
N ice outside
G ardening

Caitlyn Zampogna, Grade 3
Chestnut Street Elementary School, PA

The River

See the water drip
Slowly Softly
Swish, swash, swish
Beautiful Flowers

Kenny Gonzalez, Grade 3
Colebrook Primary School, NY

Crabs

Claws, red
Scared, running, stomping
Lots of people run
Creature

Alex Rafferty, Grade 2
Long Meadow Elementary School, CT

The Easter Hunt

An Easter bunny
Make an Easter bunny cake
A big Easter egg!

Natalya Hernandez, Grade 1
St Louis Elementary School, MA

Easter Eggs

You can cook an egg
The Easter bunny is cool
Easter eggs are fun!

Declan Sullivan, Grade 1
St Louis Elementary School, MA

Snow

Snow is white
Like whipped cream
Snow is soft
Like a kitten
Snow is cold
Like an ice cube
Snow gently
Falls from the
Soft clouds.
Dashone Eures, Grade 2
Avery School, MA

Auntie's New House

Auntie's house
All you
Can hear is
Ruff, ruff
Ruff, ruff
One small one
One big one
Barking
At people.
Liliana Miller, Grade 2
Avery School, MA

Doris

Doris
mean, cute, colorful
attacked, vicious, nip, nap
afraid of feet walking by her.
A cat
Summer Grandinetti, Grade 3
Clinton Street Elementary School, NY

Excitement

Excitement is sunset orange.
It tastes like a sugar cube.
It smells like pecan pie.
It feels like a rabbit's soft fur.
It sounds like a cannon.
Excitement is a bright sunny day.
Corbin Figueroa, Grade 3
Asa C Adams School, ME

What Is Violet

Violet is the color leaning down on me
Violet is the beautiful color
Violet can be

Violet is the color of a pretty bush
It is the color of the sunset
That sometimes goes whoosh!

You've got what it takes
To make violet for me
And I love violet and it loves me!
Julia Reel, Grade 3
Jeffrey Elementary School, CT

A True Friend

A true friend helps you
when you are sick.
A true friend plays with you
when you are alone.
A true friend shares toys and
games with you.
A true friend tells the truth
and does not lie to you.
A true friend does not say
bad words to you.
That's who a true friend really is.
John Benum Jr., Grade 3
Sarah Dyer Barnes School, RI

Juicy Apples

Apples are sweet,
Juicy too.
Brown, hard seeds
Buried like treasure hidden in an apple.
Sharing slices with my friends.
They share a slice with me.
Shiny, red,
Crunching, munching, lunching.
Apples are sweet,
Juicy too...
I'll share a slice with you.
Jessica Vullo, Grade 2
Carlyle C Ring Elementary School, NY

Soccer
Soccer
Grassy green field
Kicking, running, playing
Awesome practice, people cheering
Fun sport
Joseph Kulikowski, Grade 3
St Clement Mary Hofbauer School, MD

Birthdays
Birthdays
Presents, cupcakes
Blowing, eating, opening
Have fun at a birthday party
Balloons
William Hanna-Leverett, Grade 3
St Clement Mary Hofbauer School, MD

Nature
Nature
Grass, mountains, plants
Planting, growing, playing
Quite lovely, breezy winds, rainbows
Awesome
Alexis Prestileo, Grade 3
St Clement Mary Hofbauer School, MD

Beaches
Beaches
Sandy, wet, fun
Swimming, splashing, playing
Fun finding sea life and diving
Oceans
Preslie Coffman, Grade 3
St Clement Mary Hofbauer School, MD

Baseball
Baseball
Fun, fast, cool sport
Running, diving, cheering
Hit the ball, touch base, get dirty
Awesome
Justin Phan, Grade 3
St Clement Mary Hofbauer School, MD

Cumba
Cumba
Really fun dog
Playing, jumping, fetching
A very good and playful pet
Good dog
Dylan Ihle, Grade 3
St Clement Mary Hofbauer School, MD

Easter
Easter
Pretty, holy
Painting, hopping, praying
Eggs are painted, baskets are filled
Bunnies
Lorelle Tribble, Grade 3
St Clement Mary Hofbauer School, MD

Beaches
Beaches
Fun in summer
Laughing, swimming, surfing
Having fun playing in water
Sun fun
Savannah Hunter, Grade 3
St Clement Mary Hofbauer School, MD

Lacrosse
Lacrosse
Big net, one ref
Attacking, whacking, scoring
A good game for children to play
Fun sport
Shane Stone, Grade 3
St Clement Mary Hofbauer School, MD

Hippos
Hippos
Gray, big, round, loud
Eating, splashing, roaring
I like and find different ones
Scary
Bailey Mullen, Grade 3
St Clement Mary Hofbauer School, MD

Shorts

Teens, kids, adults too,
Wearing shorts is fun to do.
Shorts are here, shorts are there,
I see shorts everywhere.
On streets, beaches, buses and more,
A laundry pile on the floor.
If I could only have my way,
I'd ride my bike wearing shorts every day.
Nick Huffman, Grade 2
Carlyle C Ring Elementary School, NY

Flowers

Spring flowers are here.
They bring cheer.
Pink, blue and many more colors,
We can give sweet flowers to others.
Sun and water make them grow.
Look at them in a row.
Pretty petals, green leaves,
Blowing in the slow breeze.
Alicia Ramsey, Grade 2
Carlyle C Ring Elementary School, NY

Thunder

Thunder
Thunder
Thunder
Boom!
Run!
Until
It's
Over
Brendan Walsh, Grade 2
Avery School, MA

Hockey

Hockey
an awesome sport
the players try to score
everyone is a good skater
you scored
Zachary Wurl, Grade 3
Clinton Street Elementary School, NY

Sunrise

Darkness clears
a path for morning…
The Sun nearly high,
climbs up into the sky
for it has many moments to kill.
Patient the countryside waits.
Ravenous the dew seeps
into statuary grass…
Crimson the apples now.
The apple trees are seizing me
To taste…
It seems the fields are spellbound.
Warren Kennedy-Nolle, Grade 3
Bedford Village Elementary School, NY

The Backpack

This backpack is gigantic.
It has too many books.
My back is hunched, my legs are weak,
and I'm getting crazy looks.
Dolls stuffed in the pockets,
make-up in a bag,
lip glosses by the dozen,
and a blanket that is now a rag.
I don't know why I've all these things.
I really don't know why.
Oh wait… this is my sister's bag!
I think I'm going to CRY!
Micah Katz, Grade 3
Edgewood Elementary School, PA

Emma Rand

E xcellent soccer player
M arvelous personality
M agnificent artist
A wesome girl

R omantic
A ngel
N ice
D ynamite!
Emma Rand, Grade 3
Milton Fuller Roberts School, MA

Love

L ove is all about kissing.
O ur families love us.
V ote for loving people.
E veryone should have the courage to love.

Nicole Nittardi, Grade 2
Long Meadow Elementary School, CT

4th of July

I see fireworks bursting in the air
I smell the air burning
I feel surprised seeing bursts of color through the dark sky
I see the day getting darker and darker as the day ends

Alessandra Bassani, Grade 3
Meeting House Hill School, CT

Spring

It is Spring.
Children play.
Some kids sing.
Some say hooray!

Daniel Yellinek, Grade 2
Public School 205 Alexander Graham Bell, NY

Summer

Summer is pretty.
The birds sing,
All over the city.
But the bugs sting.

Anusha Panjwani, Grade 2
Public School 205 Alexander Graham Bell, NY

Baseball Player

I imagine that I will be a great baseball player
I will hit every ball so the umpire will call no strikes at all
The fans will cheer until they almost break my ear
If I was pitching the ball the other team will have no chance at all

Joseph Locurto, Grade 3
Shelter Rock Elementary School, NY

Spring Cheetahs

As the sun shines,
a cheetah lays under a tree.

The sun starts to set,
the cheetah runs around.

The moon rises and the cheetah's claws sparkle
like the stars in the moonlight.

The cheetah will start to sleep.

Grant Brooks, Grade 3
Mary C Howse Elementary School, PA

What Is Beautiful to Me

Above, above,
Stars twinkling in the moonlight
Below, below,
Bright, green grass swaying back and forth
In the mountains, the mountains,
Glistening snow on the tippy top
In the ocean, the ocean,
Dolphins doing tricks
Here ends my song,
The beautiful world.

Jasiyah Coleman, Grade 2
John L Edwards School, NY

An Awesome Friend

An awesome friend
A friend would never leave you
A friend will cheer you up when you're gloomy
A friend will accept you for who you are
A friend would respect you
A friend would listen to you even when they don't want to
A friend would tell the truth
A friend will help you fall
Just like my best friend,
Eric

Bobby Civetti, Grade 3
Sarah Dyer Barnes School, RI

Favorite Day

My favorite day
is to
have some fun
in the
shiny sun
Hang with my
friends
and family
Go to bed
Wake up in the
morning
and do
it
all
over
again.
Christopher Battista, Grade 3
Forest Park Elementary School, NY

Cousin

Nice
Cute
Funny
Golden
Tough
Sweet
Devil boy
Smart
Right to wrong
Cutie pie
Loves his friends
We laugh together
He loves cooking ware
Awesome
Scared of dogs
He loves me!
Gianna Russo, Grade 2
Helen B Duffield Elementary School, NY

Anger

Anger is a dark black cat at night
It tastes like raw fish
It smells like onions
It looks like lightning
It sounds like a bad joke
Anger feels like being pricked by thorns
Hunter Martin, Grade 2
Klein Elementary School, PA

A Dog

A dog
Mean, naughty
Brown, black, growling
Sharp claws that scratch my leg
Happy, loving, excited, nice
Angus
Erin Greenan, Grade 3
Clinton Street Elementary School, NY

Ice Pop

Colorful,
Juicy,
Melty,
Smooth,
Crunchy,
Sweet,
Icy,
Drippy,
Cold,
Sticky,
Ice pop.
Reilly Murphy, Grade 2
Helen B Duffield Elementary School, NY

When I Am Hot

When
I
Am
Hot

I feel like
I
Have
Been
Struck by
Lightning!
Liam Gelston, Grade 1
St Rose School, CT

Springtime

Springtime is here
Bringing good cheer
To every young flower
That grows in an hour
Sunshine beating down
It feels like a crown
On my little head
That after the sunset will rest in bed
Flowers growing everywhere
Soon I will put in my hair
Children beaming
And also screaming
With lots and lots of joy!
Abigail Kolyer, Grade 3
Shelter Rock Elementary School, NY

That Annoying Bee

So yellow
and black buzzing
all around the room I
tried to kill it twice, but
It stung me I tried to ignore
It but it just kept buzzing around
so…I thought of a plan I put some
honey on
the window then
the bee came buzzing
to the honey so then I
closed the window and he couldn't
get back in I'm so glad!
Dana Hinds, Grade 3
Public School 114 Ryder Elementary, NY

What to Eat*

I sniff
and sniff
I see
my prey
I run like
the wind
but I don't
catch it.
Then I
sniff
sniff
again.
Katie Morgante, Grade 2
Pine Tree Elementary School, NY
*From the view of a wolf

The Blueberry Bush

The blueberry bush
Has sweet
Juice
Inside.

I eat them
In the
Summer.

They look
Like
Blue
Gumdrops.
Susan Socci, Grade 1
St Rose School, CT

A Feather

Brown
soft
from a bird
flying in the sky
falling
down
to earth
Kyle Occhicone, Grade 2
Tashua School, CT

Angel

Angel, Angel
She is my kitty.
That pretty, pretty kitty
Angel, Angel
Come on let's play.
Angel, Angel
Yea!
Faith Gnias, Grade 3
St Maria Goretti School, PA

Shoes That Are on Sale
I am a shoe.
Clip clop!
People love wearing us!
We are so popular.
We're on sale!
For 25%.
Clip clop!
Us shoes are like dresses!
Heels, sandals, and flats!
Please buy us!
We got your back.
Flip flops!
We're 25%!
Josephine Man, Grade 2
Public School 69, NY

Earth
The Earth is a beautiful place.
It's where I was born for
goodness sakes. On Earth Day, in the
park until dark, we pick up trash
then run around, eat some dinner,
happiness found.

In my tree, in my backyard, I
climb the branches, up to the stars
I spy on the world, just a little
girl. I find stuff I've lost and go
show my mom. I run back outside,
to my special tree and hide.
Fiona Merrill, Grade 3
Our Lady of Mercy Regional School, NY

Spring
Spring, spring

Spring is a season
When the wind blows
Birds sing and the sun shines
And beautiful flowers bloom.

I can pick flowers
Eat ice cream
Listen to birds sing
Even get a tan

I love spring.
Grace Murphy, Grade 3
William Penn Elementary School, PA

Get to Know Me
My name is Katarina,
I'm not a ballerina.
I'm actually a figure skater
and a basketball and soccer player.
I like to play all kinds of sports
and build snow forts.
My mom and I sit on a bench
and speak French.
In French yes is oui
it sounds just like Nintendo Wii
the game we play on our TV.
I really like to write
and at the beach fly my kite.
Katarina Bauer, Grade 1
St Joan of Arc School, PA

My Favorite Seasons
Summer
Hot, dry
Swimming, playing, vacationing
Outside fun, inside warm
Snowing, skiing, freezing
Cold, dark
Winter
Madeleine Sloan, Grade 2
St. Madeleine Sophie School, NY

School
School
Fun, hard
Working, learning, typing
School in the day, play in the afternoon
Running, jump roping, gaming
Baseball, basketball
Play
Carson DeMyer, Grade 2
St. Madeleine Sophie School, NY

Yellow

Yellow is the color of a lemon.
Yellow is the color of the sun.
Yellow is the color of my shirt.
Yellow is the color of a sunflower.
Yellow smells like a lemon pie.
Yellow tastes like fresh corn.
Yellow sounds like birds chirping.
Yellow looks like a star.
Yellow feels like a hot, summer day.
Yellow makes me feel happy.
Yellow is the color of me.

Jessica Cusumano, Grade 3
Evergreen Elementary School, PA

King Cobras

K icking up dust
I ntelligent
N o predators
G ood speed

C ool
O utstanding
B iggest venomous snakes
R ain forest
A re the snakes that build nests
S weet

Hunter Cleary, Grade 3
The Edgartown School, MA

Fast

Zoom — a cheetah past
He is very fast

Whoosh — a horse runs by
He is very shy

Kaboosh — an ostrich is running around
He doesn't make a sound

Squeak — a dolphin jumped up high
He sings a song and says good-bye.

Seoul Moro, Grade 3
Craneville School, MA

The Sun

Red and Orange
Hot and dry

I don't have any friends
I'm too bright of a guy

They say I'm too different
To play in their games
I say that's not fair
As I walk away in shame

I sit here and watch them
All day and all night
And sometimes I think
I want to put up a fight

Nobody's around
And I'm sad about that
No friends to play with
Not even my cat

For I am
The sun

Erick Wade, Grade 3
Indian Lane Elementary School, PA

The Cat and the Mouse

There goes the cat chasing the mouse.
Whoosh! He's as fast as lightning!
To that tiny mouse
He is so very frightening.

Will the cat win?
Will the mouse lose?
Will the mouse win?
Will the cat snooze?

Yes! It has happened!
The mouse has won!
The cat lays down.
The mouse says, "That was fun!"

Jaelyn Roberts, Grade 3
Craneville Elementary School, MA

The Wind
Wish wash wish
The windy windy day
Wish wash wish
My hat my hat
Is blowing away
Wish wash wish
Athena Chalhoub, Grade 2
Public School 69, NY

August
A ugust is full of joy.
U sually it's a hot summer day.
G ardens and gardens full of plants.
U seful blue skies.
S inging chirps from birds.
T emperature is hot.
T. Clayton Schmidter, Grade 2
Long Meadow Elementary School, CT

Basketball
I bounce my ball
again, and
again, and
again
until I get a
score.
Madison Binkley, Grade 2
Avery School, MA

Chocolate Bar
Mushy and fun to eat,
A little chocolate treat;
I love it when marshmallows are inside,
It's mine!
Samantha Paura, Grade 2
Helen B Duffield Elementary School, NY

My Tree
Just in my back yard
A tree grew for many years
In the sunny day
Lisa Tran, Grade 3
Sacred Heart School, MA

Flowers
Roses are red
violets are blue
I can't smell them
because they're going to bloom

Daisies are white
they are so white
they're so light at night

Tulips are yellow
like the sun
they're so much fun.
Ashley Proteau, Grade 1
Thatcher Brook Primary School, VT

Colored Eggs
C hocolate bunnies
O n Easter morning people find eggs
L iving peacefully
O n Easter people get together
R abbits giving Easter eggs
E gg hunting
D uring the season everyone having fun

E veryone celebrating new life
G reen grass
G reen colored eggs
S pring is here!
Gabriel Samolyuk, Grade 2
St Agatha School, NY

Birthday Cake
My cake is
representing
me turning
eight. I eat my birthday
cake one slice at a time.
It tastes yummy when it goes
in my tummy. When I eat
and eat my birthday cake I
celebrate me turning eight!
Natalie Campanella, Grade 3
Meadow Drive School, NY

Winter

It started to snow
So I wanted to go...
Out on my sled.
With my cheeks so red.
Down the hill I go.
Oh no! Oh no!
Brandi Lee, Grade 3
Penn-Kidder Campus, PA

Easter

E ggs
A pril
S ugar candy
T asty candy
E aster
R ed jelly beans
Jaden Javier, Grade 2
St Agatha School, NY

Candy Breeze

Candy is a bright rainbow color
It tastes like a juicy apple
It smells like it's raining gum balls
It reminds me of a spring wind
It sounds like kids eating gum
It feels like a great summer breeze
Alexandra Tregaskis, Grade 2
Klein Elementary School, PA

Snow Boarding

fast, fun
jumping, racing, falling
jumping off a hill
having fun
Hunter Stark, Grade 2
Caryl E Adams Primary School, NY

Spring Sports

I like basketball
Like to play with my scooter
I like lacrosse too!
Brandon Grace, Grade 1
St Louis Elementary School, MA

Fan of the Year!

My name is Anthony
and I am six years old.
My favorite colors
are black and gold.
I am a Steeler fan
and this is true.
When they lose,
I feel blue.
I watch every Sunday,
hoping they win.
So I can jump up and down,
with a very big grin.
Anthony Alviani, Grade 1
St Joan of Arc School, PA

Swamp

The green, murky
Depths of a swamp.

Salamanders, caimans,
And toads live in the
Swamp.

Sometimes there is
Quicksand in the swamp.

I think the swamp is interesting,
Do you?
Max Lunievicz, Grade 2
Buckley Country Day School, NY

Tie

Oh tie,
You look like a blue tree
In the moonlight,
People praying to the sky
For peace among them,
Soft and smooth,
Silky tie with blue, sparkly water
And beautiful colors,
Where did you come from?
Tania Johnson, Grade 2
John L Edwards School, NY

Dance

Dance is black.
It tastes like moving.
It sounds like music.
It smells like fun.
It looks like costumes.
It makes me feel active.
Meghan Miller, Grade 3
Evergreen Elementary School, PA

Spring

S pring people play hide and seek
P eople play outside
R oses come out
I pick flowers to put in a pot
N ew flowers are blooming
G arden to grow plants
Ella Marconi, Grade 3
Chestnut Street Elementary School, PA

Save the Earth

Don't sit in a car when it's not far
Ride a bike.
Recycle cans, bottles, and paper.
Do your job and it will help later.
Stop pollution make it clean.
You can do it! Yes you can!
Elijah Harris, Grade 2
Public School 235 Lenox, NY

Eclipse

Sun, moon collide
Darkness appears in the sky
So far away
Once in my lifetime
Spencer Perez-Dormitzer, Grade 1
Dartmouth Early Learning Center, MA

Fun Stuff

Going in the pool
I like playing with squirt guns
Playing basketball
Kayden Diallo, Grade 1
St Louis Elementary School, MA

Spring

Trees are dancing,
Deer are prancing,
Big bluebirds are swooping by,
Clouds are drifting through the sky
Ants are crawling,
Kids are falling,
Grass is growing,
No wind blowing,
Climbing trees,
Stinging bees,
And, just as you can see,
Spring's just right for you and me.
Madeline Muldoon, Grade 3
North Street School, CT

24 Cupcakes

24 cupcakes
in
a
row
I
ate
them
all
so
I
can
GROW
Jayda Forgenie, Grade 3
Public School 114 Ryder Elementary, NY

Bored

Nothing to do
Nothing to do
I have
Nothing in my head
And can't think of
Anything to do
I do not know
What to do so…
I keep trying!
Kayla Cohen, Grade 3
Meeting House Hill School, CT

October

O ctober has many different colored leaves.
C olored leaves are sometimes bright colors.
T easing people comes at Halloween time.
O ctober is a good month.
B ees are common in October.
E agles come into people's yards in October.
R ed is a common color in October.

Haley Caraglior, Grade 2
Long Meadow Elementary School, CT

Spring

Spring, spring what a wonderful thing!
Flowers bloom! They're so great!
   You smell so nice,
   I can't resist you!
   Your colors are beautiful!
   I'm so happy you are here!
Spring, spring, you are the beginning again!

Jillian Pyden, Grade 3
The Edgartown School, MA

Water and Fire

Water
Wet, Cold
Swimming, Surfing, Diving
Splash, Cannonball, Warmth, Marshmallows
Burning, Smoking, Smoldering
Hot, Flames
Fire

Mitchell Stevens, Grade 3
Brant Elementary School, NY

Winter Is...

Winter is watching people ice skating on a frozen pond.
Winter is building a snowman and snow girl with my sisters.
Winter is having a snowball fight.
Winter is catching snowflakes on my tongue.
Winter is sipping hot chocolate.
Winter is when my whole family comes to celebrate Christmas.
Winter is fun!

Cassandra Paul, Grade 1
All Saints Catholic Academy, NY

A River

I am pure water.
I am made out of nature.
People like rivers.
Kevin Chau, Grade 3
Sacred Heart School, MA

Snowfall

The winter is nice.
Squirrels hide in the winter.
Winter is awesome.
Tony Krieger, Grade 2
The Fourth Presbyterian School, MD

Wake-up

Baby animals
Running all around in spring
Searching for good food
Chassidy George, Grade 3
Brant Elementary School, NY

Rain

Rain is very wet
Listen to the peaceful sound
It is wonderful!
Delora Jones, Grade 3
Brant Elementary School, NY

Where Kids Play

Nice waters flow here.
Fish jump all around you here.
This is where kids play.
Beth Syverson, Grade 3
Brewster-Pierce Memorial School, VT

Grass

Grass is long and green
It is beautiful in spring
Grass is wonderful
Sierra Guerin, Grade 3
Brant Elementary School, NY

The Color of My Life

Blue is my favorite color.
Blue is a color to care.
Blue is what makes me believe.
Blue is the color of the sky.
Blue smells like being strong.
Blue tastes like blueberries.
Blue sounds like birds singing.
Blue looks like I am ready.
Blue feels like I am the only one on earth.
Blue makes me feel sad.
Preston Golato, Grade 3
Evergreen Elementary School, PA

My Mom

Fun to spend time with,
a busy lawyer,
very cool to hang out with,
takes us to exciting places,
the nicest person ever,
caring and kind,
travels to New York City.
Surprises us with treats
smart and talented
we're lucky to have her.
Connor Duffy, Grade 3
Colebrook Primary School, NY

Big Old Brown Bear

Big, old brown bear
Stealing from the smelly trash,
What are you doing?
Are you hungry?
Chomping on stinky fish.
Munching on half of a hot dog.
Big, old brown bear
Stealing from the smelly trash,
Are you full yet?
Did you like our leftovers?
Izayah Jon Pacheco, Grade 2
Carlyle C Ring Elementary School, NY

Halloween Night

Halloween night, it's so frightening
In the dark I smell fear
In the streets people wear scary costumes
I smell fruit snacks
I see eye balls, I see a man's head
I got scared and I heard a ghost's voice
Woooooo! I got frightened
I love Halloween!

Lydonn Hicksman, Grade 3
Public School 115 Alexander Humboldt, NY

Fishes

Fishes can swim.
Fishes can bubble.
Fishes are proud to be who they are.
I like gold fishes, but I wonder how they talk?
When they turn so big, you can buy millions of them.
The more you buy, the more you want.
They communicate, they can swim.
But how much language can they speak?

Andres Jimenez, Grade 3
Public School 131, NY

Friends

Friends are the best!
They never take a rest.
Friends are fun.
They call me when their homework is done.
Friends are kind.
They don't make you blind.
Friends are the best!
Is your name Kess?

Amy Duverge, Grade 3
Public School 232 The Walter Ward School, NY

I Love You the Greenest!

I love you the greenest...
I love you more than the green grass that we walk on.
I love you more than our pine tree in our back yard.
The touch of my cozy green shirt.
The taste of broccoli that I eat.

Shane Kollen, Grade 3
Southold Elementary School, NY

School

School is my favorite.
I have a lot of best friends.
John is my best friend.

Mackenzie Quillan, Grade 2
Fonda-Fultonville Elementary School, NY

Boston

We saw the zoo there.
I loved the big white tiger.
The zoo is awesome.

Ethan Harding, Grade 2
Fonda-Fultonville Elementary School, NY

No Walking and Talking

No walking and talking for me
One at a time or either you see
I can walk or talk but not together
Both would make me trip over a feather

Walking OR talking; either make me gay
I do it every day
You would say that if you were me too
If you had a dog sniffing your shoe

Click click clack clack
Click click clack clack
Goes the heel of the shoe
But still no talking it's true

When I talk I don't walk
But then I talk and talk
And talk some more
When not walking I can talk galore

So you see that's the way for me
I love it that way; it's my way.
Walking OR talking
And that how it will stay.

Katherine Zimmermann, Grade 2
Memorial School, NH

Baseball

Swing and a
miss
Oh I'm
lucky
I land in the
soft
padding

The pitch
OUUUUEH!!!

The batter swung
HOMERUN!
Landing in the
stands
hitting a
bench.
A fan grabs me
As I
struggle
out of his
hand.

James Moore, Grade 3
Buckley Country Day School, NY

Donate Now

Earthquake's shock waves
And mudslides
So scary!
Less food,
Less water,
Less money.
Haitians so strong.
Donate, donate!
Under the rubble,
People trapped and scared.
They need your help!
Donate now!
Max Kreppein, Grade 1
John Ward Elementary School, MA

Chocolate

Chocolate, chocolate
It looks so good
It's a very good treat
I can eat it all week,
Chocolate, chocolate
I just wanna
munch, munch, munch
When I touch it it's kinda hard
but when I eat it it's really soft
When the chocolate is all gone
I say "Oh man"
Why did I eat it all?
Diamond Bolling, Grade 3
Public School 114 Ryder Elementary, NY

Tree Stump

Oh tree stump,
You smell like cinnamon
In mom's apple pie,
On the inside
Chips fall out of you
Making warmth for animals,
Old, rough bark
Surrounding a tunnel,
Who lived in you?
Caleigh Parmentier, Grade 2
John L Edwards School, NY

Spring Is Changing into Summer

Spring, Spring
What do you bring?
You bring fun
You bring sun
Summer's almost here
Summer is the best time of year
Rebecca Boucher, Grade 1
Thatcher Brook Primary School, VT

Cute Babies

Baby, Baby, Baby,
Cute, chubby, pretty Baby
Small, little, tiny Baby
Crying, breathing, crawling Baby
Walking, sleeping, cute little Baby
Baby, Baby, Baby
Catriona McAree, Grade 3
Our Lady of Hope School, NY

Roast Chicken

I want to eat you,
"no, no" said roast chicken
but you are tender as butter
and I am going to eat you,
yum yum,
good bye now, I'm full!
Abby Flynn, Grade 2
Tashua School, CT

Hockey

Rough, fast
Shooting, scoring, skating
Hockey is my favorite
Challenging
Max Letta, Grade 3
Colebrook Primary School, NY

Springtime

I go out today
It is a sunny day today
I play with my friends
Lily Boucher, Grade 1
St Louis Elementary School, MA

When I Look Out the Window

I see...
People that are homeless,
I see earthquakes happen,
People starve and kids too,
Droughts come and go and
leave us no water.
I see people get hurt, houses collapse.
I hear of great famines
and people long ago
that had to work to get what they want.
But that can all change
if we are not greedy or selfish
if we help them by giving them a home,
give them food and give them help.
By just being a great community.

Erika Sherwood, Grade 3
Colebrook Elementary School, NY

I

I'm a
Good looking
Kid
With spiky hair.

I have a lot
Of
Good
Friends
And
I
Love
My
Own
Life.

Harrison DellaVecchia, Grade 2
Buckley Country Day School, NY

Super Spring

It is full of rain.
Baby birds hatch from their nests.
Purple violets bloom.

Anastasia Micich, Grade 2
The Fourth Presbyterian School, MD

Spring

S unny
P lanting
R ainy
I ce melting
N ew flowers
G ardens

Eric Tudor, Grade 3
Chestnut Street Elementary School, PA

Spring

S unshine
P lants
R ain
I nsects biting
N ature
G reen grass

Ty Stahli, Grade 3
Chestnut Street Elementary School, PA

Five Senses

Baseball is gray
It tastes like a backstop
It sounds like my bat crushing a ball
It smells like I'm going to hit a home run
It looks like my bat
It makes me feel awesome

Kyle Julian, Grade 3
Evergreen Elementary School, PA

Frogs

Frogs leap on lily pad flowers
Bullfrogs have lots of power
Bullfrogs croak and ribbit too
Maybe I'll catch one for you.

Morgan Arakelian, Grade 2
Annie L Sargent School, MA

Springtime Fun

Friends coming over
We play ball in the back yard
We ride our bikes

Colton Strickland, Grade 1
St Louis Elementary School, MA

Shyness

Shyness looks like someone going back,
    but never forward.
Shyness sounds like a still emptiness
    just waiting to be heard.
Shyness tastes like something hard and burnt.
Shyness feels like something you have to say,
    but you can't.
Shyness smells like something you must conquer
    but won't.

Emily Redmond, Grade 3
West Branch School, PA

My Collection

I collect key chains
I have all different kinds
They are my favorite thing to find
Some are from places
that I have gone on vacation
My friends and family have given me more
I even got one from the NBA store
Collecting key chains is really great
In my collection I have 48!

Timothy Dolan, Grade 3
St. Barnabas Elementary School, NY

Black

Black looks like my Black Bombers softball shirt,
    Black sounds like alley cats howling,
    Black smells like dirt in the flower garden
    And feels like velvet.
    Black tastes like the blackberries
    I pick at my grandmother's house.

Philippa Harvey, Grade 2
St Anna School, MA

Winter

In winter I can make a snowman tall and round.
In winter I can go sledding on a snowy mountain.
In winter I can have a snowball fight with my sister.
In winter I can go inside to warm up and drink hot cocoa.
I love winter! Winter is fun!

Samantha Paul, Grade 1
All Saints Catholic Academy, NY

Fall
Leaves falling
to the ground
from the big tree
wind blows the leaves
onto my head
yellow, orange, green
all different colors.
Kevin Flewelling, Grade 2
Tashua School, CT

Creation
We always play, every day
When it is morning
When we play we always say
"Wow, a rainbow shining today"
It has colors like red, blue, and yellow
And many others too.
That is a creation for me and you.
Ahvani Rice, Grade 2
The Delphi Academy, MA

Fire/Ice
Fire
Hot, bright
Spreading, speeding, burning,
Flames, smoke, snowman, rink,
Freezing, sliding, cracking,
Hard, white,
Ice
Cary Novick, Grade 3
Meadow Drive School, NY

My Favorite Holidays
Christmas
Presents, Santa
Sledding, cooking, praying
Jesus is born and Jesus rose from the dead
Hopping, hatching, loving
Rabbit, eggs
Easter
Matthew Hosey, Grade 2
St. Madeleine Sophie School, NY

Night and Day
Night
Dark, cold
Shivering, freezing, sleeping
Moon comes down, sun comes up
Running, playing, learning
Bright, sunny
Day
Riley Sullivan, Grade 2
St. Madeleine Sophie School, NY

Icicles
Overnight icicles grew
Catching the stars above
My window
Shining in the dark
Like long, sharp teeth
Make a wish
Upon a star
Ayana Cody, Grade 2
John L Edwards School, NY

Flowers
Flowers are nice
Flowers are kind
Flowers can make rhymes
They can say thank-you and please
They can even say knees
Flowers love sunshine they love grass
They love water in the baths
Eliane Odefey, Grade 1
Thatcher Brook Primary School, VT

Spring
Butterflies flying in the air
Flowers blooming everywhere
A pot of gold waiting for you
At the end of a rainbow it's surely true
Children playing all around
Lots of jumping up and down...
Now everyone sing...it's spring
Sydney Paige Rohlfing, Grade 3
Shelter Rock Elementary School, NY

Things I Love About the Tropianos
Fun and laughter
Generous hearts
Smart ideas
Kind and Loving
Home away from home
Great care taking
Best of friends!
Torre Colegrove, Grade 3
Colebrook Primary School, NY

Valentine's Day
Hearts and Kisses plus XO's.
Valentine cards and a pretty rose.
Have some fun with pink and red.
Boy I'm tired, I need to get in bed.
Oh I had a rough day although it was fun.
And I got my valentines
Before the day was done.
Emily M. and Maiya G., Grade 3
Colebrook Primary School, NY

My Friends
My friends are so nice
They play with me
My friends are so nice
They help me
My friends are so nice
They cheer me up when I'm sad
I love my friends!
Anna Casey, Grade 1
Buckley Country Day School, NY

Horrible Day
You're in a bad mood,
you have nothing to do,
your face is all pinched and red.

You're not feeling good,
you've nowhere to go to,
and you wish you'd just stayed in bed.
Itai Abramovich, Grade 2
Zervas Elementary School, MA

Love Is Like a Wave
Love is like wave
It keeps coming, coming and coming.
My heart never sleeps,
Just like the ocean.
When I step into the water,
It wraps around me
And I don't want to let it go.
Sayer Weisenholz, Grade 3
Willits Elementary School, NY

Bravery
Bravery smells like smoke.
Bravery feels like a sting.
Bravery looks like a scratch.
Bravery sounds like crackling.
Bravery tastes bitter.
Bravery means you have
courage and take risks.
Hiatt Robleski, Grade 3
West Branch School, PA

I Caught...When Fishing
A string.
A beetle with a broken wing.
A catfish.
A drink
I took a sip and that's when
I found the worst thing of all...
A sharp paper clip!
Simon Scharrer, Grade 2
Wyoming Valley Montessori School, PA

Friendliness
Friendliness is a light blue.
It tastes like strawberry shortcake.
It smells like a beautiful red rose.
It feels like the soft fur on a baby bunny.
It sounds like the coo of a loon.
Friendliness is a sunset over the ocean.
V.K. Peterson, Grade 3
Asa C Adams School, ME

Recess

Running, jumping,
having fun —
That's why I like recess!
Sliding, swinging,
monkey bars too —
Recess is REALLY cool!

Chasity Collins, Grade 1
Milton Terrace South Elementary School, NY

My Dog

My dog is cute, my dog is funny.
My dog likes to chase cats and squirrels.
My dog never eats his food but when I am near it he eats it fast.
My dog I love him with all my heart and my dog can feel it.
My dog is sooooo adorable.
I will always love my dog and he knows it.

Dariana Reyes, Grade 3
Public School 131, NY

Just Because

Winter is fun just because I can go sleigh riding.
Winter is fun just because when I go down the hill, I go fast.
Winter is fun just because sometimes I like to fall off my sled.
Winter is fun just because I can ski fast down the hill.
Winter is fun just because I can throw snowballs.
Winter is exciting!

Alessandro Nardone, Grade 1
All Saints Catholic Academy, NY

Leaves

Leaves are red, leaves are brown
they fall off the trees and fall to the ground
kids play in them, kids have fun in them
leaves are not seen in the winter they fall in
the lakes I can't believe the leaves are all
over the place

Ian Butler, Grade 3
Jeffrey Elementary School, CT

My Kite

My kite can fly high,
It could fly into the sky.
I hold the string really tight
So that it does not fly away.
The wind pushes it higher.
My kite passes the birds
And flies really high
And that's my kite.

Gabriella Yarczower, Grade 3
Our Lady of Hope School, NY

Wind

Wind whistling howling
talking to me
oh this is scary
someone help me
the wind is chasing
it's chasing me
my friend jumps out
and yells boo!!!

Ashley Cohen, Grade 2
Tashua School, CT

My Mom

My mom is so sweet.
She is loving and caring too.
She is very helpful to me.
She is always there for me.
When I am sad, she cheers me up.
When I am happy, she is happy for me.
My mom is kind with everyone she meets.
My mom is the best mom of all.

Ashley Camacho, Grade 3
Public School 131, NY

Gecko

Gecko
small and scaly
running, walking, snaking
they are little cute animals
Lizard

Adam Wojciechowski, Grade 3
Clinton Street Elementary School, NY

Brownies

B rownies are sweet.
R oll them in hot fudge.
O ne is not enough.
W hen you're bored eat brownies.
N ever stop eating brownies.
I love brownies too.
E at them.
S even a day is too much.

Trevor Connor, Grade 3
Sacred Heart School, MA

Peace

Love sounds like
Light feathers
Jumping around the room.
Singing love songs
that only you can hear.
But they make no noise to anybody else
Just a joyful, light love song
That can make you go to sleep.

Thalia Feeney, Grade 3
A. P. Willits Elementary School, NY

Pure Happiness

Love,
Love is the ingredients
To pure happiness.
It's your favorite dish,
The one you enjoy best of all.
You want to eat it forever.
It's your prized possession,
Better than anything else!

Cooper Scher, Grade 3
Willits Elementary School, NY

A Dog

A dog
Colorful, cute
Running
Happy when hears food
Abby

Brandon Wrobel, Grade 3
Clinton Street Elementary School, NY

Sweet Song

Sweet song
is the thing that
makes crickets play
their song.
Without it you wouldn't dream,
the birds wouldn't sing
and the sun wouldn't beam.
The sweet song is the power of all sweet
things in the world.

Amelia Austen, Grade 3
The Tobin School, MA

Crystals Falling Down

Crystals drizzle
Flowers start to bloom.
Hearts fill me up.
I like the rain so much!
Each raindrop is special
It feels cool
I like to splash in it

Because it rules!

Alicia Walker, Grade 2
The Tobin School, MA

Monkeys

Monkeys
hairy bodies
playful
fun to watch
long tails
hang on trees
five fingers
five toes
eat bananas.

Ryan Johnson, Grade 2
Tashua School, CT

End Pollution

E nd pollution
A nd save air
R euse and reduce and recycle
T o save the Earth
H ave smiles

D o good
A nd save water
Y eah

Marc Jenkins, Grade 2
Public School 235 Lenox, NY

Key Chains

Key chains, key chains aren't they fun.
You can swing them back and forth.
They jingle and dangle all day long.
They also shine like the sun.
Key chains are fun to collect.

Erin Mullen, Grade 3
St Barnabas Elementary School, NY

Hamsters

Hamster
Cute squeaky
Eats, grooms, spins
Hamsters are cute.
Cage.

Brooke Haines, Grade 2
The Fourth Presbyterian School, MD

Anger

Anger is dark red.
It tastes like cranberry juice.
It smells like rotten apples.
It's as hard as a rock.
It sounds like howling wind.
Anger looks like a rat.

Jonah Edgar, Grade 3
Asa C Adams School, ME

Rainbow

Red watermelon
Orange lion
Yellow clock
Green leaf
Blue yo-yo
Purple quilt

Mya Corley, Kindergarten
Robert M Hughes School, MA

A Stormy Night

On a

stormy night

all alone

SPLAT!

Rain falling

BOOM!

Thunder throwing a tantrum

SHOCK!

Lightning striking

Sitting by   my

window

watching

the

storm.

Madeline Simms, Grade 3
Buckley Country Day School, NY

Trees

Trees are good, trees are kind,
Trees are very cool to climb.

I love them, I really do,
I think that animals do too.

Some are big, some are small,
But in a way I like them all.

They have roots that hold the earth still.
Some are planted on a hill.

They all have jobs they like to do,
You may not know, but they like us too.
Lee Cain, Grade 2
Carlyle C Ring Elementary School, NY

Pals

Pals
Happy, lappy
Playing, skipping, laughing
They always stick together
Friends
Maggie Laffin, Grade 2
Wyland Elementary School, PA

Spring!

Spring, spring, how I love spring!
It's when the flowers come out and sing!
Spring, spring, how I love spring!
It's my favorite time of year!
Spring, spring, how I love spring!
Birds chirp in my ear!
Victoria Scott, Grade 3
The Edgartown School, MA

Spring

S unny days in the yard
P retty flowers everywhere
R ejoice and have fun
I ncredibly colored flowers
N ature walks in the woods with mom
G reat sights to see
Emma Searle, Grade 3
The Edgartown School, MA

Ice Cream

Ice cream
Is cold
It's the perfect thing to eat
On hot and sunny days
It's my favorite
Treat
Morgan Thomas, Grade 3
Lincoln Street School, MA

Legos

Legos are neat
Legos are cool
You can play with them
At school
Nathaniel Anderson, Grade 3
Marathon Christian Academy, NY

Ice Cream

Very cold
Good for the summer
Chocolate chip…my favorite
Kaden Humphrey, Grade 2
Primrose School, NY

A Star
Shiny and little
Yellow and bright

I move my hands
As I light up the sky at night

I run and hide
As the sun comes out

The moon peeks at me
And my face starts smiling

For I am
A star
Jenna Thompson, Grade 3
Indian Lane Elementary School, PA

The Wind
Breezy and strong
Quick and cold

I give a big breeze
By waving high

The leaves fall off the trees
From above in the sky

I huff and I puff
Then you put on your jacket

For I am
The wind
Chloe Reagle, Grade 3
Indian Lane Elementary School, PA

Shopping
I love to shop
And drink pop.

I shop in the fall.
I go to the mall.

I shop for clothes.
Then I go to Lowes.

I don't shop for dresses,
Because they get me into messes.

I like to shop.
It is hard to stop!
Arielle Tyrpak, Grade 3
Ellicott Road Elementary School, NY

What Is Beautiful to Me
Above, above,
Cold wind is blowing beside me

Below, below,
Blue and yellow flowers swaying

In the mountains, the mountains,
White snow looks like a long, silvery dress

In the ocean, the ocean,
Waves look like beautiful, floating clouds

Here ends my song,
The beautiful world
Reginald Scott, Grade 2
John L Edwards School, NY

A Man Named Bob
There once was a man named Bob,
he didn't have a very good job.
He only got a dime a day,
he only had 50 cents by May!
So poor Bob started to sob.
Annie Waters, Grade 2
Wyland Elementary School, PA

Mashiach Is Coming Soon
Mashiach is coming soon
We wake up every day.
We daven and we pray,
That Mashiach is coming soon,
In the morning and afternoon.
Joshua Pomerantz, Grade 2
Yeshiva Ketana of Long Island, NY

Jaguars

They pounce! They jump! They stay!
Jaguars have lots of prey!
In the wild they can live 12-15 years.
They're bold and brave and don't have many fears.
Jaguars' fear is the human kind
On their skin you can't find a line.
Jaguars are one of the biggest cats
They eat fish and turtles but not bats.
Jaguars are all around
They grow up to 8 feet long and like to lounge around.
They live in the Amazon rain forest
In South America jaguars are the largest.
They are mammals.
They've never seen camels.
Now that you know a lot
You give a poem a shot.

Kalle Kuffner, Grade 3
Shady Grove Elementary School, PA

Summer/Winter

Summer
Hot, fun
Swimming, playing, vacationing
Beach, pool, snow shovels
Snowball fighting, ice skating, snowboarding
Cold, fun
Winter

Tara Minaahang, Grade 3
Meadow Drive School, NY

Just About Me

I am from flat screen TV's.
I am from bunnies.
I am from dirt bikes.
I am from brother, Miguel.
I am from, "If you love something, set it free."
I am from pepperoni pizza.
I am from Disney World.
I am from straight "A" tests.
I am from Selena Gomez.
I am from New York.

Giselle Marquez, Grade 3
William Ziegler Elementary School, PA

The Smart Board
The Smart Board is big.
They say I shouldn't touch.
I find this very hard,
Since I want to very much!
Donni Herskowitz, Grade 2
Yeshiva Ketana of Long Island, NY

Friends
Friends are special.
They make you laugh.
I have a lot of fun with my friends.
I love to play with my friends!
Cara Daidone, Grade 3
Our Lady of Hope School, NY

Dogs
Sniffing, barking, growling, scratching,
Running, jumping, eating food,
Rolling, chasing, playing, drinking,
Walking, loving, sleeping, is what dogs do.
Olivia Sudol, Grade 3
Our Lady of Hope School, NY

Basketballs
Basketballs are round.
Basketballs bounce.
Shoot 'em in hoop,
We got a score for you!
Justin Seetahal, Grade 2
Public School 69, NY

Spring
In spring, it's fun to play.
It gets warm.
Flowers grow in a nice way
Flowers and trees can form.
Peter Cwalina, Grade 3
Our Lady of Hope School, NY

Easter
Oh la la Easter
Chocolate bunnies, bubble gum
Easter egg hunts fun, fun, fun
Easter is awesome
Debbie Loyd, Grade 3
Penn-Kidder Campus, PA

Dog Bark
Bark bark bark!
Make it stop!
Noise noise noise!
Dogs like to do bark.
Vinci Cheung, Grade 2
Public School 69, NY

The Peach Tree
The peach trees are beautiful.
They are trees that grow peaches.
They give you shade to cool you
From the summer sun.
Laura Sutherland, Grade 3
Ridgeway Elementary School, MD

Spring
Flowers are growing.
Hard winds aren't blowing.
Animals are crawling on the ground.
Birds are chirping their beautiful sound.
Grace DeVivo, Grade 3
Our Lady of Hope School, NY

My Tree
I have a tree, it's bigger than me.
It's big, it's tall and most of all,
I love the branches it grew for me.
I love my tree and we love to drink tea.
Jessica Mimms, Grade 3
Ridgeway Elementary School, MD

Cat and Dog Fight
The fat cat was sleeping.
The dog came creeping.
He pounced on the cat
and knocked him flat.
Growl! Hiss! Bark! Hiss!
The cat fought back!
Whack! Smack! Swack!
They ran to the park
and fought till it was dark.
Bark! Ruff! Meow!
They both heard strange noises.
Creek! Crash! Boom!
The cat and dog ran away.
And to this very day
they haven't come back this way.

Katlyn McLeod, Grade 3
Emmanuel Baptist Christian Academy, PA

Wings
Through the mist darkness creeps,
But then light appears,
It makes everything, oh, so clear,
When it shines over me I say:
It is a creature with wings!
She gracefully dances,
Look how she prances!
And look at her marvelous wings!
She looks like she wants to sing,
Look at her wings,
How white and shiny they are!
She looks like a horse with wings!
How beautiful she looks in the light,
Her wings glistening with all their might,
Then she vanishes and the darkness remains,
And then, the dark clouds pour down rain.
I can't forget her wings when I try to go to sleep,
I can't take my mind off her even when I count sheep.
Her wings keep flashing through my mind,
Her wings were oh so one-of-a-kind,
And I doubt I will see that beautiful creature ever again.

Elisabeth Moore, Grade 3
Commonwealth Connections Academy, PA

Earth Day

Do not litter do not litter it will kill the trees which will stop the air from
giving us breeze and oxygen that makes us breathe so please oh please
absolutely positively do not litter then the Earth will be better

Cole Carchedi, Grade 3
Shady Grove Elementary School, PA

A Purple Eiffel Tower
(Observations on a Cap Eraser)

A straight base
then comes the strong BULKY

tip
When the storms of
mistakes
s-l-o-w-l-y
breaks down
but never
falls down
It takes some
damage
but still
stands
strong.

Kassandra Homayuni, Grade 3
Buckley Country Day School, NY

Moonset

As the moon goes down,
it's the most beautiful thing
I have ever seen.

Aujhaii Leslie, Grade 2
Simpson-Waverly School, CT

Index

Author Autograph Page

Author Autograph Page

Author Autograph Page

Author Autograph Page